JESUIT CHILD

Also by Macdonald Hastings

The 'Mr Cork' Books
CORK ON THE WATER
CORK IN BOTTLE
CORK AND THE SERPENT
CORK IN THE DOGHOUSE
CORK ON THE TELLY

Historical Novel
A GLIMPSE OF ARCADIA

War Reminiscence
PASSED AS CENSORED

Anthology
MACDONALD HASTINGS' COUNTRY BOOK

Text Books
CHURCHILL ON GAME SHOOTING
HOW TO SHOOT STRAIGHT
ENGLISH SPORTING GUNS

Biography
THE OTHER MR CHURCHILL

For Boys
EAGLE SPECIAL INVESTIGATOR
ADVENTURE CALLING
THE SEARCH FOR THE LITTLE YELLOW MEN
MEN OF GLORY
MORE MEN OF GLORY

For Little Children
SYDNEY SPARROW

For Television
CALL THE GUN EXPERT (A SERIES)
RIVERBEAT (TWO SERIES)
VOYAGE INTO ENGLAND (A SERIES)
IN DEEPEST BRITAIN (A SERIES)
THE HATED SOCIETY: THE JESUITS

JESUIT CHILD

Macdonald Hastings

ST. MARTIN'S PRESS
NEW YORK

AFFILIATED PUBLISHERS: Macmillan & Company, Limited, London —
also at Bombay, Calcutta, Madras and Melbourne — The Macmillan Company
of Canada, Limited, Toronto.

Whatever they may think of me after this
'more in the spirit of the world than in the spirit of God'

TO THE JESUITS

CONTENTS

1 *Jesuit Child*

2 *Pilgrimage*

ILLUSTRATIONS

Between pages 80–81

Stonyhurst College, Lancashire
Inigo Lopez de Loyola
Ignatius's Death Mask: Today's General of the Jesuits
The Martyrdom of Father Brebeuf by North American Indians
The Martyrdom of forty Jesuits by the Japanese
The Reductions of Paraguay
(an impression and a contemporary photograph)
'A Vanished Arcadia'
The Spiritual Exercises: seventeenth century woodcuts

Between pages 144–145

The Monastery of Montserrat
The Jesuit fathers: Robert Persons, Henry Garnet,
Edmund Campion; the spy Titus Oates
The Martyrdom of Edmund Campion at Tyburn Tree
The Jesuits at the Court of the Grand Mogul
Father Possevino at the Court of Stefen Bathory of Poland
The Jesuits at the Court of Catherine the Great
The Discovery of Jesuits' Bark (quinine)
The Discovery of the Magic Lantern
A first Map of the Moon
Father Matteo Ricci in Chinese Dress

JESUIT CHILD

Between pages 208- 209

The Wise Men of the West in China
Confessor at the Court of the Bourbons
The Expulsion of the Jesuits from France and Spain
The Popes Paul III, Clement XIV, Pius VII
Jesuit children Today
Jesuit children Yesterday:
Rousseau, Molière, Voltaire; and Pascal, an adversary

1
JESUIT CHILD

I

Apologia

'There is a saying often attributed to some Jesuit divine that if he had the teaching of children up to seven years of age or thereabouts, he cared not who had them afterwards. Who was this, and what were the precise words?' (G.H.J. Notes and Queries, 9th Series, Vol. 1, April 16, 1898, p. 308.)

I do not know who G.H.J. was who popped the question in *Notes and Queries* in 1898. Mr R. K. Browne, the librarian at Farm Street, likes to think that it might have been a kite flown by a Jesuit father named George Hayward Joyce. I myself got hold of a different version. I thought it ran: 'Give us a child at the age of seven and he will be ours for the rest of his life.' Since the notorious saying is almost certainly apocryphal it doesn't matter which form is the right one. What is relevant is that it is still widely believed that the Jesuits can bend any child, provided they catch him young enough, to their way of thinking. You may judge whether there is any truth in it from this personal history.

I was put into the charge of the Jesuits shortly before my eighth birthday. So that if a child's mind on the attainment of the use of reason is moulded by its masters, I am tainted. In the summer of my years I might, like Peter, have denied it. But now that my leaves are falling I can recognise that I am, at least, tinted.

The revelation came to me when, somewhere, sometime, I was appearing in what is euphemistically called a Brains Trust. After the programme, a member of the team I had not met before asked me if I had been educated by the Jesuits.

'Yes, at Stonyhurst. Why?'

'Everything you said on the platform tonight made me suspect it. Your attitude on any question, whether it concerned intensive farming, town planning, loneliness and whatever that silly question was about sex we had to answer in ten seconds, was predictable.'

I wondered what I had said that moved him to hazard the guess. None of the questions in the programme concerned religion. Anyhow, I am a lapsed Roman Catholic. Although I am not without spiritual hope or thought, I am unable to associate myself with any of the formal Church affiliations. Prayer for me is not words in a book, or the liturgy of a service, but an abstraction of the mind.

And yet . . . and yet . . . The sensitive antennae of my fellow brainstruster, he was a distinguished Sephardic Jew, had sorted me out. Recalling the definition in the Oxford Dictionary of the word 'jesuitical' I asked him if his reason was that he found my comments 'dissembling, crafty'.

'I wouldn't say that,' he said. 'People only call a man jesuitical when they are beaten in an argument.'

He was an enigmatic person, as Jewish intellectuals often are; a prompter who, with penetrating precision, recalled to me my lines.

I am a Jesuit child.

So at the beginning of this story of the most formidable, the most controversial, to some the most hated Society of men in the course of modern history, it is proper to underline that the Jesuits shaped the soft clay of me. I am still of them, and yet not of them. Paradoxically, I am a renegade who has never deserted their tents.

It was predestined that I should become a camp follower. My great-grandfather, a classical don, had taught in the Jesuit foundation at Georgetown in Virginia at the time of the Civil War. One of his brothers had joined an American Province of the Society, dying in the odour of sanctity a month before being ordained a Jesuit priest. He was so holy that my great aunt, Sister Philippine de la Croix of the Order of Notre Dame, wrote in her nineties that when he had to be reinterred, in a new cemetery twenty years after his death, his body was found 'in a perfect state of preservation'. Two brothers of my great-great maternal grandmother also joined the Jesuits in America. Saintly men and women in my family outnumber the sinners.

There was no call for a family consultation about which school I should go to. My grandfather, who was a lawyer; my father, Basil Macdonald Hastings, the playwright; and his elder brother, my favourite uncle, Major Lewis Hastings, M.C., who became famous as the BBC's military commentator during Hitler's war, had all been educated at Stonyhurst, the great college in the shadow of Pendle Hill in East Lancashire which the Jesuits had founded at the end of the eighteenth century.

I suckled my mother's milk in the ambience of the ancient academy. Etchings of Stonyhurst lined our dining-room walls. There was a grim steel engraving on the bedroom stairs of the eagle-towered Elizabethan mansion, cloaked in thunderous cloud, which filled my impressionable mind with foreboding. My family, staunch Roman Catholics all, taught me the tag: 'Stonyhurst is what Eton was, a school for the sons of Catholic gentlemen'. So, in the autumn of 1917, with other boys of the Old Faith, I was exiled into the misty fells of the Duchy of Lancaster, to the eerie coven-place of the Lancashire witches, to the wild environs of 'poor, proud, priest-ridden Preston'.

It was a part of England where, even in the persecutions of Elizabethan times, the recusants had never been routed out. It was too inaccessible; so much so that even in my own time at Stonyhurst it was said of the little village of Hurst Green nearby that the Catholics had persecuted the few Protestants there for three hundred years. Such are the iniquities of religious intolerance that Catholic and Protestant villagers would not go to the same pubs; and the organ pipes of the small Protestant church were under constant threat from Catholic vandals.

To travel to Stonyhurst in a two-horse brake from Whalley Station in 1917 was to rumble into a past little removed from the time when Cromwell's Ironsides, on their way to the Battle of Preston in 1648, crossed the narrow packhorse bridge, arched like a bucking horse, which still spans the Hodder.

For me, frightened enough by the chill murk of Euston Station, the journey in the dark along narrow lanes overhung with the branches of clammy trees seemed to confirm all the secret terrors I had of the gloomy picture of Stonyhurst on our bedroom stairs at home.

I was exiled, young as I was, 'because there was a war on'. Deprived of my father's control, it was thought that I needed discipline. And I got it.

I was too tender in years to start my school career in the senior foundation. I was sent to Hodder, the Jesuits' preparatory school in the river valley a few miles from Stonyhurst. Although happier times were to come I cannot pretend that my early years as a Hodderitian were other than unutterably miserable. In fairness, most boys torn from their mother's arms to be subjected in any boarding school to the savage English upper class system – even now, under more civilised conditions – have found it hell, too. Hodder, I suppose, was no worse than the rest. But it was bad.

The night I arrived at the school another boy, a year or so older than me, asked my name. My father had prepared me for that. I was to say 'Hastings'; not 'Mac' as I was called at home. He thereupon pronounced that it was a rotten name, and rooted me with the toe of his boot. Next, a gang marched me off to a horizontal ladder, a gymnastic device I had never seen before, forced me with pinpricks to climb it and, at arms' stretch, drag my way along the rungs in the ceiling. Such muscles as I had seized up, and I stuck there in a chorus of jeers.

I was lifted down by a stern man in a black gown, with false sleeves hanging from his shoulders and a Roman collar. He was the Jesuit prefect – the prefects were our masters, not other boys – whom I was to know later under the nickname of 'Bluebeard'. I never lost my fear of him from that first night at school when he slapped my face to dry my tears. I soon learnt that it was no use going to him when the older boys took away my toy soldiers, and broke the blade of the penknife which was an advance present for my eighth birthday. I learnt early that, from now on, I was out on my own.

I kept the blubbing for bedtime in the dormitory. I forced myself to bite my lip when the formidable Bluebeard roused me from bed one evening, and thrashed me for various unknown offences. Luckily, he let me keep my combinations on. Physical violence, so it seemed, was the way of life. I had greater fear of the boys' committee, five of them, than my Jesuit masters. Little monsters of ten and eleven were given the authority to call us into a classroom, and kick us until they were tired of the exercise.

While I can write with affection in future chapters, I make no excuse for the bitterness in my pen now. Those early days at Hodder were awful. The headmaster, the Rector, was a bald-pated man, with a hot potato in his mouth, whose favourite phrase was 'You old hypocrite'. I was certainly a young hypo-crite.

I could not understand, what was admittedly a personal quirk of one of our masters, that there seemed to be some merit in making chalices out of silver paper, and setting up altars in miniature inside our school desks. I was carried along with preparations for First Holy Communion, and given a book called *Garden of the Soul* which I found unreadable. I went to confession, in a little box separated by flywire from the priest, in which I had to invent my sins. The important sins seemed to be dirty thoughts. Dirty thoughts, or so I imagined, must be something to do with my sister who hadn't got a tail like me. Bottoms were clearly unthinkable. I hadn't got round to breasts and navels, never mind the more complex perversions of humanity. In truth, it wasn't until I was about fourteen that I discovered what my third leg was made for. Nevertheless, we were taught to feel wicked. I felt very wicked.

The round of daily mass and daily prayers in the school chapel was hateful to me. I was never one of the elect who was appointed to flame the candles and distribute the prayer books. I played the game because I would have been frightened to do anything else. Erratically, I was religious. I parroted the words, I fingered the rosary. But deep down inside, even then, I was wondering what it was all about.

Those of us in the Preparatory Class were taught by a woman, who also played the harmonium in the school chapel. She was the only feminine thing I recollect at Hodder, a frail creature made of strawberries and cream, who ought to have been a nun. If a man had touched her she would have broken like a piece of fine bone china. I remember her, in the mist of a mantilla, bowing over the altar. She died young, almost certainly of consumption.

At Hodder, the Jesuits only taught the elder boys, but they kept a stern paternal eye on all our activities. The house was gas-lit, the heating was erratic and the food, in wartime, execrable. We had no days out from term's beginning to term's end. Parents, even if they could make the long journey to the un-welcoming landscape, were discouraged from visiting us.

Below the school building, made in bogus chateau architec-ture, there was a delicious vale in the Hodder valley called 'Paradise'. My own recollection is that Paradise was out of bounds to us except on a 'Good Day' once a year. When the Day came round it rained all day; and the 'Good Day' was cancelled. We dewed our exercise books with our tears.

In retrospect, most of my memories of Hodder are misty. I was so lonely there, and bored. It was characteristic of the place at that time that the way we celebrated the Armistice in Novem-ber 1918 was to be given the privilege of sliding down a fire escape chute fixed to a first floor window. I was permitted at impromptu races to be the timekeeper.

I would have begged my parents to take me away except that our letters home were censored. When I confessed all during my holidays my father simply impressed on me how much tougher it was in his generation when they were all sent to school in September and didn't come home again until the following

August. He loved to tell me that, one Christmas at Stonyhurst, the only present he got was an orange which was stolen from him by another boy who subsequently became a distinguished Dominican.

It was small comfort. But my father buoyed my hopes with how different it was going to be when I was promoted to The College. In my last days at Hodder a good man raised my expectance of the future. In the great tradition of the Jesuits, he introduced me to amateur theatricals. I played Morgiana, the slave girl, in *Ali Baba and the Forty Thieves*. The knife, a piece of cardboard wrapped in silver paper with which I had to kill somebody or other, was one of the most exciting things I have ever held. With that, I began to have a clue, however slight, what Jesuit education was about.

I began to realise that I was a child in a plan; that the Jesuits wanted to exploit me, not necessarily as a child of their own, but as an individual. Constantly, they were judging my mettle; testing, in firearms terms, whether I stood proof. It was a hard upbringing in keeping with the Jesuits' own training. Slowly, like a raw recruit in the Guards' Depot at Caterham, I got into their ways.

Somehow, the Jesuits would never have thought it very wrong that, on a first night of term at Hodder, another boy, the son of a famous wine connoisseur, offered to share with me a half bottle of champagne his father had put in his overnight bag. He is now a Jesuit priest himself. The Jesuits, quick to punish, quick to forgive, allow that boys and men are venal.

If I have subsequently failed, by the Jesuits' own exacting standards, they can only blame themselves. The streak of iron in me, the questioning attitudes, the rebellious spirit, the taste for lonely action, the sheer obstinacy of so much of my life, are born of Jesuit training. By contrast I owe them my love for cultural things, for theatre and elocution, for argument, the joys of conversation; and the awkwardness of individuality.

It was at Stonyhurst, after the pap of the preparatory school at Hodder, that I learnt to relish the wine, some of it plonk, of

Jesuit education – that same education which in Europe had thrown up way out people like Voltaire, Rousseau and Corneille, the same idiosyncratic education which, at Stonyhurst, had produced such dissenting and differing men as Arthur Conan Doyle, Charles Laughton the actor, Bernard Partridge the *Punch* artist, Oliver St John Gogarty, the great Irish patriot, writer and wit, and that eminent lawyer of our own time, Lord Devlin.

It was at Stonyhurst that I came under the spell of the Hated Society, 'dreaded and detested on all sides as the worst species of knaves'. 'They care for no man, so that it may gratify and please the Pope, though it may bring confusion of all the world and the betraying of their own country.'

Although thousands of books have been written about the Jesuits, in which they are described with every scurrilous epithet, this is a time for reassessment. Now, when institutions throughout the world, not just religious ones, are in disarray, the Jesuits, 'the right hand of the Church', have problems, too. After four hundred years in which they have been the militants of Catholicism they find themselves putting their heads, not into a hangman's noose any more, but a soft pillow.

When my grandfather was a boy in their charge the Jesuits were scarcely tolerated in polite society. When my father was a boy it was still considered slightly suspicious in England to have been one of their scholars. From the awakening eyes of a child to a time when some of the most eminent Jesuits of our own day were my contemporaries at school, I find myself not the devil's advocate but one who hopefully believes that, if the Jesuits can get on course again, the world will.

II

Alma Mater

'Old Alma Mater, here's to thee
Stonyhurst, old Stonyhurst.
Long life and all prosperity
Stonyhurst, old Stonyhurst
Though generations come and go,
Though boyhood doth to manhood grow
We aye the same we used to know
Stonyhurst, old Stonyhurst.'

WE sang the words of the school song, in my time, to the music of *The Red Flag*. The Socialists have no prior claim on the tune because their own wordy rubbish is based on a German song about a pine tree called *O Tannenbaum*. As boys in the prison, as it was then, of Stonyhurst, we were almost in open revolt when we were told by the Jesuits that we had to sing the words with a different noise. I don't know what the tune of the school song now is; or even if there is one. Stonyhurst today has changed so much that I scarcely recognise it, except in its stones. Let me tell you how it was when I first encountered the ancient academy; and how subsequently I was one of those rebels who protested loudest at the change in the school anthem.

Except that it was an institution with its footings deep in the past there was nothing to parallel Stonyhurst, apart from the savagery of its scholars, with Dr Arnold's Rugby, or any of the venerable places in what are called in England the public schools.

Stonyhurst was an anomaly. Fr Bernard Vaughan, the Jesuit who won himself an effigy in Madame Tussaud's waxworks by

storming at 'The Sins of Society' from the pulpit of the Church
at Farm Street in London's Mayfair was right when he coined
the words: 'Stonyhurst is what Eton was . . .' In Protestant
England, Stonyhurst was an enclave of the recusants, the sons of
the Old Faith.

The school had burgeoned, in the late eighteenth century, in
an isolation in which its scholars were barred from the old
universities, a self-contained world in which for many years the
Jesuit priests, fugitives from the Continent, wearing lay clothes,
dared call themselves no more than 'The Gentlemen of Stonyhurst'. The Jesuits remembered the persecutions of Elizabeth I
and James I. The Protestants could see 'no good reason why
Gunpowder Treason should ever be wholly forgot'. The Jesuits
were alleged to have fermented it.

In my generation, the Gentlemen of Stonyhurst had long
since boldly assumed the gown and the Roman collar. The
number of boys had grown to about four hundred. The buildings had swelled to house about five hundred.

When I arrived I knew little of Stonyhurst's history; or the
Jesuits' history. I was only overwhelmed by the size of the
place. Between Preston and Whalley in the train, an elder boy
pointed out to me the greened copper domes of the eagle towers
striking through the trees. When we dragged our trunks into the
Elizabethan quadrangle to be carried off to the dormitories, I felt
as small as a brick in the structure of the ancient walls.

Because I was overwhelmed by its draughty grandeur; the
long corridors, the wide oaken staircases, the vast refectory, the
glimpse of old libraries with ladders to get at the books, the hint
of museum mysteries beyond, I have no clear recollection of that
time apart from the minutiae of my own existence. I learnt that
my number at the school was 5; that the private place in my life
was a wood-lined cell in an iron-bed in a communal dormitory;
and that I had to put the clothes out of my trunk into three
drawers of a community chest in the centre of the room.

Those first nights at Stonyhurst were a sort of drunkenness,
with the euphoria of drunkenness and the hangover that goes

·with it. The patter of hundreds of boys passing through the building was the orchestration. The tune was the clatter of a huge oak-rattle, summoning us at six-fifty in the morning to wash and dress and get to mass in the school chapel. We paraded, under the watchful eyes of the Jesuits, in single file to the washing-place where, in cold water, we got through our desultory ablutions. We went to mass, and thence to breakfast in the refectory, in which the light was dimmed by blocks of armorial bearings in stained glass. I forget what we had for breakfast, but it was inadequate. Parents who had money to spare paid for 'extras'. The boys who had 'extras' got things like bacon and eggs. I wasn't one of them.

After breakfast we had private studies at our desks to learn verse, and complete exercises. During that period, class by class, we were sent to the common-place, as it was called, to perform natural functions. Even there we were overlooked by a Jesuit prefect.

From 9.30 to 11 we were in class. From 11 to 11.30 we exercised ourselves, in any way we knew, in a gravel playground enclosed in high iron railings. From 11.30 we were in class until a quarter to one o'clock when a bell called us for dinner.

The midday meal could have been good. All the meat was homegrown on the college farms, but through some witchcraft in the netherworld of the kitchens it was often uneatable. Our most hated meal was a hash we called 'gravy only' because the meat was inedible. It was followed by a blancmange, which I could never stomach, we called 'baby's bottom'. Truthfully, the Jesuits didn't eat any better than we did. They could never get round to organising good catering. Once, years later, when they were kindly giving me a dinner in the parlour at Stonyhurst, they produced a wild duck soup of which the memory makes me retch to this day.

After the midday meal we had the horror of compulsory ball games in wet Lancashire fields. I am sure that some liked it. I was among those, I think the majority, who didn't. There was class in the afternoon, except on half days, and tea in which we were offered what generations of boys had christened 'shouting cake' because the currants in the bread were so far apart that they had to shout to make the next one hear.

There was an interval after tea in the playrooms, followed by supper – we only had dry bread and cocoa for supper – and night prayers. The older boys then had studies from 9 to 10 p.m. before the rattle stirred us again at 6.50 the following morning.

Personally, the order of the day made me dreadfully tired. I never got enough sleep. But the life was not without its compensations. After that fearful place, Hodder, there were greater freedoms. There was a tuck shop where on a shilling a week pocket money, I could buy at my choice whipped cream walnuts and milk chocolate bars. In the summer the college bottled pop of different colours, with a glass ball in the neck, for tuppence a bottle. If you didn't want to drink it you only had to shake the bottle, and push down the marble, to shoot a satisfactory jet of fizzy stuff at any boy nearby.

Such was the day to day curriculum at Stonyhurst while I was there. In effect, we were kept behind the bars of the routine. The Jesuits looked over us, at every hour, like warders. We were forbidden to pass the iron railings of the playground; go beyond the playing fields, or the playrooms. We were not even allowed to wander in the libraries, the gardens or the old part of the mansion.

My uncle Lewis told me that, in his time, when he had broken bounds, he was told he would be thrashed if he did it again. He did, on principle; and celebrated it by carving his initials on the stone pillar where he jumped the wall. He did it so well that his carving shows in the stone to this day.

For that, he got twice nine. The phrase is meaningless to anyone who doesn't know the system of Jesuit scholastic discipline. Now, it is very nearly a thing of the past. In my time, my father's and uncle's time, and my grandfather's time, it ruled our lives.

It is a system of corporal punishment which, in afterthought, I believe to be one of the best systems ever devised. A boy who was guilty of a misdemeanour – not only at Stonyhurst but at

.all Jesuit colleges – was ordered by his master to get six, nine, a dozen, or twice nine of a strap called a ferula. The ferula was a thick bit of gutta percha which generations of boys used to say was made for the Jesuits by the Sisters of Mercy. It wasn't; the type that was used on us was made by the bootmakers at Stony-hurst. It was administered, with very rare exceptions, on the palms of the hand.

From its shape, narrow in the middle, thick at both ends, it had none of the cutting effect of a cane. While it was painful at the time, the soreness soon passed off if you pressed your hands into a hot water pipe. There was never any danger of lasting damage. Why I have always admired the system is that the sufferer need never lose his dignity. It even invited a boy to show what he was made of.

The way it worked was this. If a boy was ordered by one of his masters to get so many strokes, the master concerned had nothing more to do with the matter. The boy was on his honour to go to any one of the four Jesuit prefects of his choice, at four different times of the day, to secure punishment within the next twenty-four hours.

A boy who funked it risked the contempt of his fellows. A boy who faced it had to take it at a time when almost invariably the whole school was passing by the cadet corps armoury where punishment was administered. The cracks were laid on by a Jesuit who did not know what they were for. He asked the culprit the name of the master, the number of strokes, and wrote them impersonally in a punishment book. The test of character was to walk out afterwards, hands in pockets, and join the crowd of other boys as if nothing had happened. There was no future for cry-babies. Speaking for myself, I have had little difficulty in riding uncomfortable situations ever since.

It may have been a year or two in the strict curriculum before I knew enough to assess what Jesuit education was about. In the early years I conformed. In the latter ones, I was altogether ten years under Jesuit control, I was a rebel under a benign influence which I came to admire.

At that time I was too engrossed with what I could do with my own future to embrace a sense of history in the way of which Hilaire Belloc wrote: 'It adds to a man, giving him, as it were, a great memory of things – like a human memory, but stretched over a far longer space than that of one human life. It makes him, I do not say wise and great, but certainly in communion with wisdom and greatness'. History was still a classroom lesson for me. But in due course the Jesuits, in their inimitable way, pointed a finger into the living past.

One term, when we came back to Stonyhurst, we discovered that all of us were divided into four groups for the purpose, of course, of wretched competitive games. The groups were called 'St Omers', 'Shireburn', 'Weld', and 'Campion'.

I was in 'Weld'. I would have far preferred to have been in 'Campion', named after the proud Jesuit martyr of the Elizabethan persecutions who was a hero I could admire. But we had no choice. In 'Weld' I did my best to keep my distance from slimy leather balls on muddy fields. But the division of us all into groups with their strange names stirred my imagination. Why 'St Omers', 'Shireburn', 'Weld', and 'Campion'? The answer explains the uniqueness of Stonyhurst.

The College owed its origins to an English Jesuit of the Elizabethan period named Father Robert Persons. He was a controversial figure of whom it has been said that he would cheerfully have condoned the assassination of Good Queen Bess. He encouraged Philip II of Spain in the trust that the Great Armada would bring back Protestant England into the arms of the old Roman Faith. To foster his aims he founded, in 1593, in the Netherlands, a seminary for the sons of Catholic families denied the rights of the Church in their own country.

He was in many ways, wrongheaded, fanatical, and unwise; but he was a formidable man. Against all the odds he established an Academy, starting with a mere handful of English boys, which grew into an institution housing, in favourable times, up to two hundred. The boys who attended the school committed, under English law, high treason. On their way from England some were arrested, and even thrown into prison. But the recusants, the people who would not send their children to Protestant religious services, took the chance. The boys were almost all of the old families, the nobility and landed gentry, who had the money to smuggle them abroad. For one hundred and seventy years St Omers, its name pronounced phonetically by the exiled English schoolboys, flourished.

It flourished, in spite of the political upsets inside the mainland of Europe, in spite of the spies who infested it from England. Many of the boys were there under aliases, their parents either detained in prison at home, or else suffering exile abroad and proscription of their property.

But Father Persons had a gift, one in which the Jesuits excel to this day, of finding powerful patrons. King Philip II of Spain, in whose dominion St Omers then lay, gave the academy a pension of ten thousand crowns. The Infanta Isabella and the Archduke Albert, her husband, then governors of the Low Countries, supported the establishment. Father Persons even overcame a troubled phase in which it was suggested that the outlaws of St Omers, from their preparatory school at Watton three leagues away, were strategically placed to send signals to the English Fleet in the Channel. The magistracy stipulated that the Rector must never be an Englishman. But after three Spaniards had ventured the task of mastering English boys, an Englishman he always was; and, in 1760, the Academy obtained from Louis XV the coveted title of 'College Royal'.

With the passage of the generations the buildings at St Omers grew more and more stately. But there can scarcely have been a time when the Jesuits there felt truly secure. Titus Oates, the English spy whose mendacious plot is one of the nastiest episodes in English history, was a scholastic there when he was already a man. The catholicity of Maryland in Virginia, 'a colony overrun with Jesuit and secular priests' was sending over 'Popish youth to be educated'. An alumnus of St Omers, the Jesuit Father Emmanuel Lobb, put his finger into the fire of Protestantism by receiving into the Church the Duke of York, afterwards James II. Another Jesuit was chaplain to one of the last of the ill-fated Stuarts, an infant who became known to history as the Old Pretender.

Over more than a century and a half, there was no golden age of serenity. In 1635, when a siege was threatened in the interminable European wars, the boys had to be released from studies to work on the ramparts. In 1640, when some of them were out walking, they were surprised by bandits. In trying to escape, three were drowned. In the Civil Wars in England, the Academy almost died because so many of the scholars returned home to fight, and no doubt fall in the Royalist cause. Twice, in 1684 and 1725, the establishment was burnt down, and rebuilt again.

In the political pattern of his times, Louis XIV was outraged when he learnt that the boys of St Omers had thrown up their caps and cheered at an English victory over his forces. The Rector of the College had to make an abject apology. In 1688, the news of an heir to James II induced the College authorities to sound the bells and set bells ringing elsewhere in the town. The ringers were fined, and the College authorities had to make another apology. Plague and smallpox, familiar enemies of the period, interfered with the work of the school as surely as the regular approach of various warring armies. How the boys were educated, separated year in and year out from their families at home, largely unaware of what had happened to their own parents, always conscious of being in a foreign and ever threateningly hostile land, would be beyond explanation without an understanding of the indefatigable determination of the Jesuits, the stern paternalism, even the arrogance, which made them so many enemies and such loyal friends.

In the end it was inevitable that their meddlesome hands in the affairs of Christendom played the cards too high. In 1762, word reached the Superior at St Omers that the Parlement in Paris had decreed that the Jesuits were to be kicked out. Calling the boys together, he told them that the Jesuits were to be banished. At St Omers, they were to be replaced by new masters of the French

Parlement's choice. Predictably, the boys voted unanimously to migrate with their old ones to Bruges, then in the Austrian controlled Netherlands.

Together, masters and boys planned a pretty piece of undercover work. Sad though they must have been to leave what was the only real home which most of them had known, they were accustomed to the hardships of isolation, and warmed to the thrill of adventure. In the knowledge that the parochial authorities had no clue what was afoot, fifty-two of the smaller boys were sent to march it to the frontier. As a cover, the regular supply of provisions was sent to the house. Ninety boys were spirited away, and valuable articles of property, before the local authorities got wind of it.

Partly in canal boats and waggons, which had been made ready for the purpose, the whole school made the journey in two days to Bruges. A Jesuit chronicler of the time records that the move was made with satisfaction – that the parents in England, 'when informed of the strong measures which had been taken, expressed the highest approval – not one scholar being withdrawn in consequence'.

For the English Jesuits, the brief period at Bruges was one of the dimmest in their chequered history. There, the candle of the Society of Jesus all but expired. After the spacious and cultivated surroundings of St Omers, they moved into a derelict dwelling house where the first comers had to eat without knives and forks, and slept on straw palliases laid pell-mell on the floor. As others came, there was not even room for them in the shapeless ramshackle place. Boys had to be lodged in the inns of the town. But the Jesuits purchased another building, a great and noble structure, called in English 'The House of the Seven Towers', which had been judged fit to be the quarters of the King of France when he was campaigning in Flanders. Although the old stables had to be used as a study place, and the mice made havoc with the boys' books, there were soon over two hundred scholars, including the children of the newly-revived preparatory school, resuming the traditional curriculum. The Austrian Empress,

Maria Theresa, was graciously pleased to grant a charter to the new establishment. With renewed hope the Jesuits started to dig in again.

But the gloom of 1762, when they were banished from St Omers, was only the prelude to the dark ahead. The Bourbon sovereigns, jealous of the Jesuits' power at court, and elsewhere, had banded together to throw them out of their various realms. They demanded that the Pope should suppress the Society; and in 1773, Clement XIV did. The Austrian Government complied with the rest of Christendom.

Officially, with the Pope's seal to confirm it, the Jesuits were now secular priests. A commission seized the English College at Bruges, put their own seals on the doors, and introduced a Flemish priest as the new President of the establishment. A guard of soldiers stood over the place while avaricious officials searched it for the hidden treasure which the Jesuits were popularly supposed to have smuggled out of St Omers. Somehow, the disestablished Rector of the Jesuits managed to keep some form of order. It is even said that the regular course of studies was resumed. But the school was doomed.

The design of the Supreme Junta at Brussels, once they had got rid of the Jesuits, was to put English Dominicans from Bornhem in charge with a view to keeping the College alive, and looking after the lining of the pockets of the tradesmen in the town to whom it brought such good business. The notion may have seemed sound in committee, even though the Dominicans did not want the onerous responsibility; but the biggest mistake of the authorities was that they reckoned without the boys. No doubt, then as later, the boys, as boys do, had reservations about their masters. In different circumstances they might have smirked at the Jesuits' discomfiture. Not now. The Prefect who had hotted their leather breeches was their own father. The others were interlopers.

When the soldiery assembled one night to carry off the community of ex-Jesuits to confinement, the boys to a man rose in rebellion. They charged the muskets and bayonets of the soldiers posted at the doors. They wrecked the furniture and the windows. Some escaped to arouse townspeople shocked by the harshness of the authorities. The culprits were ordered to bed at the point of the bayonet; but the mutton-headed soldiers could not deal with them. The uproar and confusion kept the burghers of Bruges awake. In despair of silencing the rebels the officials had to yield to the ignominious expedient of bringing back some of the senior Jesuits from prison to restore order.

When the Jesuits were again incarcerated the boys took hold again. The Dominicans, when they arrived, could not control them. Lay teachers, brought in from madhouses and houses of correction, were even more at a loss. Parents came from England to reclaim their rebellious sons. Numbers dwindled until, accepting the inevitable, the authorities declared that the establishment was closed. The boys were fading away. Under Papal edict, the Jesuits, as an Order of the Church, no longer existed. The great venture, inaugurated at St Omers in 1593, might well have ended in 1773 at Bruges. It would certainly have ended if the Jesuits were lesser men than they are.

Looking into the bleak future, a future as bleak at that time as the flat Flemish landscape, the Fathers surmised that there was one place, even if they were disinherited and disowned, where there was a haven. This was their English College at Liège where, before the suppression, they had trained their scholastics in theology and philosophy. Liège was ruled, not by the civil authorities, but a Prince Bishop, who welcomed the late Rector of Bruges, as the first President, and bade him 'continue his work for the good of England'. A new Pope, Pius VI, gave his approval to the institution. Behind the political scene, the Jesuits, in lay clothes, continued inflexibly to obey the Society's constitution, their ordered mode of life and system of education.

For more than twenty years, the English students at the Liège Academy enjoyed 'a period of unbroken peace'. It flourished under the benevolent patronage of the Papal Nuncio, and the principal citizens of the town. The lovely countryside about seemed to promise a happier future for the Jesuits, a time when they might flourish again after the sour and stagnant years in Flanders' fields.

Decisively, the peace was shattered in 1794 by the approach of the French revolutionary armies. In all the two hundred years, and more, in which generations of boys of the Old Faith had been educated in exile, they and their masters had never relinquished their loyalty to England. They might have been less passionate about it if religious intolerance had not prevented them from being educated at home. As it was, encompassed by the enormities of the French Revolution, none wished to remain.

For a time it was mooted that Bavaria might be the next place of refuge for the school in exile. There were anxious deliberations. Then some brave soul, I wish I knew who he was, tentatively suggested: Why not go home to England? For two centuries it had been the country, their own, where the fugitives could have no hope of security. But times were different; and the pressures of unrest in Europe demanded fundamental change. Boys and masters decided to take the chance.

They had no clear notion where their new home in England was to be. Refugees in front of the advancing Revolutionaries, they started down the Meuse in boats which had been held ready for the emergency. They took what valuables they could move; but much had to be left behind because transport had been commandeered in Liège by a beaten Austrian army anxious to secure its own line of retreat.

At Rotterdam, the party put to sea, back to an England they had left behind so long before, an England which had almost forgotten them, on board the *John of Yarmouth* bound for Hull.

III

Quant Je Puis

DISCONSOLATE, weary, homesick and seasick, unutterably miserable and lonely, the exiles of Liège, masters and boys, made a landfall at Harwich. Some of the youngsters who had parents in England took their way across the grain of the country to their own homes. The residue, a few of them French, whose families were emigrés from their own land in the Revolution, stayed with the ship and their Jesuit masters. There was nowhere else for them to go.

But in the vacuum of flight there was a feather of hope. In an age without telephones, a post carried by horse, communications with the Continent winded by sail, news still travelled with astonishing speed. The predicament of the exiles had reached England. It is possible, even likely, that they had a promise of a safe retreat before they left France. They can scarcely have guessed what it was, or where it was. On their arrival, Thomas Weld of Lulworth, a landowner with extensive properties, a man who himself had been educated by the Jesuits during their brief sojourn at Bruges, was waiting to greet them. The Fathers Marmaduke Stone and Charles Wright – wearing like so many Jesuits splendid English names – were escorted to London where Mr Weld's eldest son attended to take them to the family seat in Dorset.

Mr Weld offered them as a haven his mansion of Stonyhurst Hall in the valley of the river Ribble in East Lancashire. In afterthought he wasn't giving away much. Stonyhurst was a property which had come into his possession through marriage.

Formerly it had been the seat of the Shireburns, a distinguished and wealthy family who had inherited the estate almost in direct descent from the time of the Norman Conquest. It took the Normans nearly fifty years to penetrate into that remote part of East Lancashire. In the late eighteenth century Stonyhurst was still as inaccessible as anywhere in England. The Welds, their main properties in the south, had never lived there. The mansion was a derelict, a place to which their agent made only occasional visits.

The two Jesuits, in the misguided hope that better times were coming when they could return to their beloved Liège, were hesitant. But, for the present, they had no choice. At least, Stonyhurst seemed to be a place which was sufficiently remote to enable them to pursue their mission of education free at last from political interference. In the event they were nearly wrong about that.

They accepted the gift horse without as much as looking it in the mouth. Word was sent to the main body of the exiles to make their way, any way they could, to a dot on the map in the wilds of Lancashire. They had no friends except their patron Thomas Weld. A few years later, in the desperate strife of the Napoleonic wars, a writer in the *British Critic* was to comment: 'The nation, struggling for its existence with the military despot of France, has little attention to spare for the proceedings of an obscure body of men, keeping an obscure school, in one of the rudest districts of the kingdom'. Men and boys, the Jesuits and their scholars were out on their own.

The fugitives on board the *John of Yarmouth* finally disembarked at Hull. There the little party, which had dwindled at every coastal port as boys flighted home like sparrows to their nests, hired a barge to tow them up the Ouse to Selby. Everywhere they travelled the boys, in their Liège uniform of grey coat, buckskin breeches and black stockings, the Jesuits in semi-ecclesiastical garb, were mistaken for foreigners. And to the English at that time all foreigners were Frenchmen. Just as at St Omers the English Jesuits and the English boys had been suspected of being spies so, in their native land, they were welcomed as French ones; deserving all they got, as one soap-box orator observed of them when they were on their way, for having killed their king.

From Selby they coached it to Leeds. Then they pushed on by horse-drawn canal boat to Skipton, twenty-three miles from their destination. From there, some of them boys barely in their teens, they footed it. The roads were little more than tracks. They were in strange country. It is told that, in Clitheroe towards the end of their journey, exhausted children in their strange uniforms collapsed on the doorsteps of the astonished townspeople. One of them told later that the soles of his shoes had parted from the upper leathers. He made the last few miles by fastening them like sandals with string.

Like all great adventures there is some doubt how it ended; or, more properly, how it all began. It is generally accepted that the first boy to make the distance to the bleak mansion of Stony-hurst was one George Lambert Clifford, the same who recorded the disintegration of his shoes. He was the eldest; and therefore one of the strongest. But even he must have been dismayed by what he found.

At the great iron gates he tolled the bell; but there was no answer because there was nobody there. After his weary walk through the empty fells of Lancashire he entered an Elizabethan quadrangle with a flight of broad half-circular steps leading up to the main entrance. He banged on the door, again and again. Getting no answer, except the dull echo of emptiness, he found a bit of iron railing. Using it as a crowbar, he forced an entrance. The door fell bodily inwards on its tired hinges, and he stepped into the Great Hall.

If he was alone, and the weight of evidence suggests that he was, Clifford was an intrepid young man. He ranged fearlessly about the old house, dismal and dark with the accumulated cobwebs of forty years. In parts the place was roofless, the structure altogether so dilapidated that much of it was unin-habitable. The wind whined through holes in the windows, the floors and the doors. It had the dank smell of the tomb, evoking bones that rattled and ghosts who couldn't sleep.

When the Shireburns were there Oliver Cromwell had called it 'the best half-house in England' because the grand plan of it had never been completed. Now it was a relic, a leftover of history, with nothing to commend it except memories of Papist plotters, Jacobites, and remnants of Plantagenet and Tudor history.

In the wilderness of house and landscape, boys and masters straggled in. Twelve boys who, says Clifford, were afterwards known as the Twelve Apostles, 'of whom I was nominated Peter', founded the new establishment. It is told that the first comers celebrated their dismal prospect on the night of their arrival with a 'Te Deum'. The boys knelt one behind the other. Swaying with exhaustion some of them dropped to sleep. To remind them of their duty a monitor gave the back marker a push. The whole line collapsed to the floor, one over another, like a pack of cards. If ever there was a school with no future, however glorious its past, it appeared to be this one.

Deep in their hearts the Jesuits believed that they were again in a temporary home; that they had to hold their children together until, in happier times, they could return to the Continent. A lesser body of men than they were, suppressed by the Pope, exiled from the mainland of Europe, might have thrown in their hand. That they didn't is one of the remarkable stories of this ever remarkable Society. In the early days, in the desolate ruin of Stonyhurst, time was when the Rector, calling himself President in the period when a Jesuit could scarcely reveal his identity, had to announce again and again to his community that there was only bread for dinner. The boys were reasonably fed. For themselves, he reminded them that their founder, St Ignatius, had always deemed it proper that his sons should suffer tribulation. But St Ignatius never intended that they should take it lying down. The Jesuits never did.

The motto of the family of Shireburn who had built Stonyhurst was 'Quant Je Puis', bastard French which means roughly,

'As much as I can'. The Jesuits adopted it as the motto of their new school. It is not clear whether the Shireburns, like the Welds, were all recusants. In the days they lived in, men in positions of power and influence had to be circumspect to keep their heads on their necks. But it is probable that, over the generations, they were more or less constant in the Old Faith. There is evidence that at least one Shireburn was educated by the Jesuits on the Continent; and that a Jesuit priest was chaplain to another. In the Civil war the Shireburns were Royalists; in the Jacobite Rebellion they were on the side of the Stuarts. Certainly Cromwell didn't trust them.

In August 1648, when as Lieutenant General he came into the country with his cavalry, he invited himself for the night into Stonyhurst Hall. There is a story, popular among generations of schoolboys, that to show his skill as an artilleryman he fired a roundshot between the twin towers of the house. It is nonsense because at that time the twin eagle towers with their cupolas did not exist. And, anyhow, the sort of crude cannon which Cromwell used were too inefficient for accurate marksmanship. It is even questionable whether his artillery train was with him when, on the eve of Preston, after picketing his cavalry in the park, he demanded hospitality at Stonyhurst Hall. But the word of mouth story which is probably correct is that, having imposed himself on his unwilling hosts, he wouldn't risk sleeping in a Papist-Royalist bed. He chose to take his rest, with his sword and pistols beside him, on a refectory table set in the centre of the Great Hall, guarded at its four corners by his Roundheads.

The memory survived him at Stonyhurst as a kind of joke. Subsequently, if a boy misbehaved in the refectory he was punished by being ordered to eat his meal alone on the very table on which Cromwell reputedly slept.

On the night of August 29th, 1794, when the outcasts of Liège first occupied Stonyhurst, it is questionable whether there was even a bed for any of them to lie on. Letters survive, from boys to their parents, of the discomfort they suffered crowded in outbuildings with flagstoned floors and tiny fires. The

Jesuits, usually such industrious letter writers, are strangely silent. They were probably too desperately busy.

Their predicament is not difficult to imagine. Their first need, after starting fires, must have been horses. It is likely that there were carriages and wagons, whatever their state of repair, in the coachyard of the old house; but horses were needed to pull them, to open communications and to bring in provisions from the outside world. I am sure that boys were sent out to hump wood for the bread ovens; that the fallow deer in the park became more culinary than decorative. Years later, 'rogging' for brook trout and salmon in the Hodder river became a Stonyhurst custom. I guess it began when the boys cornered the fish for a Friday meal.

The fugitives from Liège had carried some property with them, although much of it was lost loading one form of transport into another. In practical terms what was saved can scarcely have made life easier at Stonyhurst. It is said that one object was a sacred vessel, a monstrance, which was broken up and divided, bit by bit, among the boys. One boy lost his bit. The monstrance is at Stonyhurst now. On examination, it is complete enough for me to think that the story is questionable. But, at Stonyhurst, you never know. Only a few years ago, an elderly Jesuit discovered that, among the cutlery tossed about the house, was a collection of Georgian silver, marked with the monogram of the English College at Liège, which had never been recognised. When I was there recently the Rector showed me a miniature behind a miniature which seems to be the work of the Elizabethan master, Nicholas Hilliard. The Jesuits, with all their virtues, have always inclined to casualness about their treasures. Never worldly wealth, although they have often been suspected of it; but beautiful cultural things that have accidentally come their way. In their troubled history they have always had more urgent matters to think about.

Never more than in those early days at Stonyhurst. Where they had excelled in Europe was in winning the support of wealthy patrons. In the wilderness of East Lancashire, as it was then, their coming brought nothing but unremitting hostility. The local people viewed them with the ingrained suspicion of all countrymen towards strangers. The closed village communities, many consisting of little more than a bare half-dozen of illiterate incestuous families – there was a sprinkling of 'village idiots' in all of them – isolated the newcomers in a conspiracy of rumour. It travelled.

It was not long before the Jesuits were given to understand that they were unwelcome in England, alien and probably traitorous. It is fair to add that, in the fever of war, such things happen; and England, in the French wars, was stretched to the uttermost. It was true that the exiles had brought Walloon servants with them. There were Spaniards and French among the boys. It was undeniable that some of the masters, some of the boys, had adopted aliases to secure themselves in a dangerous world. But the claims made against them were demonstrably untrue.

A clergyman, one Collins of the Anglican Faith, who was also a magistrate of the little town of Whalley nearby Stonyhurst, summoned the exiles to appear before him with their foreign servants and their foreign scholars. Hectoring and bullying he called them spies using the coast to signal Bonaparte. He imposed the limitations of movement which are put upon internees. It was freely said in the public prints that 'a plot had been discovered, and that the College of Stonyhurst was to be suppressed'

In effect it was a hundred years before prejudice began to lose its voice. In 1795, the Jesuits had been summoned to take the oath of allegiance which they took willingly enough, although it occupied two days. In 1817, they felt it necessary to inform Lord Castlereagh 'that greater care cannot be shown than is done at Stonyhurst to impress on the infant minds entrusted to them both the moral and the religious obligation of loyalty, reverence to the Constitution, and dutiful submission to Law'. In 1829, the year of the Catholic Emancipation Act, the Jesuits, alarmed by the clause in which it was expressly forbidden to enrol new members in any religious order, sought an interview with Sir Robert Peel. He told them: 'You Jesuits, and not see through that! We must throw a tub to the whale, and this is it. But observe, no one can proceed against you except the Attorney-General – and I can undertake that he will have something better to do'.

In between, a meddlesome member of Parliament who began, as meddlesome members of Parliament do, by presenting himself as a champion of the Catholic cause, adopted Stonyhurst under his special protection. Sir John Coxe Hippisley decided to mould Catholicism in England upon the Gallican model; free that is in many aspects from Papal control. He proposed that a system of theology which he prescribed should be taught in its schools. Paradoxically, he was a Protestant. After being damned by the Jesuits he became their most bitter enemy. In 1818 he attended the Congress of Aix-la-Chapelle in the hope that he could break them. Of course, he failed.

It is all old hat now, not even much interesting to a new generation; but it is important to remember how hot tempers were a little more than a hundred years ago. But even at that time the Jesuits, in their loneliness, found champions. Looking into the past it is surprising that one of the first of them was the great old admiral of the Royal Navy, Lord St Vincent. I cannot understand what drew him to these men. It may well have been their courage and the discipline which, as a sailor, he so much admired. He wrote to a friend of his, then at Rome: 'My dear Madam, I have heard with indignation that Sir J. C. Hippisley is gone to the Congress at Aix-la-Chapelle, with the view to obtain the extinction of the Jesuits. I therefore beseech you to cause this letter to be laid before His Holiness the Pope, as a record of my opinion that we are not only obliged to that Order for the most useful discoveries of every description, but that they are now necessary for the education of Catholic youth throughout the civilised world.' The message was brought to the Pope. With others it combined to give Papal support, with the unofficial support of the English constitution, to the Jesuit establishment in England. It is remarkable that, at the close of 1809, when the Gentlemen of Stonyhurst appealed for benefactions for the advancement of science at the school, the Lord St Vincent was one of its first patrons with a contribution of five hundred guineas. He was joined by others like the Duke of Northumberland, the Marquis of Buckingham, the Lords Moira, Kennan, Southwell, Stourton, Petre, Arundel, Clifford and Arden. The Jesuits, after years in the wilderness, had again found their touch.

They had dug in at Stonyhurst with a fond eye on Liège – Liege as the boys called it in the English pronunciation of 'liege lord'. They never thought that they would stay in England, or be allowed to. But, from hopeless beginning, the Jesuits pressed on regardless. Against all the odds, in the conviction that it couldn't last, they set the place in order.

It is surprising that, within months, the number of boys rose from a mere twelve to fifty. A whole day's holiday celebrated the hundred. Within two months of their arrival, classes were organised again. A part of the Elizabethan garden, known as the 'Labyrinth', was ruthlessly uprooted to make a playground. 'The President', with a vandalism for which he had no regrets, boiled down the wealth of lead statuary in the gardens to re-roof the house. The hostility of the villagers, Papists by tradition, was overcome when they were provided with a chapel. They returned, as they had been under the Shireburns, as servants of the house.

Over the years renovation continued. Old buildings were demolished, new ones took their place. The College acquired new farmlands. The first gas works in a public institution in England was established at Stonyhurst. The first McAdamised road, under the patronage of the Jesuits, was built between the Hodder river and the village of Hurst Green. In 1894, when all thought of Liège had been forgotten, Stonyhurst celebrated its centenary on English soil.*

* The substance of this historical account, although not the comment, is derived from the *Centenary Record of Stonyhurst College* (1894) by Father John Gerard, S.J. I have also borrowed from a latter scholar, Father Hubert Chadwick, S.J., who has corrected some of Gerard's findings.

By that time the College had grown into one of the most astonishing establishments in the land. Like a mediaeval monastery, it was almost self-contained. The buildings, added to over the years, were so vast that they accommodated in comfort perhaps five hundred people, boys and men. The house had its own power supply and its own farms. It had carpenters' shops, bootmakers' and tailors' shops, its own abattoir and market gardens. There was even a brewery where weak beer was made for the boys, stuff known in my father's time as 'swipes'. With a dash of Jesuit showmanship, Stonyhurst also instituted what became in its time one of the most famed astronomical observatories in the world.

It was a long haul from the days when, at the tail of the eighteenth century, the Gentlemen from the English Academy at Liège advertised in the old *Catholic Directory: 'The annual pension is 40 guineas, but for children under twelve only 37 guineas will be required. Scholars in Rhetoric and Philosophy pay 45 guineas, on account of extraordinary expenses and some particular indulgences. The Sunday or holy-day dress is uniform, and consists of a plain coat of superfine blue cloth, with yellow buttons, red cloth or Kersemere waistcoats. The use of silk is not permitted. The scholars are taught Latin, Greek, and all the branches of classical education, sacred and profane History, Geography, Arithmetic, and when sufficiently advanced, Algebra and Geometry, with all the other parts of the Mathematics, in the respective classes. Particular care is taken that they read well, and write a good hand, and that they speak and write French with accuracy. All the pensioners live and sup with their masters, and have the same table. No distinctions are allowed in diet or clothing. As long experience has convinced the directors that a profusion of pocket-money is very prejudicial, not only to good order, but even to study and application, they request that parents will not be forward in indulging their children in more than a guinea at most per annum; and this must indespensably be placed in the hands of one of their masters for their occasional little wants. The Vacation begins on the 15th of August and ends on the 15th September. Absence from school at no other time will be permitted. Finally, the College is a large building, capable of lodging an hundred and fifty persons conveniently. The garden and court adjoining, where the young gentlemen play, are very airy and spacious; the situation very pleasant and healthy.'*

From its earliest days it was a stern school; so severely classical that senior boys were required 'to translate from one language into another; not only from Greek, Latin and French into English, but from an English version of an author back into the original tongue, from Greek into Latin, from Latin into French'. There were playtimes in which the boys were only allowed to converse in French. To enforce it a system called the *Signum* was devised. Any boy found talking English at a forbidden time was ticketed. He could only get rid of the ticket by passing it on to another boy who offended in like manner. And so it went on until the final offender suffered punishment for all. A Jesuit Prefect of Studies at the time lamented 'the growing habit of reading modern poetry, attributing to this pernicious practice the alarming increase of false quantities'.

The classical rule was so strong that it is recorded that the Jesuits tried to change the memorable English name of Stonyhurst to 'Saxosylva', 'Collegium Saxosylvanum', or 'Saxosylvenvense'. Over their dead bodies I applaud their failure; although I can understand that, in the hostility in which they lived, they were tempted to introduce an unworthy name in this England. In fairness, when the centenary of Stonyhurst was celebrated in 1894 none of the contemporary Jesuits would have contemplated such a change. The Englishry of the place was by then firmly rooted.

It is pleasant to recall that one of the earliest pupils at Stonyhurst was Charles Waterton, the eccentric Yorkshire squire whose 'Wanderings in South America' is a minor classic; and who, incidentally, invented the modern pastime of birdwatching. At school, Waterton broke all the rules. 'By a mutual understanding,' he wrote in his autobiography, 'I was considered rat-catcher to the establishment, and also fox-taker, fourmart-killer, and cross-bow charger, at the time when the young rooks were fledged. Moreover, I fulfilled the duties of organ-blower and football maker, with entire satisfaction to the public'.

In after years, Waterton performed the astounding feat of climbing to the top of the Dome of St Peter's in Rome – I still cannot understand how he had the agility to achieve it – and placed his gloves on top. When the Pope, not unnaturally, was shocked Waterton climbed up the following night, nobody else could get there, and took his gloves down again. He had perpetrated much the same sort of outrageous things at Stony-hurst. In his old age he had become a beloved son of the school and still wore the uniform of his boyhood. In his eighties one of his party tricks was to wrap his leg round his neck and bite his big toe. But, in retrospect, I believe that the old eccentric gave Stonyhurst its now essentially English character. He loved it dearly; and, when he died, he left to the school the remarkable collection of his preserved tropical birds and natural history exhibits. It is a pity that, quite lately, Stonyhurst has sent them on permanent loan elsewhere. In my day they were one of the features of the old house.

It was men like Waterton who brought home to the English Jesuits, based so long on the Continent, that their place was England. But, for two hundred years and more, persecuted and distrusted, England seemed the last place on earth to be. Only slowly the Jesuits realised that it was the best place to be. Understandably, because nothing had gone their way for a hundred years, they were slow to settle down, reluctant to change a curriculum of education they had developed during three hundred years.

It was the system which had disciplined the sons of the nobility in all the old courts of Christendom throughout generations when the Jesuits had cultivated Europe by the throat. Severe, but responsible, it was in their opinion proven.

My great-grandfather, a scholar who kept his daily diary in Hellenic Greek, was in no doubt of it. On September 20, 1862 he wrote to his homesick son at Stonyhurst: 'What then but out of love for you prompted us to send you where you are now?

Bear this pain because we know that your going is for your good here and hereafter. Remember that you will have not only a good secular education but that your religious instruction will be completed. Your superiors are kind and careful of you. You have everything provided for you; it rests only with you to be attentive, obedient and diligent. Remember what I once said to you; "Beware of stumbling on the threshold of life". Try for my sake, for your mama's sake, for your own, to bend yourself, my son, to the loving yoke that is upon you . . .' There is much more of the letter in the moral middleclass Victorian manner. My great-grandfather, who seems otherwise to have been a sweet man, was convinced in his generation that it was the privilege of small boys to be put through the hoop. The Jesuits shared his opinion.

In example of the closed world in which he had confined his son, I treasure another letter of his – my grandfather copied all the pater's letters in copperplate into a notebook – which begins: 'I should send you a paper now and then but I think you would not be allowed to have it. There are so many objection-able things published in journals now. You never received the number of Dickens's *Pickwick Papers* that I sent you for the reason I suppose that your superiors think it objectional reading. If it did not reach Stonyhurst the Post Office must be in fault. But for the latter supposition it would not be worth while to ask about it. I will try to get the *Universal Register*,* and send it to you instead. Give my affectionate compliments to your President and believe me your affectionate Papa.'

Sixty years on my father wrote to me at Stonyhurst: 'Have you read *Pickwick Papers* yet? I know that you have glanced at it here and there. But it is important that you know it from end to end.' In my day Dickens passed the censor; but times hadn't changed all that much. Boys on holy days were no longer required to wear a tail-coat of blue cloth, buckskin breeches and red waistcoat, but the bigger ones still dressed in a morning coat. We had holidays at home, four weeks at Christmas, three at

* Now the London *Times*.

Easter, about seven weeks in the summer. My father considered that, unlike him and his father, we were mollycoddled. But in the words of the school song, Stonyhurst, even in my time, was 'aye the same we used to know'. Because so much of the Jesuit system of education is lost now, it is worth recording how for hundreds of years it worked; worked for better or for worse, according to your persuasion, and made its mark on history.

Stonyhurst was just one of the Jesuit Academies in Europe, just one of the missions of the Order scattered throughout the world. In global terms it can still be called a relatively unimportant institution in the hierarchy of the Jesuit Curia in Rome. But knowing Stonyhurst, you start to know the Jesuits. The importance of Stonyhurst, the difference which divides it from other great English public schools, is that it derived from a form of education, invented in isolation in three different academies on the Continent, largely by Englishmen for exiled English boys. In its methods it followed the example of Jesuit teaching in what at one time made a count of a thousand establishments throughout Europe. But it preserved a special identity – a European Common Market attitude one might call it today – which survived and flourished in, of all places, the terrain of the Lancashire witches.

Call Stonyhurst just one piece in the jigsaw of the Jesuit story. The total picture is the more rewarding after the telling of the shape of this one bit.

IV

Ascensio Scholarum

'Syntax is empty, Poetry is empty, Rhetoric is empty.'

IT was a world without women, unless you included the hags. The hags were what we called the College servants, many of them no doubt desirable young women from the local village whom we were discouraged, probably deliberately, from regarding as females at all. The Chief Hag, an outsider, was the College matron. For a large part of my schooldays she was the terror of my life, a creature whose familiars were Black Jack, an enema and a bowl of soapy water. With her broomstick manner, her rooty hands, her cruel starched bonnet and apron, I reckoned as a boy that she had no femininity at all.

I am prejudiced because, when I went down with pneumonia in my early teens, before there were any drugs to beat it, the hag did her sadistic best to see me off. The Jesuits conferred on me the last rite of the Catholic Church, the Sacrament of Extreme Unction. Years later I recollect laughing to myself when the dear old priest who had administered it told, in unctuous detail in the boys' chapel at Stonyhurst, how I was for the dark. He thought I was long since dead.

If, after the passage of the years, I have a criticism of Jesuit education as I knew it, it is of a satiety of spirituality and the unnatural absence of a tender female touch. Understandably in their celibate lives, although not unforgivably, they eyed all women in the context of the Biblical Eve. They also devoted an unconscionable amount of time getting us ready for the next world before we were even ready for this one. I believed

47

enthusiastically that I was for this world; and early in years I was sincerely doubtful of a packaged deal in the next. It is proper to add that most of my contemporaries seemed, to use a boss word of the confessional, to be in no 'difficulty'. Perhaps, like Cassius, I thought too much. More likely I was so much a Jesuit child that I could not bring myself to conform without conviction.

It is a fallacy that the Jesuits stamp children into an assembly line pattern: on the contrary, they have promoted more formidable, perverse and prickly men – for a throwaway, Cardinal Richelieu – than the offspring of any other system of education. Hanging on their wings, I learnt from them in my way to question, and to reflect.

It is another popular delusion that the Jesuits are all diabolically clever. They are not. They have as many ordinary men in their number as the House of Commons, or Congress. I remember one of them telling us in a history class how the coffin of the odious Henry VIII burst open and dribbled pus which was licked up by a mongrel dog on the flagstones of the chapel of the monastery at Sion. When I raised my hand and suggested that if a saint had been in the coffin, after being charioted six weeks in a poorly made lead box, the result would have been the same, I was ordered to get a dozen for insolence. In fairness the idiot in charge of the class was not typical. The best Jesuits are the best and most sophisticated people I have had the fortune to meet in my life. But it is important to underline that a black gown with a pair of false sleeves does not confer wisdom much more than the black coat and pin-striped trousers of a politiican.

But a genius invests the Society as a whole. Over the years at Stonyhurst I came to admire the Jesuits, whatever I may have thought of individuals. I found lifelong friends among them. And I am grateful now for the physical discipline they inculcated, the intellectual stimulus they injected into my own mind. I may have been an odd man out; but I was in. I suppose it had something to do with my genes.

My great-grandfather was convinced as a historian, a geographer and a classicist, that the touch of the Jesuits was the key to life hereafter and civilisation here on earth. My grandfather, a shatteringly pious man who produced eleven children, and elected throughout his life to wear a semi-ecclesiastical suit without collar or tie, brought up his family in a strictly Stonyhurst tradition. He even administered corporal punishment to his brood at fixed hours, in the Stonyhurst way, when his temper had cooled. My father, a Pickwickian figure, was altogether a more easy-going person. Owing his loyalty to Catholicism his world, as a playwright and journalist, was more largely in the West End theatres, Fleet Street, the Savage Club and the Coal Hole of the Savoy. But he believed that I should go through the Jesuit hoop, as he had. He never tired of telling me how much tougher it was in his day.

It was tough enough in mine. An Elizabethan schoolboy would not have been surprised by the jargon we used, or the order of our days. It was the boast of the English Jesuits that Stonyhurst was founded in the tradition of their sixteenth century academy.

At St Omers there was a line in the boys' playground indicating the areas which could be used by senior and junior scholars. So at Stonyhurst we were divided according to age into the Higher Line and the Lower Line. At St Omers classes were designated, not by form numbers but, starting at the top, with the beautiful names of Rhetoric, Poetry, Syntax, Grammar, Rudiments, Figures, or Little Figures. At Stonyhurst the rule prevailed. At St Omers the boys who in troubled times couldn't travel to their own homes went for holidays to a villa within a short walk of the school. It was in a village named Blandyke (Blandecques today). At Stonyhurst all monthly holidays were thereafter known as 'Blandykes'. There were other similarities.

In exile the English boys played a primitive style of cricket. Up to my own time, with a stone for a wicket and a stick for a bat, we still played it. We called it pot-stick. In the playground there were two walls, mounted at the ends with Georgian finials, designed for a simple form of fives. Up to a little before my own time, Stonyhurst played its own peculiar form of football, a game regardless of the number of players on each side, in which, with a national flag at the goal ends, the teams were defined as 'The English' and 'The French'. Such were the leftovers of history.

There were no entrance examinations for new boys. The Jesuits, to quote Father Bernard Basset, 'accepted any boy at any age and gave their full attention to the task of fashioning him into a social, balanced and well read Christian'. The emphasis in our education was on the classics and the humanities. We took the then regular Oxford and Cambridge examinations, the Lower and Higher certificates. There was a science laboratory, stuck somewhere over the gymnasium where a lay master – I think I am right in saying that he was then the only non-Catholic on the staff – taught what it is that makes litmus paper turn blue; or is it black? No boy of any ability in my time at Stonyhurst was allowed to learn the answer. The Prefect of Studies ordered our ascension through the school. Those who didn't shine were relegated to the study of science.* The rest of us polished our haloes in the grandeur that was Rome and the glory that was Greece. There was even a special class for the muddied oafs and flannelled fools who played for the school's first XI and first XV; chaps who were too muscular for the Lower Line, and too dim to rise to the dizzy heights of Syntax, Poetry, and Rhetoric. The class was called Higher Line Grammar.

In theory the Jesuit system was a seven-year course. At St Omers, there's no getting away from St Omers, the custom was born that at the end of each scholastic year each 'school' announced to the lower one: 'Rhetoric is empty', 'Poetry is empty', and so on; and with their master all the boys, leaving behind one may presume only the 'Higher Line Grammar' types, moved up one. The tradition survived at Stonyhurst. At the beginning of each school year the *Ascensio Scholarum* was posted on the notice boards.

* It was an uncharacteristic phase. Throughout the centuries Jesuits of brilliant attainment have cultivated the sciences. It just happened that, in my generation at Stonyhurst, the Prefect of Studies was a dedicated classicist.

ASCENSIO SCHOLARUM

In its barest terms Stonyhurst was a secluded Spartan place, in an unwelcoming climate, which might have disconcerted any child. The Jesuits hovered over our daily activities, hour by hour, with hawklike watchfulness. Even when we went to the lavatory, had our weekly bath, or got our hair cut, a Jesuit was on guard. Single filing through the long corridors, queueing at the tuckshop, keeping our place on the right side of the playground, there was a Jesuit with flowing wings on duty. It was a part of the jargon of the school. Continental origin again, that we referred to most of the rooms in the College as 'a place'. Thus we talked of the shoe-place, the washing-place, the common-place (the lavatories) and the study-place. Wherever we were, we were overlooked.

Separated in four playrooms we were overseered by four masters. At Stonyhurst there was no 'fagging'; and it was all the better for that. There was a committee of head boys; but, mercifully, their powers were strictly limited. Schoolmasters, whether they wear Roman collars or bow ties, are bad pickers of future leaders of men. In my own time, my masters, like so many schoolmasters 'men amongst boys, boys amongst men', picked too many Steerforths by half. But the Jesuits kept ours under control. The discipline was theirs. It was enough for one of the four Jesuit Prefects to say quietly 'get a dozen' to keep the place running smoothly.

Telling of my boyhood, it is a lump of history that what I recollect of Stonyhurst sent another one who couldn't recollect to prison. The trial of the man known as the Tichborne Claimant, the longest and most famous case in English legal history, rested largely on his memories of his schooldays at the College. If he was indeed Sir Roger Tichborne, Bt., as he claimed – his mother had identified him as her son – he was heir to vast family estates. In cross-examination the most damaging evidence against him was how little he remembered of his old school. I am a little on his side. He came to Stonyhurst in his late teens with not much English – he had been educated heretofore in France – and, at best, he wasn't very bright. The Jesuits bust him. He couldn't remember the system, the buildings and the jargon of the school. He couldn't recall in any detail three years which, in mine, I could never forget. It is the most powerful argument against the Claimant, whose coffin was labelled 'Sir Roger Tichborne, Bt.', that he remembered so little of what should have been the most impressionable years of his life. If he was who he said he was, he must have been an incredible fool. In fairness, in the English nobility such people are not unusual.

Under the disciplines in which we lived it was inevitable that there was an undertone of mutiny. Wrongly, we were not even allowed to wander in the museum, the library, the old gardens, or the Elizabethan quadrangle. We were moved, by bell, book and candle, every session of the day. My father told me that in his time it was customary for two boys who had had a quarrel to raise their hands at morning studies and request permission to settle the matter in the gymnasium. In mine I went it alone; and I usually lost. In mine I was more conscious of the undercurrent of adolescent rebellion which was endemic in the sort of society in which we lived. The older boys, bursting with energy and new found masculinity, were again and again on the point of bursting their tops. At intervals they challenged 'The Crows', as generations of boys had called the Jesuits, to control them. Of course, 'The Crows' won.

I recollect sitting at my desk, with my name and year engraved in brass next to the ink bottle, in the huge study-place when the Rector climbed the rostrum and, thin-lipped, announced to us that 'Christopher Devlin is now being birched'. Devlin had challenged the establishment in some trifling way. But it was a challenge; and the Jesuits, properly, judged it a time to teach us all a lesson. I have no hesitation, although I have left out so many, in mentioning Christopher's name. In due course he himself became a distinguished Jesuit; and had as his brothers, Lord Devlin, the lawyer, and William Devlin, the actor. I admired Christopher prodigiously because, after his punishment, he ostentatiously appeared in the study-place carrying a cushion on which to rest his sore bottom. It was the only occasion, so far as

I know, on which the Jesuits, a little rattled, hit a boy's backside. Normally that was something they were reluctant to do.

There were occasions when we were all 'kept in'. I attributed the trouble largely to 'the dagoes' which was the name we had for the boys of Spanish and Latin American extraction who came to the school from abroad. They were more excitable, in ways more mature, than we were. I remember one who blinded my eyes, at the end of term, by appearing in a grey Homburg hat, carrying a silver mounted ebony cane. Predictably he disappeared, after he left school, into the wilderness of a gigolo world in the South of France. Looking at him, so much more grown up than I was, I was mixed with admiration and contempt. At that time I couldn't be sure who were my heroes and who my villains. I wasn't at all sure about myself. When I nearly kicked the bucket I heard the Hag saying that I was highly-strung. I was ashamed of the verdict. It seemed that I wasn't like ordinary boys.

For one summer term I was absent from Stonyhurst. It was decided after my illness that I should stay at home to recuperate. I enjoyed the halcyon days of my life. By the sea I fished, I swam, I hunted; and flourished in strength and confidence. I learnt the ways of the country from, improbably, the manager of the Gaiety Theatre at Hastings who, besides teaching me how to find plovers' nests and catch dormice, introduced me to the joys of the living stage. When I returned to Stonyhurst, I was a different person.

Without regret I heard that the Hag was dead; or, anyhow, gone with the wind. The old Rector of the school had served his term of office. I was glad about that as well. He had castigated me, fairly, for stealing a pound from my father. I had pretended that a postal order that my father had sent me for travelling expenses had not arrived. I was ashamed of what I had done; and more ashamed that the Rector should know that I had done it. Now that he was gone I felt that I was back again with a clean sheet. I was blessed, too, on my return with a much beloved pedagogue, who boosted my own morale. At the end of my first term with him I was first in class. I was made Roman Imperator, another Jesuit thing for which we were awarded a barbaric medal with a purple ribbon which we wore on Sundays in the lapel of our black suits. A year later I was promoted to the Higher Line.

From that time Stonyhurst was altogether a happy place for me; and I savoured the sweets of Jesuit education. As kids we were disciplined as the untamed animals we were. As adolescents the Jesuits introduced us, by little steps, to a cultivated world. The rule was still strict; but we were encouraged to think of ourselves as individuals, and the Jesuits brought out our own bents and personalities. They were always watching amongst us for potential recruits to the Order. But although they must early have decided that I would never be one of their number they made it my pleasure to be one with them.

Without much experience of other schools I fancy that the social structure of Stonyhurst was unique. The J's, forty or fifty of them in my time, occupied an area of the building known as the West Wing. It was traditional that, in the eleven o'clock morning break, we could visit any one of them. They welcomed us, sometimes dozens of us, into their simple rooms, equipped with an iron bed, a prie-dieu and a crucifix, a desk loaded with books and an ashtray heavy with stubbed-out cigarette ends. They saw us, too, with fatherly interest, alone. Every boy, whatever his station in the school, had the right to queue up, whenever he felt like it, for a talk with the Rector. It was usually to ask the great man to sign a bill for running shoes, blazers, or pocket money. Boys flocked into the West Wing for the company of their masters, or just for fun. It was one way in which the Jesuits learnt to know us. They had others.

One of the most civilised things they cultivated was the classical peripatetic. A master, who was informed on a specialised subject, would take about a dozen of us who were interested on a talking walk. With favoured boys hanging on his wings, some dear old Jesuit expatiated on what he knew. It might be an expedition in which we were shown birds' nests, the splendid architecture of Stonyhurst, the manuscripts in the famous library; or how the world went round in the observatory in the garden.

There were also 'Good Days', dating back inevitably to the past. If we sang in the choir, played in the cadet corps' band, or made any special contribution to the society of the school, it was celebrated in the Lancashire vernacular as a 'do'. We were guided out by a master, no doubt as hungry as we were, to stuff ourselves with tea-cakes, jellies and buns. It was theoretically the only time we saw the outside world.

But as we grew bigger and subtler some of us 'bunked'. It was a psychological need sometimes to escape the atmosphere of the closed school. I fancy that the Jesuits knew all about it. They must have winked an eye at what we were up to, because we weren't so cunning that we couldn't easily have been caught. The ploy was to climb the railings in the playground, drop down into the wood outside, and make for the river Ribble in the valley. There we crossed the river in a rowboat for an enormous tea in what we regarded as no-man's land. All I ever knew of the extent to which the Jesuits were aware of our mischief was that one day I was ordered to get twice-nine from the First Prefect who didn't even tell me what I was suffering for. But I could read the wink in his eye. I opted to take punishment from him personally. He laid on the strokes very gently.

Almost the worst crime we could commit, before it became fashionable to condemn it, was smoking. In this matter the Jesuits were strangely inconsistent. Although to bunk and smoke in the ordinary way was a corporal offence, there were times, feast days and what-have-you, when the Head Boy approached the Rector for permission to smoke. It was sometimes granted. The result was that, from eight to nine in the evening in the playrooms, the place was a fog. Where the cigarettes came from I haven't the faintest recollection. The Jesuits, strict as they were in most matters, smoked themselves. They also enjoyed drinking. We were brought up on bad beer and, on party occasions, a glass of negus, to respect the cup that cheers as a civilised custom.

What, for my part, we had too much of was prayer. I some-times wonder whether I would be a better churchgoer now if I had not had such a bellyful of it at Stonyhurst. Every morning at school we attended mass and prayers, grace before and after meals, evening prayers in the chapel with regular hymn services thrown in. In addition there was Benediction twice a week; and, on Feast Days, High Mass. In the Christmas term there were three days of Retreat in which we were bashed with spiritual exercises from morning to night; forbidden to speak together, or read anything except sickeningly pious books. I dreaded Easter when, unlike other schools, we were not sent home. We had to live through Holy Week in which, on top of the normal services from Palm Sunday to Easter Sunday, we had the chant of Tenebrae for three days. Much of it was beautiful. The Jesuits are masters of liturgy. The young boys, piping trebles, sang like thrushes. I liked listening to the basses sounding the lovely Latin words of the movement of the stone from the Tomb: 'volventes, volventes'. I loved the drama of the service, the fat beeswax candles, the glorious vestments of the celebrants, the full-throated music of the organ, and the discipline of the acolytes in their cherry-pink cassocks and laced surplices. But I couldn't pray.

In hope for me the Jesuits at one point put me in charge of the Lady Altar, the statue of the Madonna which was a centre of Stonyhurst life. My job was to clean the candelabra, see to the flowers, and oil the woodwork. I loved the responsibility because what went with it was a cell, containing the impedimenta of the altar, to which I could retreat. I kept white mice, which were subsequently assassinated by the rats who swarmed through the old building, in a cage on top of a cupboard. I played about with blowlamps. And, to my discredit, I used it as a hidey-hole to duck mass, snatching forty winks on the altar cushions in a corner. Of course I was ultimately caught. I was not punished for it; but I suspect that it was then that the Jesuits agreed that I was not of their spiritual world. If they did, they never let on.

I had an impression in my later years that the rule of the place was not exerted as firmly as it used to be. The Jesuits, perambulating shoulder to shoulder at night in earnest private conversation in the school corridors, exercising in the Dark Walk, an Elizabethan avenue of yews in the gardens, seemed gentler and more fallible. With the selfishness of youth I often distracted one of the J's from his breviary to talk about my small affairs. I was tolerated with a patience and kindliness which, I suppose, is the difference between a career schoolmaster and a spiritual one.

It became increasingly easy, with official permission, to avoid the compulsory competitive games which I detested. I liked bowling at the nets at cricket because, being left-handed and tall, I was not bad at it. I hated the matches because, bespectacled and shortsighted, I couldn't time bat and ball. I preferred to slip away, when my side was batting, to dig for pignuts and tickle brook trout in the beck behind the pavilion. I loathed football and opted, whenever I could, for cross-country runs because it was always possible, in open country, to slip away for a forbidden cigarette.

And there were joys which still stay with me. None greater than the summer ones, when we were taken to the bathing-place on the river Hodder. It was a deep salmon pool with a funnel of white water at its head which generations of boys had used as a chute. I suppose that, rising in the Lancashire fells, it must have been very chilly; but we were of an age when we didn't notice it. On the banks of the river there was a row of stone bathing-huts put up in Victorian times when nakedness, even amongst a party of boys, was unthinkable. We wore little drawers supplied by the College. But at some period, I think in my father's time, the boys had torn the wooden doors off the huts and used them as surf boards in the rapids. Above the bathing-place there was a row of foot-stones across the shallows of the river called 'The Philosophers' Stones'. It was another watermark of Stonyhurst history. The stones had been laid there by men of undergraduate age who stayed on at Stonyhurst for university teaching before Papists were admitted to Oxbridge. In fact, the Philosophers survived at Stonyhurst, with heavy moustaches to confirm their new found masculinity, until shortly before my own time; although long earlier, the way had been open to them to Oxford and Cambridge. I imagine that the Jesuits, in their Lancashire retreat, could not quite bring themselves to believe it.

There was recreation for me, too, on the miniature rifle range. At that time I never suspected that in after years I should write books on sporting arms. But I got the taste when, by kind permission of my friend the Regimental Sergeant Major of the Officers' Training Corps, as it was called then, I was allowed to count out .22 ammunition for the range. The O.T.C. was compulsory, two parades a week. As Juniors we were uniformed in a blue suit, a sort of Norfolk jacket with a slouch hat derived from the Boer War period. We were equipped, in our small teens, with cavalry carbines. On promotion to the senior corps, we changed to khaki and short Lee-Enfields. I learnt the improbabilities of setting Fox's puttees left and right, so that they didn't gape; and was introduced to army training in the ridiculous period in which asses on the staff of the War Office determined that officers, and cadets who were expected to become officers, wore a ridiculous form of khaki plus fours. At first I hated the O.T.C. Latterly, thanks to an affectionate C.O., not a Jesuit, I enjoyed the discipline of arms' drill. I even became a fair shot on the rifle range.

Unholy son though I was, Stonyhurst won my heart. I acquired the tricks of the place, the way to make marbles out of the clay which lined the ambulacrum, the vast indoor playground, big enough to play a football match, which was surrounded by the rifle range, the indoor swimming bath, the carpenters' shop, the cobblers' shop, and the common-place. My masters sometimes took me to 'Maggies'. Maggie was a dear old thing shaped like a cottage loaf who occupied a College lodge and specialised in bread buns and strawberry jam. I was invited to be the carver in the Refectory for a table of fourteen boys. It gave me a little power and the certainty of shaving off the most tasty bits for myself. I was sometimes even given permission to follow the otterhounds; to go to Bolton's, the Stonyhurst Post Office, of which a contemporary of mine wrote the doggerel:

> *To Bolton's we go every day*
> *If we get leave that is to say*
> *To buy their vegetables so nice*
> *Either Post Toasties or Puffed Rice.*

He is now a Jesuit, and the man who has written what is perhaps the definitive history of the English Jesuits. As I knew him he was a boy with a sure vocation for the priesthood who teased his masters by threatening to become a Benedictine. I was never in danger of joining him in any of the venerable Orders of the Church. And yet the Jesuits pointed the way to my own subsequent career.

From early boyhood, I showed a certain gift for elocution and amateur acting. I was a show-off, and I had a clear voice. At Stonyhurst I won a prize in an elocution competition by reciting, in a treble trill, Edgar Allen Poe's onomatopœic verse *The Bells*. The performance, how I would hate to hear it now, was thought so good that they wouldn't give a prize to the boy in the senior class above me.

My gift, such as it was, went to the roots of Jesuit teaching. From way back in the sixteenth century theatricals had been a keystone of their form of education. Plays in Greek, Latin and French, with splendid scenery and candlelights, had illumined their 'Good Days' in the academies on the Continent. The memory was as green at Stonyhurst as it was then. Every summer we had 'Academies' in which the boys played classical plays. Every 'Blandyke' we had concerts in which we sang songs and acted out scenes from music hall sketches. The school orchestra thumped out *Light Cavalry* and excerpts from the D'Oyly Carte operas.

After the Church and the Boys' Chapel, the most important room in the house was the Academy Room. It was furnished with a beautifully plastered ceiling, a carved oak proscenium arch with red velvet curtains, and the walls were lined with the colours of regiments of long ago. It was fitted with full stage lighting equipment; there was a Green Room, used as a classroom on non-theatrical occasions; and, underneath the benches in the auditorium, a fascinating scenery store. I spent some of my happiest hours in the Academy Room. While I was always keen for the opportunities when I could appear on stage I was content enough to play with the lights, shift the scenery and make-up the other actors. I had acquired from Gamages a japanned tin make-up box loaded with Leichner's greasepaint. I still have it, without the greasepaints. Latterly I have found it ideal for storing fishing tackle.

As far back as I can remember I would tell anyone, who was interested enough to enquire what I hoped to be in after life, that I was going to be a dramatist like my father. I was wrong about that, and he was wrong about me. When I got the make-up box and, every holiday, persecuted my family and their friends with after-supper recitations (Tennyson mostly), littered with flourishing gestures starting at the belly button, my father became alarmed enough to think that I was heading for what he called 'the baboon business'. To knock the notion out of me, one of his favourite admonitions was to remark: 'Take your hands out of your pockets, you are not an actor'.

Nor was I, nor likely to be. I was much more anxious to measure up to his own, at that time quite remarkable achievement. The Jesuits judged me with greater subtlety than he did.

They gave me my head; but they kept their hands on the bit. They appointed me reader in the Community refectory. It was another peculiarly Jesuit custom. Traditionally, the Society sat down to luncheon in their own refectory in silence. One of the boys read to them. My stint was the second sitting. The exposure was the more exacting because, if you mispronounced a word or faulted the composition of a sentence, the Jesuit in charge corrected you, and made you read it again. How much I owe to good and holy men, who can scarcely have enjoyed their own meals with ears cocked to spot my own cock-ups, who taught me the art of reading aloud; how to look ahead on words and punctuation, how to anticipate lines and paragraphs.

Individual Jesuits took time off to coach me in my bent. The earliest was one who marched me to the Hodder Valley, where there was a tumulus, a remnant of some ancient battle, to practise speech, like the old Greek Demosthenes, with pebbles in my mouth running uphill. When I was at the summit he walked away, yard by yard, testing whether I could throw my voice after him. I only once came a cropper in the elocution competitions; and it was also one of the rare occasions in which one of my Jesuit masters misjudged me. He got me to recite the passage in that turgid play, Flecker's *Hassan*, the one which begins 'They have changed our guard for the last time, it will be sunset in an hour', in which Rafi and Pervaneh have one night of love together before their death with, was it a thousand tortures?, on the following morning. Utterly innocent of the undertones of sex I hadn't a clue what I was being emotional about. Correctly I was relegated to third prize. I was beaten by Henry John, one of Augustus John's vintage family, who recited Thompson's *Hound of Heaven*.

The Jesuits placed emphasis on the prizegiving which took place every summer at the Great Academics, virtually the only time in the year when, reluctantly as I thought, they welcomed parents, entertaining them in a marquee behind the yew hedges on the bowling green. To my disappointment my own parents were never amongst them. But I had my hour of glory in the Academy Room when the prizes were distributed. Books, always books. It was another Jesuit custom. In my library now I have *Great Bowlers and Fielders* by C. B. Fry stamped with the College crest which I won '*in arte eloquendi*'; *The Second Jungle Book* awarded '*in Comp. Angl: et litteris*'.

I was writing by then weak essays, parodied from Chesterton and Belloc and my own father. I won a prize for a play on that much maligned Yorkshireman, Guy Fawkes. I pinched the idea from something my father had written. Copying my betters seemed no bad way to start. In the last days at Stonyhurst I even composed a rhyming pantomime – it was *Babes in the Wood* – for which my father contrived to get telegrams sent to me from distinguished people in the theatre to give me first night wishes. It was a good ending.

Not long later my father contracted a fatal illness. I was taken away from Stonyhurst. I missed the days when senior boys had their own private rooms. I missed Poetry and Rhetoric. Counting my luck, the Jesuits had given me a warm understanding of the classics. I had become an omnivorous reader, almost a book a day. I had learnt how to speak; and a useful acquisition, as I have found ever after, is that, from my experience in the refectory, I could carve a joint which is something that so many of my better educated contemporaries cannot do.

V

Vale Atque Ave

IN the Sodality chapel at term's end we school-leavers were given a harangue by the Rector to prepare us for the battle with the outside world. The Sodality was a sort of Jesuit order of spiritual chivalry for the older boys. All I remember of the Rector's parting admonitions is his telling us how careful we ought to be to stay clear of the underworld of 'Red Light' districts. But although I have subsequently travelled in most of the seamy, steamy, sordid places of the earth, I have never come upon the wicked invitation of a 'Red Light'. Brothels must have changed their illumination since the Rector's time.

Of course, he was an innocent. We called him 'The Wonder Worker' or, because of his bald head, 'The Egg'. A good and pious man, it was predictable that he had entered the Jesuit novitiate without seeing anything of the world at all. So much for the popular belief that all Jesuits have the sophistication of the fathers of Mayfair's Farm Street. Among the community in my time – it happens in all enclosed societies of man – there were those who were simple, desiccated, neurotic, and even sexually perverse. There were others, nearly all displaying endearing eccentricities, who had come to terms with the life that they had chosen.

I have warm memories of a father, we called him 'Bouncy', who introduced me to tap-dancing in the style of Jack Buchanan of musical comedy fame. It was one of his lovable eccentricities that he also taught Greek declensions to the steps of the tango. Another, a Hellenic scholar, had a theory that men are shaped like the letter 'V', and women like 'S's'. Aesthetically, he preferred the 'V'.

A third, of American origin, was fond of telling that he had given away a fortune, collected after investing his money in Bethlehem steel at the outbreak of war in 1914, because he realised that, if he had stayed in the world, he would have become a cad; albeit, in his own judgement, a very successful one. Latterly, when I left school, he used to get me to invest money on the classic races for him (he was good at picking winners); and there was nothing that he loved more than to bury his Roman collar under a scarf and to drink improbably mixed cocktails at the Savoy; or real absinthe at Berlemont's in Soho. Once, when the then Rector of Beaumont at Windsor had been reluctant to let him off the collar for the evening, he greeted me in a rage, to say: 'He asked me what time I was coming back. If I had not known that he was speaking for Jesus Christ, I would have strangled him.'

I was at an age when I was devouring a surfeit of books; among them the sea stories of Captain Marryatt. So many of the odd characters in his wooden ships could so easily have been transported into the enclosed world of my masters. There was the dear old Luxembourger who was reputed to speak forty languages; and of whom it was generally conceded that he could not make himself understood to a native in any one of them. There was the happy father whose fun it was to make skilful imitations of shaving sticks out of turnips and silver paper; and pass them off on his unsuspecting brethren. There was a puce-faced priest, with arms like iron bands, who taught cricket to the under-sixteens. Holding a bat with one arm on a short handle he could slog a ball from boundary line to boundary line. With a box full of balls at his feet he hotted our hands by making us catch them. There was a cricket fanatic who had an improbable friendship with the great batsman, Jack Hobbs. One summer's afternoon, Hobbs, with his Surrey colleagues, Peach and Sandham, came to demonstrate the game. On to him an un-familiar pitch I bowled Hobbs first ball. The great player gave me an autographed photo of himself to prove it. There was the prefect who, hour in and hour out as he was watching over us, wound balls for Stonyhurst cricket, the guts of the balls made out of ancient Jesuit gowns. There was the distinguished Jesuit astronomer who kept vigil in the observatory in the garden, forever waiting for the tremors of earthquakes, who, dying at a great age, spoke the memorable last words: 'Now I shall know whether the moon really is a green cheese'.

Like officers and men in the army I suppose that, masters and boys, we all thought we knew everything about each other. We boys probably sensed more than they suspected; and they certainly knew more than we would have cared to be told about us. It gave a lift to our exuberance to sing a doggerel, based on a hymn tune, exploiting the nicknames of some of our masters, not all of them Jesuits, which ran 'G. G., Popo, Q. Q., Gano, Gus'. We invented nicknames like 'Splush' of a man who salivated when he spoke; 'Minus' of a choirmaster with a high tenor voice which suggested the castrati; and 'Poop' for one who under pressure rolled nervously from one foot to another like a sailor on a ship's deck in a swell. The mannerism was particularly evident when he suspected, as subminister in charge of the refectory, that one of us was secreting a bottle of sauce. For some reason the use of sauce was counted an offence; although if ever food needed a relish it was ours.

But we accepted the hazards of breaking the rules. In a closed society we all knew our place like men on a ship of war. The Captain was the Rector, the Vice the Minister in charge of housekeeping and the needs of his brethren in the Community. Then followed the Procurator, a sort of Minister of Works and Agriculture, who was responsible for the college buildings and farms. Then came the Subminister who presided over refectory, dayroom and infirmary. Finally, there were our warders, the four playroom prefects, who administered punishment and divided amongst themselves various responsibilities, from common-place to dormitories, at different times of the day. There was also a spiritual father whose function was vague, because all our masters were our spiritual fathers; but one who was always one of the nicest old things in the place.

In a strictly masculine society it was remarkable that the incidence of homosexuality, that wretched nuisance of the public school system in England, was rare at Stonyhurst. If it occurred I was scarcely aware of it. We had some silly business of calling the prettiest among the younger boys 'tarts', exchanging notes, holding hands and sometimes kissing. I remember a little bottom-pinching; and not only by the boys. But we seemed to be mercifully free of the evil. In his autobiography, Sir Arthur Conan Doyle, an alumnus of Stonyhurst, and no friend of the Jesuits, wrote of his time there in the seventies: 'The Jesuit teachers have no trust in human nature, and perhaps they are justified. At Stonyhurst we were never allowed for an instant to be alone with each other, and I think that the immorality which is rife in public schools was at a minimum in consequence. In our games and our walks the priests always took part and a master perambulated the dormitories at night. Such a system may weaken self-respect and self-help, but at least minimises temptations and scandal.'

Conan Doyle's assessment of Stonyhurst life, made in 1924, was written from a hostile attitude. But I can echo him in all but sentiment. I wonder now whether it was such an entirely good thing that we were allowed to know so little about human relationships. In my own case I confess that I was clumsy in the company of women long after a man ought to be.

In the generality of the education other men, who didn't share Doyle's ardent rejection of religious convention, in his case in the cause of spiritualism, also resented the fierce discipline of the Jesuits. My uncle Lewis was one of them. Late in life he told me that, as a boy, the Rector wrote to his father accusing him of some homosexual irregularity. It was untrue; but his father chose to believe the Rector rather than his eldest son. As a consequence, Lewis ran away from home, working his passage on a sailing ship to South Africa. He told me of it, with a shame-faced wrinkling of his nose, in explanation as to why, throughout most of his life, he had been a rebel. A successful rebel, although he didn't say so, who became organising secretary of the Unionist Party of South Africa, an athlete in the international class in boxing, rugby and running; and, finally, a public figure. It is ironic that one of the frontispieces of the *Stonyhurst War Record* of World War I is of Major Lewis Hastings addressing seven thousand people, without benefit of microphone, in a personal recruiting campaign in which he raised that number of volunteers in a fortnight.

Lewis was typical of an individualistic type of man which, again and again, the Jesuit system has thrown up. Looking at the records Stonyhurst can claim no great statesmen and few scientists. The classical teaching was no encouragement for scientists. Roman Catholicism was for so long a barrier to politics. What Stonyhurst has produced, with the Jesuits' great theatrical tradition, is a succession of distinguished actors; about my own time, Charles Laughton, Colin Clive (who created the lead part in *Journey's End*); William Devlin, Peter Glenville and Francis Sullivan. And characteristically, from men who had tasted the terrors of the ferula, it became known as the V.C.'s school. The first Victoria Cross of the Kaiser's War was won on the bridge at Mons by Lieutenant Maurice Dease, a Stonyhurst man. The first Victoria Cross awarded to the army in Hitler's war was won by Major Andrews – a contemporary of mine we knew as 'Bummy' – in the retreat from Dunkirk.

Although I have vivid memories of my masters it puzzles me that my memories of most of my own contemporaries are so vague. Perhaps they were conformists, and I was not. I remember Peter O'Flaherty. He was my bosom pal at the age when boys first make close friends. He ultimately became a Southern Irish rebel, second-in-command of the I.R.A. He posted his name with others on the door of Southwark Cathedral in 1939, a time when the I.R.A. were laying bombs in suitcases about London. He came to see me; but I am grateful that he went before Special Branch came to see me about him. Poor chap, he spent most of the war in prison, first in Belfast and then confined by his old hero, de Valera. When he came out he was as broken as prison makes a man to be. He died soon after; someone who in only slightly different circumstances, and with a bigger cause, might have had his portrait in the line of heroes, one of those on the walls of the refectory at Stonyhurst who were decorated with the Victoria Cross.

The best of us, it must have been the first hope of our masters, entered the Society of Jesus; in my time about ten a year. Stonyhurst has produced some of the most distinguished of the English Jesuits: Bernard Vaughan, Martin D'Arcy, Charles Plater, and my own contemporaries Bernard Basset, Philip Caraman and Christopher Devlin.

I left it, as a schoolboy, not without affection but without regret. I hungered, few boys don't, for a larger and, under my breath, more wicked world. Not the world that the poor 'Egg' tried to tell us about, but one which was waiting to be cracked. For a time I dutifully attended Sunday mass, associated with a handful of friends surviving from schooldays, even had a passing acquaintance with the Rugger lot. But I knew that I didn't belong. The last positive religious thing I did was to serve at mass for my father's requiem at Farm Street Church. Soon after, it all fell away.

Not that I lost contact with Catholicism, and its attitudes. But what I learnt only made me more eager for the fatted calf. Hilaire Belloc had something to do with it. Aggressive in his faith as he was, he was also greedy of the joys of this life. My first encounter with him was at a dinner party in Douglas Woodruff's flat in Lincoln's Inn. Another of the guests was my late Prefect of Studies at Stonyhurst, a man who had seemed so formidable a few years earlier, shrunk to size in the presence of Belloc who was wearing a cloak with the manner of an old toad squatting at the entrance of his hole. I was still a boy but impetuous enough to ask the great man whether, when he took 'The Path to Rome', he really walked forty miles in a day. In his clipped voice, he replied: 'I am a journalist, young man, a journalist'. I remembered that. I have remembered a story of him which came to me years later.

At the Saintsbury Club, a dining club which meets twice a

year at the Vintners' Hall to commemorate George Saintsbury, the historian and wine connoisseur who wrote *Notes on a Cellar Book*, I heard the tale of the night when Hilaire Belloc was called upon to deliver the traditional oration, 'In Praise of Wine'. It is a formidable experience for lesser people, addressing the most knowledgeable experts among the vintners, and in the company of some of the best writers of the day. The task demands careful preparation. Belloc forgot that he was expected to do it. Pushed to his feet, he began: 'Gentlemen, I am drunk.' Those who heard him said that, struggling through the mists of wine, he got better and better. His peroration, although I heard it repeated only once, lives with me: 'When I depart this world, and appear before my beloved Lord at the Last Judgement seat to account for my sins upon this earth, which have been scarlet, I shall say to him: "Lord, I cannot remember the name of the village, I cannot even recollect the name of the girl; but the wine, my God, was Chambertin!" '

Shortly after my father died I had tea at Beaconsfield with G. K. Chesterton. He had no cause to be bothered with me except for a friendship with my father. That meeting was memorable because, although he said much more, hugging his great belly in amusement, he advised me that, as I went out into the world, I would meet two sorts of great men; there were the little great men who made everybody else feel small, and there were the great great men who made everybody else feel great.

Two great men sent me on my way. With the animal brashness of youth I went back to Stonyhurst, sporting an old school tie, a few years later. It gave me pleasure to smoke where hitherto I wasn't allowed to; to stroll into the local pub, the Shireburn Arms, where none of my masters could interfere with me. I was a beastly young man without benefit of manners.

I think of myself with so many regrets: perhaps who doesn't? I was swirled into the world to pick out 'the little great men from the great great men'; to decide what I would say at the last Judgement seat.

VI

Sic Transit Gloria Mundi

I SUPPOSE that it had something to do with the surfeit of spirituality at Stonyhurst that, when I left it, I went for the world. It was accidental that my introduction to it was its seamiest side. It happened that an uncle of mine was a civil servant with special responsibilities inside Scotland Yard. Although I was hell-bent to get into Fleet Street my father, in the last months of his life, decreed that it would be safer if I started my career in a Government office where I couldn't be sacked unless I stole the petty cash. He also determined that, going out into the world, I ought to have a bowler hat and an umbrella. In his young days, when he had been for a time at a desk at the War Office, correct dress was a frock coat and a top hat. So I potted my head in the hated bowler and, contriving to leave as many umbrellas as possible on buses, I went to work.

My own function as a clerk was to check the forage returns of police horses and the reports of police surgeons, which seemed largely descriptions of delinquent teenagers emphasising 'pubic hairs well developed'. I did my best, without stealing the petty cash, to get fired. Whitehall is probably still trying to unravel nonsense of mine on matters which I found unsavoury. Fortunately, within a few months, a friend of my father's offered me a job in the publicity department of the caterers, Lyons. It didn't seem an ideal choice; but the address was 61, Fleet Street. From the underworld of police work to the Philistine area of advertising, I passed on my way.

I make no apology for this diversion. It is related to my upbringing as a Jesuit child. I was on an edge when I said goodbye, or I thought I had, to the Jesuits. I was saying goodbye to my father; and to all the people about me who wanted to keep me within the Roman Catholic faith. It would have been so much more comfortable to have adopted an outward conformity. But I have never been able to take an attitude in which I have not believed. It is a measure to a large extent of my subsequently essential penuriousness that if I find a man a four-letter man I cannot refrain from telling him so. An odd thing in me, although I love this life so much and have so little hope of what can come hereafter, is that I have scarcely any fear of death.

It would certainly be nice to believe in a metamorphosis from this world to another one. It is entertaining to speculate that, when we die, we pass on like the caterpillar from the chrysalis to the butterfly. It is ludicrous to imagine that we rise to a pasteboard world of holy pictures, pantomime angels, and God sitting on a cloud. How lucky other animals are who cannot count the years, or consider the inevitability of death. Yet, to some extent, we are one with the animals in which the only immortality which is certain is the genetic traits in our progeny.

A great Jesuit has argued with me that people who cannot believe that this world, in the words of the rubbishy old melodrama, 'is just a stepping stone between two vast eternities', are simpletons. In his own ethic such people are without values. I wonder. Speaking for myself, no virtue in it, my life has been ruled by values. It seems to me that a sort of stoicism creates its own satisfaction. One discipline is work; not for the love of work but for the delight of attainment. It does not matter what the work is; planting a row of potatoes, polishing a car, painting a picture, washing a window, or selling a pup. It can also exist in the discipline of prayer. But to me, with memories of nuns in an aura of Madonna lilies and waxed floors, that seems an empty way of existence.

How difficult it is to worry it out. A rhyme sticks in my mind which runs:

> *There goes the little moron*
> *He doesn't give a damn*

71

JESUIT CHILD

I'm glad I'm not a moron
My God, perhaps I am!

I wonder whether some deep truth has evaded me, as I often wonder whether something that everybody else knows has escaped me because nobody has got round to telling me what it is. It is possible that I arrived at my own thinking, however fallacious it may be, in that holiday from Stonyhurst when the theatre manager brought me to terms with the life of the countryside where, in simple truth, death is life and life is death. The story of green places is of creation to kill, of killing to live and living to kill. It is a tragedy of our times that today so many people in great cities believe that milk, meat and bread are things that come out of a supermarket. It is even fashionable to suggest that in an industrial society we don't even need to grow food which may soon be manufactured on a machine.

I write at the age of sixty, filled with a mess of thought. I believe that the Papacy will be condemned by posterity for banning the pill at the price of a population explosion in which human beings will have to live like battery hens. It seems that Rome still belongs to a time when people were intolerant because they believed. It appears not to know that we are tolerant because we are disbelieving. The ultimate disaster threatens, the disaster of which the superstitious have said will come when the second Peter assumes the triple crown, the fall of the Papacy. If that happens Western culture, as we know it, will vanish.

My gloom, my dark anticipation of the future, may well be the measure of my years. I am not the first old man to say good-bye to youth without complaint. So many have promised, in the words of the Western Brothers' song: 'It will never be the same again'. And of course it won't. I am not too worried. In the pattern that emerges for my children I am confident that they will cope. But the crisis, another crisis in human affairs, is here. The old religions, the old convictions, are on the run. Concrete is winning over grass. Electronics are beating the printed word. Too many damned inventions are running ahead of the human capacity to digest them.

As a child of the Jesuits, it seemed that everything was predetermined. As a man I have blamed myself for my reservations about formal religion. I reckoned that if it was appointed that I appear at the Last Judgement seat to account for my sins on earth, with Hilaire Belloc as my first witness, I might be forgiven; my crime that I seized all the splendid things it had to offer.

It wasn't until forty years later that I went back to the beginning. Meantime, I looked at the world. It was absurd but true that my introduction to it was a close family society as disciplined, dedicated and paternalistic as the Jesuits themselves. It was a society with the same memories of persecution, the same gift for showmanship, something of the same stern conduct in its affairs. It was even organised, if not in voluntary poverty, in total obedience to the communal need.

Formal dress was not a black gown. In those days it was white tie and tails. Ceremony on my new masters' part was conducted in the incense of cigar smoke, in wine which was certainly no altar wine; and in venerable places like the Trocadero, the Strand and Regent Palaces, the Royal Palace off Kensington Gardens; and that latter example of the late baroque, the Cumberland, flourishing on the site where so many Jesuit martyrs met their end on Tyburn Tree.

From Stonyhurst I was swept into the world of the Salmons and the Glucksteins (with a sprinkling of Josephs), that remarkable and prolific Jewish family which has contributed so much to English life. The firm was J. Lyons & Co., who developed the teashops. Joe Lyons, who gave his name to them, was a nominee. The reason was that the Salmons and Glucksteins identity was then associated with a chain of tobacco shops. But it was the Salmons and the Glucksteins who unquestionably created the great catering business. And they kept it a family matter. It was their boast that their sons started their careers washing up in the kitchens. It was their pride that every department of the vast business was controlled, at all its levels, by a member of the family.

It was the only board of directors that I have ever heard of which met every morning. At midweek every week the senior members of the family collected in a private room at the Trocadero Restaurant to settle its domestic affairs. Wives and daughters lunched downstairs until such time, if and when, they were required to give their own opinions. The elders decided every detail of the family's business. If young so-and-so was going to be married, and it was agreed that he had made the right choice, everything was arranged for his future wife's trousseau, his best man, his wedding reception, his honeymoon hotel, and his future home. Motor cars, clothes, accommodation, hospitality, were all arranged. I couldn't for the life of me work out how the young men spent the very modest incomes they were paid. I fancy that they worked them off selling dud shares to their relations. The Jesuits couldn't have managed it better.

The firm has little outward individuality now. In those days it hummed with personalities. In the publicity department in Fleet Street I started in humble jobs like making the tea for senior members of the staff, carrying the copy to the printers and writing display advertisements for unimportant trade papers. But over the years I came to the notice of Major Montague Gluckstein, who was then director in charge of Lyons publicity. Inside the company he was known as M.I.G. I formed a respectful, albeit affectionate, relationship with him. I had already had some success as a journalist. He sent me on my way.

He was never inclined to throw money about. What M.I.G. preferred was to give it in kind. Again and again he would send for me when he was being shaved in the morning at the barber's shop at the Royal Palace Hotel, in the hope I think that I could make him laugh, to instruct me to go to his Savile Row tailors to order myself a suit. He ordered that I was to lunch or dine at the Trocadero, the Royal Palace, Strand or Regent Palace not less than three times a week. I was paraded for the oyster choosing and the wine tastings. The managers of the firm's restaurants, and the chefs, were told to introduce me to the arts of good living. One of the jobs I was appointed to was the publicity of C. B. Cochran's midnight cabaret in the Trocadero Grill Room. It was soon my boast that I knew not only all Mr Cochran's Young Ladies, the top dollies of their day, by their Christian names; but, more important, they all knew me by mine.

It was a personal business in which my bosses were withdrawn; but warm, ever present, and forgiving. I recollect an occasion when I was summoned by M.I.G. to account for a dinner bill for a press party which I had signed in the name of the firm. By any standard it was excessive. We had run through the lot from cocktails to champagne, from claret to burgundy, from Château Yquem to vintage port, brandy and cigars. Sure that I was about to be fired I could only offer the weakest defence. At the end of the interrogation Major Monte – it was our other name for him – put down the bill with the remark: 'When you leave this firm, Hastings, I sincerely hope that you will remain one of our customers; because, God knows, you are the sort of customer we want'. I have remained one of their customers.

The job wasn't all jam. I had to work all hours in the office writing advertisements for swiss rolls, designing menu cards for gala occasions, turning out press hand-outs in the varying styles of different newspapers. I was on call at any hour of the night to deal with the suicides in the company's hotels. It is a fact of life that people who kill themselves usually do it in the small hours of the morning, and away from home. It is a constant concern of hotel proprietors, catering for people who want to see life, that they are regularly embarrassed by people who have seen too much of life already. I was cursed with telephone calls in the small hours of morning from cool Continental types who invariably began the conversation: 'We 'ave 'ad a bit of trouble 'ere'.

I came in because it was important for the firm to keep the name of the hotel involved out of the papers. If it was named, worse if the room number was quoted, people cancelled their bookings. The trick was to give the reporters all the bloody details, and ask them to refer to the case as happening 'in a West End hotel'. The crime reporters thought we were nice to give them the works without demanding a *quid pro quo*. My job was to collect the facts.

I have a vivid recollection of an early morning at the Regent Palace Hotel when I was brought in on a case in which, when the chambermaid arrived with breakfast, she couldn't get into the room. Two electricians, summoned to help, offered to knock down the door. The manager demurred. He said that there was an empty room nearby; and suggested that one of the young men should climb over the outside balcony to see what was going on. The boiler-suited electrician enthusiastically agreed. He performed the gymnastics all right but, coming back to inform us, he fell in a faint: 'He's still living, sir,' he said, 'but he's bleeding something awful'. After that, we broke down the door, which had been jammed with a wardrobe. After one look at the mess, the character had cut his throat with a safety razor blade, the manager seized a towel, and tying it round the victim's neck, remarked: 'He's ruining the carpet'.

I learnt a lot from the hotel business. There was a time when, in horrific circumstances, some poor woman killed her children and killed herself by drinking Lysol. I arrived as a member of the Salmon family was saying: 'It's just like Madame Tussaud's upstairs'. The manager gave a slight bow with the comment: 'I understand, sir, no bill outstanding'.

In my meeting with the world it is improbably true that almost my first engagement was to arrange a photographic session with a model named Marjorie Robertson who posed as the advertising symbol of the Lyons teashop waitresses called 'Nippies'. She is better known today as Anna Neagle. At the end of my years with Lyons I was given special responsibility for the publicity in connection with the launching of the new thousand-room hotel, the Cumberland at Marble Arch, the first hotel in Britain with a private bathroom to every room. Every room a bath was made possible by a change in the Victorian law requiring that every bathroom had to have a window.

The launching of the Cumberland Hotel, then one of the new wonders of London, had a climax when, the day before it was opened to guests, King George V and Queen Mary asked for a private visit of inspection. Their Majesties did not want the press following around with them, but the King agreed that a representative of the company could attend, and tell afterwards what happened. It was me. I feared that it would be a testing assignment. But the King was rather deaf. The interior decorator of the hotel was very deaf and, hanging behind, I heard every word of the conversation. Listening at the door of one of the bedrooms I heard the King ask: 'Now, tell me, is this a double or a single room?' The chairman of the company explained that it was a double room. There was a thoughtful pause. The King enquired in a puzzled voice: 'Then where does the woman undress?'

The huge hotel opened the following morning and, after the enormous advertising campaign, never mind the patronage of royalty, it was packed out within the hour. Lyons had brought their key men from all their established hotels to organise it. On the first morning, I stood in the hall with the hotel detective, innocuously known as the enquiry superintendent, as the place was beginning to run like oil. With a portfolio of police photographs in his pocket, he was identifying the international hotel thieves, the confidence tricksters, the expensive prostitutes who were arriving in droves, mostly from the Continent, in the hope of easy pickings. I believe that not one slipped the net. Politely they were eased away from the Reception Desk, and sent back to the capital they had come from.

The opening of the Cumberland was one of the most massive triumphs of the Salmon and Gluckstein family, one of the most carefully prepared operations in business I have ever seen. It started when the steel skeleton of the hotel was still going up. A line of bedrooms and sitting-rooms in different designs was built, complete in every detail, inside the frame. Communications were linked with the Regent Palace. Inside them, with all service provided, you could believe that the hotel was operational. The only difference was you had to climb up a ladder through the scaffolding to get into it. There the decisions were made on the definitive decor.

One afternoon, as the whole structure was taking shape, I attended a conference, at which a senior director presided with a number of junior members of the family in attendance, to decide how the upholstery of the furniture would be done in the public rooms. The young men were asked for their opinions. One suggested the lasting advantages of real leather; another said that imitation leather was so good that it was impossible to ignore the economic advantages of employing it. A third said that he would prefer a cotton material because fashions change, and chintz would be cheaper to replace. At last the chairman spoke: 'Now that you young buggers are finished I'll tell you what the chairs are going to be covered with. They are going to be covered with the bottoms of the British public six times a day'.

They allowed none of us to think, not even the least of us, that the success of the project was a foregone conclusion. We were never allowed to forget that what we were spawning could well be a white elephant. There were alarms when, sinking the foundations six storeys underground the builders hit the old Tyburn ditch. Anyone who goes down to the bottom of the building can see the dregs of the Tyburn River, washed through with so much blood, through a culvert in the foundations now. I thought at the time how odd it was that I should be drawn back to a tree with so many associations with the Jesuit martyrs.

But I did not think much about them. I worked hard; and my bosses gave me the good life. M.I.G. decided that I must learn ballroom dancing. The University of Dancing, as it was called, was centred at the Empress Rooms, another of Lyons places. The teachers were then numbered among the champion ballroom dancers of the world, including Willie Maxwell-Stuart, another alumnus of Stonyhurst, who I think I am right in saying was never defeated in an international championship. It was said that he was unbeatable because, in the formal ballroom dancing of the time, 'he was a gentleman who danced like a gentleman'. For my part, I danced like a clown, and I soon gave it up. But I was pleased enough with myself.

In my early twenties I was initiated into the luxurious existence of pre-war London night life; the mysteries of fine cuisine, the potent magic of the cocktail bar and, to a young man, the disturbing glamour of cabaret and suppers for two. I revelled in midnight blue tails, and the armour of starched white waistcoat and bow tie. I could interpret the abracadabra of a French menu rather better than I had ever learnt my French grammar. I was 'known' in the West End night spots. Altogether I thought myself a helluva fellow.

Then, one evening, when I was waiting for a girl friend in the foyer of a restaurant, fingering the red carnation in my buttonhole and remarking to myself how much more elegant I looked in my evening clothes than the other diners-out, a stranger came up to me and said: 'Have you got a table for two?'

I had begun to look like a head waiter.

That night, in my chagrin, I promised myself that I would never wear full evening dress again; and I have very nearly kept the promise ever since. Now, tieing a bow tie is as much an anguish for me as it is for most other people, and the end product is reminiscent of the sails of a ship in a storm.

I got another part-time job within a few weeks, leaving the Salmons and Glucksteins with an affection for that great Jewish family which stays with me now. It was flattering that, years later, M.I.G. asked me to come back to them. But by then I had adopted a new life. For a brief period, before I had established myself as a journalist, I recollect that I organised the first public demonstration of frozen foods in England. I arranged an enormous banquet at the Savoy in which everything on the menu was 'Birds Eye' foods. Afterwards we sent home the guests with samples sufficiently surprising at that time that they dropped them on the floor to establish how frozen they were. I also tried to exploit canned beer; but I came to the conclusion that the English would never accept it!

The war changed everything for me, as for most other people. At Munich time I was asked to write for a new magazine. I delivered my first two pieces before it was published. It was *Picture Post*. I became the paper's war correspondent. At the end of the war, when I was a casualty in a car crash when there wasn't a German in sight, I became the last editor of the *Strand* magazine; and one of the first contributors of a new magazine for children. Again, my first articles were written before the paper was published. Boys, now grown to manhood, will remember the vintage years of *Eagle*.

When I tired of city lights I searched out the countryside. I have dedicated myself to the green places, with the fanaticism of an anchorite, ever since. Oh yes, I still love the fatted comforts which the town has to offer. But for me the most fulfilling years of my life have been passed in lonely places with a gun or a fishing rod in my hand; or a horse between my legs. I became so dedicated to country life that, with A. G. Street, I founded the magazine *Country Fair*. I ran it for eight years; but by that time it was evident that the general magazines were done for. *Picture Post*, *Lilliput*, *The Strand*, all national institutions in their day, had folded. Television, the child of the electronic age, was brooming them away.

In early 1939, at New York in the *Queen Mary* on one of her very early voyages, I remember the pressmen coming aboard to ask if there were any interesting personalities in the passenger list. They had interviewed the Hollywood types. I remarked that there was one other passenger worth talking to, a man called Gerald Cock who, for B.B.C., was running the first daily television programme in the world. The boys, over

Stonyhurst College in East Lancashire – the grim engraving which pointed a finger at me in early childhood. My father, who had inherited the picture from his own father, hung it in an honoured place on our bedroom stairs. This 'Old College of the Eagle Towers' is where three generations of us went to school

Inigo Lopez de Loyola

Today's General of the Jesuits

Ignatius's Death Mask

The living appearance of St Ignatius is lost. All that exist are posthumous idealised portraits. But the founder of the Jesuits seems to live again in the profile of the present General of the Order. Pedro Arrupe, himself a Basque, is cast in the same mould as the death mask of the soldier who became a saint

LA MORT DE QVELQVES PERES DE LA COMPAGNIE DE IESV
& de quelques autres perfonnes arriuée en la Nouuelle France dans la publication de l'Euangile.

The story of the Jesuit martyrs in America and Japan – and, later, in England – is the saddest in their troubled history. The American Indians, with
their love of torture, condemned many to prolonged and terrible deaths.
The symbolic representation of many executions (*above*) recalls the ritual
killing of the heroic martyr, Father Brebeuf. The Japanese killed many
more. They learnt of death by crucifixion, of which they had previously
been unaware, from the missionaries who told them the story of the cross

22

Augustinus Ota Iappon, Societ. IESV, capite
truncatus medium Fidei I Kinoximi 10.
Augusti 1622.

S. Iacobus Kisai Iappon, Societ IESV, crucifixus &
lanceis transfixus propter Fidē Nāgalachi 5 Febr. 197

Leonardus Kimura Iappon, Societ IESV, vivus concrematus
lento igne propter Fidei Nangasachi 18. No. an 1619.

Nicolaus Kean, Iappon, Soc IESV, pedibus suspensus,
et in foueam cingulo tenus depressus in odium
Fidei, q. die moritur Nangasachi. 31. Iul. 1633.

Photo: British Museum

THE REDUCTION OF SAN JOSE IN CHIQUITOS

.21.

D ILIGENTER colunt terram Indi, eam ob causam ligones è piscium ossibus parare no-
runt viri, quibus manubria lignea aptantes, terram fodiunt satis facile, nam mollior est:
ea deinde probè confracta & aequata, feminae fabas & milium sive Mayzum serunt,
praeuntibus nonnullis quae defixo in terram baculo foramina faciunt, in quae fabae & mi-
lij grana iniiciantur. Facta semente, agros relinquunt: nam eo tempore hiemis fugiendae
causa, quae satis frigida est, utpote regione inter Occidentem & Septentrionem sita, & circiter trimestre
durat, nempe à 24. Decembris ad decimum quintum Martij, ij nudi incedentes in sylvas se abdunt. Trans-
acta hieme, domum redeunt, expectantes sementis maturitatem. Messe confecta fructus re-
condunt in totius anni usum, nullum mercimonium ex ijs facientes, nisi
forte ob vilem aliquem supellectilem permuta-
tione facta.

R. B. Cunninghame Graham called it 'The Vanished Arcadia', the ideal state
which the Jesuits created in South America. The Paraguay Reductions, as they
were called, flourished in communal prosperity for one hundred and fifty
years. They provided a settled and prosperous way of life for the nomadic
Indians. The Reductions were reduced to ruins, overgrown by the jungle
(*opposite*) when the Jesuits were suppressed by colonists and misguided sovereigns

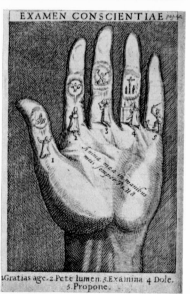

These woodcuts, from the seventeenth century, were the first illustrations of the Spiritual Exercises. The exercitant, in total retreat, was called upon to use these symbolic representations to concentrate his mind on eternity

their crack of dawn whisky on the rocks, gave me the brush-off: 'Television, shucks'.

In its early days television was as pathetic as sound radio in its own early days. But I had done a couple of pieces at Alexandra Palace, as I had begun my own career in the heyday of radio at Broadcasting House. It was plain what was coming next.

It waited, during a long period of what amounted to little more than technical amateur theatricals, until 1957. I came into it, on the sidelines, over a lunch in some awful pub in Notting Hill Gate. The producer said that he had been asked to do an experimental series for six weeks. Could I manage six spots on the countryside? The programme was 'Tonight'. It went on for eight years; and changed the face of television for ever.

As a freelance writer generally finds himself in the middle of his life my feet were in different camps. I was writing novels, I was doing 'spots' for 'Tonight', I was editing; and fighting monstrous demands for income tax.

It was a demand for income tax which moved me, at a lush lunch with the Editor of *The People* to say that I had always had an ambition to cast myself away, like Robinson Crusoe, on a desert island; and to find out how I would make out with the boy scout's traditional knife and piece of string. He took my offer with a handshake across the table. On a desert island in the Indian Ocean I nearly lost my chips. I lost thirty-two pounds of my normal twelve stone weight. It is incidental that I paid my income tax out of the expedition; and that they got me off just in time. The important thing is that the physical experience changed me.

Whatever I had been before I staggered home with a new outlook. I found that I did not want to prove anything any more. In practical terms I discovered that, while I had always been a butterflies in the belly performer in front of television cameras, I had a new serenity. I was thinking less of what I was doing, less of what I had done; and more of what I am. After sucking where the bee sucks, the experience on the desert island brought me back to the start. I suppose that I underwent a sort of conversion. In truth, I have never had any regard for my own importance; nor, least of all, the promise that I am for immortality. In faith, luckier ones can believe. In the fun of living I can only tell what has happened to me; what I have thought searching better minds than my own.

I have come back, and back again, to the Jesuits. Wrong or right, right or wrong, the Society stands for principles which cannot be ignored. So much is a mystery to me, so much exasperates; but I want the Jesuits to be right. Myself, I am of no matter. Other people can fight the battle which I have lost; but which, with fascination, I tell again. It is a worldly view but, deep underneath, the Jesuit Child in me remains.

VII

Ad Majorem Dei Gloriam

AT school we began every exercise in our theme books with the letters A.M.D.G., the initials of the Latin motto of the Jesuits meaning 'For the Greater Glory of God'. At the end of the task we wrote L.D.S., 'Laus Deo Semper', which can be translated as 'Praise God for Ever'. I did it by rote. I am surprised that, as a schoolboy, I thought about it so little.

I remembered that we had had whole holidays on the feasts of Jesuit saints. I remembered that, on his special day, we had kissed the relic containing a piece of the rope which had bound Edmund Campion on the hurdle on his way to the scaffold at Tyburn. I remembered a ludicrous sermon on an Italian Jesuit saint, named St Aloysius, which was delivered by a worthy but simple Yorkshire priest who managed the College farms. He began: 'The life of St Aloysius may be summed up in three phases. He was born, he lived and he died'. For a farm animal it could have been a reasonable epitaph.

At Stonyhurst I had never had any patience with the spiritual library loaded with pious and largely unreadable devotional books. I was happier with Caesar's armies and Caesar's wars. But forty years on, when I had come to terms with my essential inability to conform I came to Stonyhurst again. It led me to revise the thoughts of a lifetime.

As so often happens it was a fluke. Working on a series of television programmes in the north I proposed that we might do something at Stonyhurst on Charles Waterton, the York-shire squire. One of the technicians in the unit asked me who

Waterton was; and who the Jesuits? He might not have known about Waterton; to me it seemed inconceivable that he had never heard of the Jesuits, those people of whom it had been said: 'You can hang Jesuits until you are tired, and there are always others to take their place'. As I searched my mind to enlighten him, Jesuit child that I was, I realised how much I scarcely knew myself.

A little later I did another programme for B.B.C. television called *The Other Lancashire*, a documentary on the county, the larger part of it beyond the grim industrial belt. I went back to Stonyhurst again. I trust I told people in the south something of the hidden wonders beyond Manchester in the north. But I was the one, returning to my old stamping ground, who got the sock in the jaw.

Stonyhurst had changed: the most remarkable change that, when I was invited into the common room for morning coffee, I saw women. The stiletto heel was not just in the door, but established in what I had always believed was an exclusively male environment; more than that an environment, with rare exceptions, dominated by the black gowns and Roman collar of the J's. What I found were traditional schoolmasters, in gowns over sports jackets, pretty women being pretty; and the Jesuits, a mere handful of them, standing like sidesmen at a football match.

I reluctantly discovered how many of the traditions I grew up with had been dismissed as remnants of the past. The new school-masters talked of 'Forms' rather than the ancient class names which gave so much glory to the school. The study-place had been abandoned. The poor J's had given up their quarters in the West Wing. The Astronomical Observatory had been forgotten; the Elizabethan gardens were running riot. It was a bigger school, no doubt a better school, but not the place I knew.

Initially I felt a sense of betrayal, like a soldier who finds that his old regiment has lost its individual identity. I had never thought of Stonyhurst as other than a centre of Jesuit command.

It had seemed to me that it was one of the citadels of the Order. I was wrong; it never was. In the world-wide disposition of the Society it was an outpost. Many Jesuits, thirty-three thousand of them in eighty-five countries, had never even heard of the place. Even in the English Province they had other, if less spectacular, missions. In the Jesuit headquarters in Rome, Stonyhurst rated no more important than a slit trench.

In the guests' parlour, sumptuously lined with portraits in oils of the Stuarts, I heard about it from the holding force of Jesuits who still remain. Later, in the house at Farm Street, the message was the same. I listened in much the mood in which, in a very different context, I learnt that Lyons had decided to close their Corner House in Coventry Street in London; that gilded twenty-four a day people's palace for which I had invented the advertising slogan 'Open for Ever'. The Jesuits told me that they were short of recruits, their commitments too heavy, their men too thin on the ground. With the rest of the Catholic Church they themselves were in a phase of rethinking and retrenchment. I couldn't escape the hint that Stonyhurst, which had seemed so permanently endowed, might not last much longer as a Jesuit school. It was already more than half way to becoming a secular one.

To what loss?

I had sipped the wine of Jesuitry; but only from a small vine-yard on a northern slope. The Jesuits, on their own admission, were looking for new grapes to press. It concerned me how little I knew of the largest religious order in the Church; a Society, like so many at the present time, which feels that it has lost its way.

From Stonyhurst I went to the London Library where the list of books on the Jesuits was so long that the librarians had to Xerox the pages in the subject catalogue to guide me. At Farm Street, 114 Mount Street now, the Jesuit headquarters in London, the father archivist helped me in the hunt. For a year it was something of an obsession with me, the search to find what had made the most militant order in the Church tick; and why it isn't ticking so sweetly any more. Finally, B.B.C., still the greatest patron of the arts, financed a pilgrimage.

On the trail of a television programme, I trod in the footsteps of Ignatius from Loyola in Northern Spain to Barcelona and Rome. In the pursuit, with a film unit in attendance, I went to places which have scarcely altered since scribes in peace lettered and illuminated glories on parchment.

At the Jesuit house in Barcelona, a stern place, as such Spanish places are, with curved iron bars over the windows and heavy-headed nails encrusted in the doors, I met a priest who put into my care an old sword wrapped in newspaper. Its guard and scabbard were lost; but it was still a sharp weapon. What I collected so casually was the veritable blade which, four hundred and fifty years ago, Ignatius Loyola, the founder of the Jesuits, dedicated to the Black Virgin at the Monastery at Montserrat. I put it in the back of the car as I went on my way to salute her again.

2
PILGRIMAGE

I

Inigo

THE country of Inigo Lopez de Loyola, known to history as St Ignatius, is on the Atlantic coast of northern Spain. The region is quite unlike most of the peninsula. It is wet, often cold, and the landscape is more reminiscent of the lowlands of Scotland than the parched hot earth of the south. As Tacitus observed of Britain, 'the soil does not afford either the vine, the olive, or the fruits of warmer climates'. The timbered hills are painted in misty blues and greens. A vein of the Ebro, the Arga, which runs across the neck of the country, sparkles with white water in refreshing contrast to the sluggish yellow streams of the Mediterranean littoral. 'Oak and iron' are the stuff of the province of Guipuzcoa. It is no wonder that the Basques, blue-chinned, bullet-headed, barrel-chested men in black berets, count themselves a different race from the flamenco people of Andalusia, Castile and Aragon. Inigo, the eleventh child of an impoverished and quarrelsome family, was one of them. With claims to nobility its conduct was generally barbarous. So in his youth was his.

His ancestral home, Loyola, was a grim square fortress, pierced for cannon, sixty-four kilometres east of the seaport of Bilbao. Inside their gloomy stone walls, three feet thick, Inigo's forebears held their ground with slow-match for their culverins and the quick point of their swords. Earlier, in his grandfather's youth, the place by popular request, and with the approval of Henry IV of Castile, had been reduced by the burghers of the neighbouring towns. They spiked the cannon and razed the upper walls. Inigo's grandfather was only permitted to rebuild, after serving four years on the frontier against the Moors, on the understanding that the upper part of the house was re-erected in vulnerable brick; and that the gun embrasures were unmanned.

So it stands today: a square house, its top storeys reconstructed in Moorish style, overwhelmed by the embrace of a baroque basilica. Every room in the once brigands' den has been converted into a chapel. The devout, debouching from droves of motor coaches, make their obeisances to the great saint. The less devout salute him in a row of cafes opposite the Church while beret-capped Jesuits, busily reading their office, pass by. There are the usual souvenir shops where St Ignatius is commemorated in plaster, metal, pasteboard and plastic. There is a subterranean radio station, manned by Jesuits who are the disc-jockeys of the district. Inigo never dreamt what he had started. But, from the beginning, he dreamt of glory. At first, it was pride of family represented by the Loyola coat-of-arms, a silver cauldron on a chain flanked by two black wolves rampant, which is carved in stone over the entrance to the house.

In the humble little hotel where we stayed in Azpeitia, his home town, wondering how we could film the Loyolas' house without the basilica creeping in, it occurred to me that no man in history, apart from St Paul, had such a remarkable conversion as Inigo Loyola.

In his latter years, he was fond of confessing to his community what a horrible young man he had been. The evidence is that he was right. He came from a country where men are coldly arrogant, hot-tempered, and inordinately brave. He came of a family with a long, if disreputable, history whose pride was the more obsessive because they were concealing poverty. Physically, Inigo was a small man, with the determination that small men have to impress their personalities on others. As a child I can believe that, with ten unruly elder brothers and sisters spread over twenty-four years of wedlock, he was an unholy handful.

It was surely a relief for the family when, at the age of seven, a kinsman took him off their hands. Don Juan Velasquez de Cuellas, the governor of the royal residence at Arevelo, admitted him into his service as a page. Tidily-made, with long fair hair, flashing eyes, inborn belief in his social place, Inigo was an ideal choice. The appointment introduced him to the elaborate etiquette of the Castilian court. The Governor's wife was one of the queen's ladies-in-waiting. It can't have been much of a life for the little page when Ferdinand the Catholic was married to the austere Queen Isabella who ran the court on a shoestring; and who was buried, at her own request, in the coarse habit of a Franciscan. But, a year later, it was fun. The king married the young French princess, Germaine de Foix. Suddenly the court became frivolous and gay. For a time the Spaniards were to forego their constant preoccupation with black and death, their taste for human relics; their relish for bannered funerals followed by hot chestnuts and rough wine. Inigo, permitted on occasion to offer on bended knee a golden goblet of wine to the young queen, elected her his queen-of-hearts.

It was a period of history, four hundred and fifty years ago, when the nonsense of chivalry reached a ludicrous popularity. The best seller of the day, when printing itself was still a comparatively novel invention, was *Amadis of Gaul*, in which gallant knights rescued maidens in distress, got kings out of trouble, and in which magic was the order of the day. It was the type of writing which Cervantes satirised in *Don Quixote*, the sort of tomfoolery which is represented in our own time by folk heroes like James Bond. *Amadis* was one of the books which moulded the mind of the young Inigo. A boy with a dagger, a long sword, a pistol and the toss of the head which is Spanish pride, he dedicated himself to the cause of knight errantry. An abject slave to his superiors at court, he consciously played the hidalgo to those he counted his inferiors. Although he had named Germaine as his queen-of-hearts in jousts with blunt lances when his reward was perhaps a kerchief from her lily-white hands, he laid the women in his native town of Azpeitia with contemptuous disdain. He strutted about, with a skinful of wine under his dagger, looking for trouble and getting it. A contemporary told of him that 'he was reckless in games, in adventures with women, in brawls and deeds of arms'. An official document, a minute of the correctional court of Guipuzcoa to the episcopal court in Pamplona in 1515, records him as 'bold and defiant, clothed in leather trousers and cuirass, armed with dagger and pistol, his long hair flowing from beneath his knight's cap of velvet'. The judge described his character as 'cunning, violent and vindictive'. Inigo himself told, after his conversion, that he had had no scruples about allowing a man to be sentenced for a theft which he himself had committed. It is significant that the description of any contemporary juvenile delinquent would have fitted him like his own dogskin gloves.

The easy rebellious life wasn't to last. A court scandal, in which surprisingly he had no part, brought his patrons into disfavour with his queen-of-hearts. His hopes of a glorious career at court came to an end. He was forced to look for another calling. In nepotism another relation, the Duke of Najera who was viceroy of Navarre, offered him a commission in his guard. Inigo, after the frippery of court, had the unpleasant surprise of being recruited as a footslogger. But his ambition was undimmed. Hell-bent on heroism he reckoned that, if he could not be a royal favourite, he would anyway distinguish himself in the unsettled border province as a gallant soldier against the French. To his disgust, as he stamped the parade ground, peace reigned in the country.

But in those days even an impatient Basque had not to wait long. It was a phase of European history in which national borders were undefined and nationalism, with all its grim implications for the future, was beginning to find expression. For some dim reason, in that age when Castile, victorious, drove the Moors out of Granada, the French king, Francis I, decided that Navarre must be taken back from Spain. In 1521, an army of twelve thousand men advanced on Pamplona. The city was undergarrisoned, and the artillery inadequate. The townspeople were for surrender. Inigo, when he got the news of war, force-marched his men from his own province. At Pamplona he denounced the Mayor of the City for his cowardice. For Inigo it was death or glory, and honour before all. 'His nightly excesses, serious and grave misdemeanours' hadn't sapped his passionate loyalty to the throne of Castile. His reputation as a troublemaker hadn't diminished his power of leadership and persuasion. Against hopeless odds he inspired his faltering companions to face the foe. As there was no priest inside the citadel, Inigo confessed his sins to a brother officer. Then he posted himself in the breastworks of the fortress where the battle was hottest.

There was to be no gallant sword play for him, no equestrian feats of arms. The French bombarded the inadequately guarded citadel for six hours. When they moved in, they found Inigo in a welter of blood. A wayward cannonball had shattered one leg and damaged the other. After the surrender which, in the bread-and-butter of history, proved nothing and changed nothing, the French commander allowed the surgeons, as best they could, and it was a pretty bad best, to set Inigo's leg. A fortnight later they allowed him to be littered home to Loyola.

From the victor it was a chivalrous gesture to a fallen enemy which he surely forgot as Anatole France, in a short story, suggested that Pontius Pilate in his old age might have forgotten the trial of the King of the Jews. Neither of them could have imagined, Caesar's procurator or the general of the French King, that what had seemed an end was a beginning. A stone ball, lobbed by a clumsy cannon in Pamplona, helped to win a transient battle. The soldier who fell to it was destined, as a direct result of his wounds, to change the course of history.

The citadel in Pamplona where Inigo fell has gone with the wind. A group bronze on the site, a twin casting of one at Loyola, commemorates him on his litter with his helmeted henchmen at his side. A fragment of the old city walls, and the bridge over the Arga where the victorious French stormed into the city – only to be thrown out again within the year – sur-

vives. Like most of Spain, Pamplona is still riddled with relics
of the past. Better to look at the living people, the Basques in
their black berets with their big noses, square bodies, grave
comportment and proud charm. Citadels fall, stones crumble;
but in the immortality of genes nothing changes. Bernard
Shaw wrote that, in the study of history, it is important to
remember that the people of the past were people just like us.
You can see 'Inigo Loyolas' running bulls, playing pelota,
listening to pop music, in the Basque country today. Looking
at them it is strange to reflect that if Inigo had fallen in our own
time scale, instead of his, his leg would almost certainly have
been properly set; and that he would have passed by as just
another unknown soldier.

That he didn't is one of the mysteries of this life. At first, and
later, all he was determined about was how soon he could get
his leg into a well-cut riding boot again. He stiffly paid his
respects to the Frenchman, who had given him parole, by
surrendering his sword. In his pain he gritted his teeth for the
long march to Loyola.

He was littered for a fortnight. His people thought it too
dangerous, with French skirmishers on the hoof, to carry him
through the river valley which is the easiest way. They dragged
him over the mountains. After the heights of Lizarrega, the path
descended to Ozaeta where, in high fever and near to death, he
had to be rested. In Arzuelan, they stopped at the house of one
of his sisters. When, at painful last, they reached the bridge at
Loyola – ninety-two kilometres at footpace with a wounded
man – it was his sister-in-law, Magdalena, who welcomed him
home. His brothers were still at the wars. She made ready for
him the finest room in the upper storey of the castle.

Inigo, whose courage was astounding, was confident of his
recovery. The doctors, whose ineptitude was calamitous, did
their wretched best to kill him. They were brought from all
over the place. With pompous nods of the head they agreed that
Inigo's broken leg had grown crookedly. The bone would not
heal. Proudly, Inigo told them to break it again, and set it

properly. He endured the torture, without anaesthetic, for a second time. He suffered it, with only white clenched knuckles to show his agony. He was expected to die.

When he recovered, it was discovered that a piece of bone beneath the knee of his right leg had pushed itself forward over the other and was projecting uglily. It was more than Inigo could stand for. In a horseman's age women judged a man by the turn of his leg. With his heart bent on chivalrous achievement he demanded that the lump of bone must be sawn away. He let them do it in grim silence. He submitted to being put on a primitive surgical rack in which it was attempted to straighten the limb. Of course the barbarous process failed. He was doomed to a short leg and a limp for the rest of his life. In exquisite pain he stuck it out on his bed at Loyola, month after month, refusing to believe that he couldn't draw his sword and ride for Castile again.

His brother brought him news that the invading French had been defeated. Old drinking pals warmed his heart by visiting him on his sick-bed. His patron, the Duke of Najera, had not lost interest in his welfare. Inigo was convinced that new glories, but not the glories he expected, awaited him. As he recovered his vigour, although he could not yet put his damaged leg on the ground, he asked his sister-in-law for copies of the romantic books of chivalry which had inspired him at court. There were none at Loyola. But what she found were four leather-bound volumes in which, long before, a German Carthusian monk had written a life of Christ. She also produced a thick book of pious legends called *The Flowers of the Saints*. With nothing else to engage him the young knight, at first reluctantly, plodded through the wooden type.

He read of hermits, of ascetics, of mystics who scourged themselves to blood. He read of men whose joy was penance, who had dismissed wordly thoughts; and who had found fulfilment in beggarly poverty and spiritual glory; of saints who were elevated from the ground, fed by angels, and worked miracles; of knights of the faith who set out on their errantry without

INIGO

armour or plumes, with a pilgrim's staff instead of a sword, and
without as much as a groat in their pockets. On his lonely couch
Inigo slowly conceived himself as a soldier not of his queen-of-
hearts, but of the Queen of Heaven. He began to think of himself not as *Amadis of Gaul* but as a Knight of God.

With a shortened leg and a limp he couldn't cut a dash any
more with a lance in his hand. But he could bring heroic fame
to his family in Loyola by carrying the standard of Jesus. In
imitation of the old saints he would vow himself to God even
more fervently than they had. He would subject himself to
greater suffering, dedicate himself to greater mystical achievement.

Contemporary psychiatrists know that it is almost impossible
to undergo a terrible physical experience without a change of
personality. Many men become wrecks. A few, Inigo was one
of them, are diverted from one stream of enthusiasm to another.
At first his conversion of spirit was a muddled one. He modelled
himself, in a different cause, on Amadis, the wandering Knight.
He got it into his sick head that he was called, as a penitent, to
reclaim for Christendom the holy city of Jerusalem from the
Turks. He would achieve it by preaching, poverty and prayer.
He swore, in bitter memory of his past, perpetual chastity. He
couldn't wait to get on his legs to find a new future and a new
mission.

He undoubtedly surprised his numerous relations. After expecting him to die, they discovered him sending a house servant
to Burgos to bring back information about the rule of St Bruno,
of the monks who preserved holy silence. He told his family
that it was his intention 'to abandon everything in starkest
poverty, to walk unknown as a pilgrim through the world, to
be treated with contempt'. It is reasonable to suppose that they
thought him mad. So, in a sense, he was. How often lunatics
have changed the world.

When, after a year, he recovered his health, with a short leg
and a limp, Inigo, in his knightly finery, made family visits.
He told them of his ambition to change his way of life. He

95

revealed to them his intention of going with a begging bowl to Jerusalem. It seems that they treated him with affectionate patience. His brother showed him the charms of his estate at Loyola, reminding him of all the goods things he would inherit. His old patron, the Duke of Najera, insisted on paying his wages as a soldier, which the Duke at that time could ill-afford. Inigo used them to pay debts out of his frivolous past, and to restore a picture of the Madonna in his parish church.

As a person, in that phase of his life, he must have been exasperating. He was to realise before long that, although he could read and write, ride a horse and cross a sword, he was a simple provincial. In due course he was to regret so many of his extravagances as, in the early years of his conversion, he regretted the extravagances of his youthful life. He is probably the most attractive saint in the calendar because he was so essentially human, so wilful, so precipitate in conduct, so persuasive, so full of sin and forgiveness, and so splendidly brave. I envy the women who knew him in his wild youth. I envy the men who, in his maturity, he led. The silly asceticism of his middle age is understandable; it was socially fashionable at the time. The fact that, after years of folly, he attained a Roman gravity, and an art of worldly management, is one of the wonders of history.

When he left Loyola on his chivalrous pilgrimage Inigo was accompanied on the first part of his journey by his retainers and relations in the manner in which the crusaders went to war. After parting from them, he directed his mule towards Barcelona; to Montserrat, the ancient Benedictine monastery hanging like a swallow's nest on the walls of the mountains outside the city. On the way he exchanged his knightly dress with a beggar who must surely have been puzzled to know what to do with the raiment. He kept only his sword. In pilgrim's clothes, he kicked his mule up three thousand feet to the monastery. The new life to which he had dedicated himself was beginning.

After weeks, in which Benedictine monks instructed him, he kept vigil, in the way he had learnt in *Amadis of Gaul*, before the venerated statue of the Black Virgin there, and in the style of the knights of old. He hung his sword on an iron grille in dedication to the Madonna. He gave his mule to the hospitable monks. And then he went on his footsore way.

A traveller in Spain can readily imagine today that he has adventured beyond the barrier of time. Past is particularly present; present has made relatively small impact on the past. When it fell to me, in a television programme four hundred and fifty years after, to offer the saint's sword to the Black Virgin again, Inigo might have been beside me. Television cameras with their sound recorders, lights and cables, confer on the man standing in front of them a mystic and lonely experience of their own. Hearing my voice at night when the basilica was empty, speaking so loud in such a quiet and venerable setting, I was awed. Earlier I had listened to the monks, their heads buried in their black cowls, chanting plainsong with the same timeless beauty that the votive candles in the chapels spilt their wax. I had wandered in the old cloisters where Inigo had walked and talked before me. The Angelus bell sounded a summons to serenity.

The monastery at Montserrat must be as near to heaven on earth as men can reach. It has all the appurtenances of tourism; shops, funiculas, cabled railways, restaurants and bars; and, these days, even a hotel. But the edifice, first carved by the Benedictines into the composite rock of the mountains thirty-six years before the Battle of Hastings, the place in which Inigo dedicated himself in the time of King Henry VIII to the Mother of Christ, has the aura of a prayer in stone.

To an Anglo-Saxon the queue of pilgrims insanitarily kissing the orb in the hand of the Black Virgin, beautiful as she is, is distasteful. But the Latins like it that way. A journalist is more interested to observe that, although numerous writers have declared that the Virgin's face has been blackened by the votive candles of the faithful over the centuries, the fact is that her face was black in the first place. There are mysteries about the statue, said to date from the late eleventh century; but my own guess is that the face was made of black wood in the Biblical tradition of 'black but beautiful'. Never mind. Inigo wouldn't have bothered himself, when he was filled with his conversion, with enigmas like that.

The pervading sweetness of Montserrat today is the vision, every day, of girls in bridal dresses who have come to the monastery to be married, leaving behind their white veils and bouquets as a pious tribute to the statue; of light-footed priests leading their flocks in Catalan dances in the piazza which has been sliced out of the rock; of black-robed monks peering down shyly from the windows of the monastery on the gay scene. The Benedictines are more reluctant to expose themselves than the Jesuits. The world outside the monastery is evidently not for them. But they provide taped music for the folk dances.

Fenestrating, as Max Beerbohm called it, at my hotel window I thought, as I had thought in India when I saw the Hindus uproariously taking one of their Gods for a walk on his feastday, how much fuller religion is when it is part of the fun of life; how empty, at its worst, the dire horror, for example, of Sabbatarianism in the north of Scotland. And yet Inigo, at the beginning, in imitation of the early Christian hermits, was fired with the same hell-raising zeal as a 'Little Minister'. Looking out over the piazza at Montserrat down the drop from the monastery over the fingered rocks into the blue valley three thousand feet below, I tried as an exercitant to follow Inigo, in the folly of his life, on his way.

It was a folly he himself was to recognise many years later. His first aim was to emulate, even outdo, the ascetism of the early Christian saints. When he left Montserrat, after keeping vigil 'according to the ancient and solemn rites for a nobleman', he was in a half-world in which he was at once Amadis, the romantic knight, and one of the band of legendary saints, armed with cowl and penitential girdle, who had achieved the Kingdom of Heaven.

Such was his confused state of mind that on his way to Montserrat when he encountered a Morisco, a Christian Arab, who debated with him whether the virginity of Mary could have survived after the birth of Christ, he reached for his dagger. Sensing danger, the Morisco galloped ahead leaving Inigo reflecting, in the manner of *Amadis of Gaul* whether, in the name of chivalry, he ought to kill the fellow. In keeping with a pagan custom he looked for 'a sign'. He gave his mule free reign; but the mule disdained to give chase to a baptised heathen.

In keeping with a mediaeval conception of religious devotion, the pious rubbish he had read in the lives of the saints, he left Montserrat determined to do bloody penance. In the act he nearly killed himself.

For his retreat he chose a cleft in the rock on the banks of the river Cardener at the religious town of Manresa, today about half-an-hour's drive from Montserrat. I travelled there, apt for grace, to discover that the slit in the rock had been converted in the seventeenth century into a baroque chapel, lined with alabaster plaques and bad paintings. About it is a Jesuit house. All that is left of Inigo in his 'primitive church' are the crosses which he reputedly carved in the stone. In the dreary little industrial town which is Manresa today, his cave deserves a better fate. The pilgrim walks in the footsteps of Inigo more closely up the road which corkscrews its way to Montserrat, down the bubbling course of the Arga to Loyola; in sleepy villages where the peasants wear the same kind of sandals, *alpergatas*, which Inigo wore on his tortured way.

He apparently intended to stop in Manresa for only a few days. In his abstraction he punished himself there for ten months. He flagellated himself, he fasted, he denied sleep. He sprinkled ashes on black bread to make it more unpalatable. He wouldn't comb his matted hair, or trim his broken finger nails. When he permitted himself rest he pillowed his head on a lump of wood. In rags, carrying a rough calabash, he begged for alms, which he then distributed to the poor of the town. He rejoiced in his lowliness and his loneliness. An 'Inigo' in our own times would certainly have been removed to a public institution. In his time, as in India now, holy men commanded superstitious respect.

For the mercy of God, people put alms in his begging-bowl. The religious communities opened their doors in Christian charity.

But there was more to Inigo than that. Though he consorted as he did with the poorest of the poor, they recognised that he was not one of them. The people in the little town realised it too. Inigo's proud head, however filthy his body, gave him away. However much he wished to deny it, his fascination for women never deserted him. His life was saved at Manresa, and later at Barcelona, by devoted women who mothered him back into something like health. He did his best to undo their ministrations. He scourged himself daily, even beating his chest with a stone. Once, carried unconscious to the house of one of his patronesses, when the doctors dsepaired of his life, there were found in the cupboard of his cell his weapons of mortification – a girdle worked with wire, chains, nails strung together in the form of a cross, and an undergarment interwoven with small iron thorns.

Of all the saints, the life of Inigo is probably the most thoroughly authenticated. In latter years he told so much in confession to his community, wrote so much that is extant. He recorded his struggle at Manresa; how after a few weeks of penance and fast, he saw diabolical images; how there were times when he contemplated suicide; how at last he achieved a spiritual elation in which he had visions of Heaven. It is unnecessary to seek a miraculous explanation. It is not belittling, or irreverent, to look for a human one. Ultimately, albeit painfully, the penitent evolved into a leader of disciplined sanctity and true greatness.

It is absurd but also true that, out of worldly accident, I myself have had a faint taste of what went on inside Inigo de Loyola. In 1960 I was cast away on a desert island, a thousand miles from anywhere, in the Indian Ocean. I did it, not to find erusalem, but in the mundane cause of a journalistic assignment.

I deliberately undertook for a popular newspaper to test my capacity for survival on an isolated island. None believed in that mad part of the world, that I could achieve it. I was filled with doubts about myself. In the event the experience tested me to the limit.

I made a landfall after a nightmare in high seas battened down in the fo'cs'le of an Aberdeen trawler half-filled with seawater and swimming with a cargo of shark meat. For forty-eight hours without food in the bucking boat I was certain that we were going to the bottom. In semi-delirium, although I willed hard to control myself, I saw in the blackness the devilish things, the grinning gargoyles, the obscene shapes which Inigo belaboured with his pilgrim's staff in his cave. I hung over 'terrifying abysses', a familiar phenomenon of children's nightmares, a nauseous experience which is not confined to holy men, nor far removed from a bilious attack.

In the enforced solitude, when I got to the island, the next symptom – it showed itself after a few days – was that an impersonal disc jockey started working in my head. Although I know no note of music, and have little ear for it, I found myself reluctantly listening to orchestral scores which, in normal times, I could scarcely hum. But, insistently, they filled my brain. I didn't want it. I wanted to listen to the mewing of the seabirds, the whisper of the palm-fans and the music of the sea. But the noise wouldn't go away. I was told by medical men later that this is a normal phenomenon in a man who deprives himself suddenly of regular meals and an even moderate alcoholic intake.

Soon I was filled with a great gloom, a fear that I couldn't see through the mission I had imposed on myself. I notched the passing days with my knife on a palm tree. I had no terror of solitude; indeed I largely welcomed it. In my case it wasn't surprising. In my calling as a writer, I am accustomed to self-communion. For Inigo, brought up in the gregarious environment of court and military camp, it must have been more difficult. Indeed, he later showed that he was essentially one whose personality required a company of men about him.

Like me he exercised his mind in writing; fumbling at first, seeking the way to gain God. I, the professional, made the record for the popular prints. Undernourished, physically over-stretched, I subsequently had to rewrite most of what I had put down. Inigo later admitted that he revised the Spiritual Exercises he first composed at Manresa again and again over the years. I can guess how vague and indecisive the first version must have been.

Inigo told how, in his ecstasy at Manresa, he fell to tears, a habit which persisted through his life, and caused his eyelids to remain permanently red-rimmed and inflamed. In the night watches, spearing fish in the lagoon, I laughed and sang. The two emotions are closely related.

Like Inigo I grew a nest of uncombed hair and developed a straggling beard. My finger nails also were black and broken, and there were tropical sores weeping in my legs. I was emaciated as Inigo clearly became in his cave at Manresa. And I, too, as the weight fell off me, felt a wild elation. I, too, like Inigo, had hallucinations and extrasensory perceptions.

When they came to take me off the island, I could move only on hands and knees. I was speeded in my recovery, stage by stage on my way home, by the ministrations of devoted women. Any man, or castaway, an escaped prisoner of war, any off-beat figure in society, comes upon them – women who, without asking questions, will look after him. In my case, stage after stage as I made my way home, they appeared – Ignatius might have said miraculously – to nurse me back to health.

II

Master Ignatius

THE fantasy Inigo had conceived on his sick bed in Loyola was that he could succeed where the Crusaders had failed. He became obsessed with the quixotic notion that single-handed, armed with piety alone, he could throw the infidel out of the Holy City. His retreat to Manresa was a spiritual preparation for his encounter with the windmills of Islam.

As a knight errant he could scarcely have made a worse start. Weakened by fasting and self-mortification, it was a wonder that he could walk. After my own experience at sub-subsistence level, it was weeks before I could struggle in and out of a bath without help. And I hadn't flagellated myself, as he did day after day; denied the call of sleep, or scorned good food. In motoring jargon Inigo, astonishingly, ran on an empty tank.

In contemporary terms what he set out to achieve was a 'Wosbee', one of those initiative tests devised by the British army in which a cadet, on a ration of something like sixpence and a raw potato, is required to solve a problem, make a difficult cross-country journey, and achieve an aim. None has set himself a more formidable 'Wosbee' than Inigo.

The females, fluttering about the holy man, tried to dissuade him from undertaking the wild adventure. They did prevent him from sailing on a small brig to Italy which foundered on the voyage. They pressed money on him, but it was useless because he gave it away to the first beggar he encountered. But the women, who clearly adored the courtier of Heaven, persuaded him to get his nails cut, and his hair trimmed, for his journey.

PILGRIMAGE

In a grey-brown cassock, with a wooden cross and a begging bowl about his neck, leaning in his limping walk on a pilgrim's staff, Inigo went on his way; regretted, we may be sure, by the other sex looking over their shoulders at what might have been. So much nonsense is written in the name of piety. The nuts and bolts of existence never change. It is told of Inigo that, after his brave trudge to Barcelona, a woman saw him kneeling in the cathedral in prayer. She felt compelled to speak to him. She took him into her house, and mothered him. There was no marvel in it; although she later imagined that she saw a light like a halo over his head. All she did was a natural feminine thing in a man's crazy world. Something like it has even happened to sinners like me.

What was incredible, in the face of all the odds Inigo stacked against himself, was that he got to Jerusalem. He left Manresa on February 18th, 1523. He was in the Via Appia in Rome on Palm Sunday. He was there to ask the new Pope, Adrian VI, for his papal visa. At that time, the crisis in the Church – Rome in its second decline in the decadence of the Renaissance – made no impact on him. He couldn't look left or right. The eyes of the raw recruit were lifted towards the Holy Land, and Heaven. With the obstinacy of a Spanish bull, almost as stupidly, he was charging the red rag.

With papal authority to make the pilgrimage, for what the paper was worth, he set out for Venice at a time when the Turks, who had just seized the Island of Rhodes, were threatening Rome itself. Islam was in glory: Christendom was in a mess. The holy simpleton didn't know; or perhaps even care.

He made his way through a countryside riddled with bubonic plague. People locked their doors against the emaciated man whom they reasonably supposed was a victim. He slept rough, and went hungry. At Chiozza he learnt that Venice, as a plague precaution, was closed. Other pilgrims went to Padua to collect health certificates. Inigo was too exhausted to march again. He counted it a miracle that, the following morning, he was allowed to enter the city without question. It was no miracle. The

Venetians were commercial travellers who, plague or no plague, weren't going to shut out any tourist at the time of their Great Spring Fair. Inigo's miracle is reminiscent of the story of the Great Exhibition in Paris in the nineteenth century when it is said that a woman was struck down with plague on the eve of the opening of the show. The authorities conjured her away and made sure that nobody would admit, even to her daughter who accompanied her, that her mother had even existed. Inigo's journey is best regarded, not as a miracle, but football pool luck.

Indifferent to money, 'prompted only by love, faith and hope', he listened disinterestedly to other pilgrims haggling for a passage with the shipowners on the waterfront. He himself had no money, so the matter didn't concern him. In company with the pigeons, he pillowed his head on the stones in the arcades of St Mark's Square. He was discovered by a rich Venetian, no doubt his unusual appearance and courtly manner stood him in good stead again, who offered him hospitality in his palazzo. Not long after he encountered an acquaintance, a wealthy Spanish merchant who, under the old pals act, promised to use his influence with the Doge to arrange a free passage to Jaffa. Inigo, not unwilling to accept what today would be called a public relations ride, sailed in a well-found caravel, probably a similar vessel to the one on which Columbus voyaged to the new world, in company with the Venetian governor of Cyprus.

Although the Turks were again on the rampage with Christendom, they didn't permit religious scruples to interfere with the profitable tourist trade in Jerusalem, any more than the Venetians cared to put off their Fair to keep out the plague. From the time the pilgrims came ashore, fervently kissing the soil of the Holy Land, up to the gates of Jerusalem, they were subjected to a monstrous series of government levies. Herded like cattle, prodded by armed soldiers, cheated of every ducat that could be extracted out of them, treated with the sort of contempt which is the especial horror of bureaucracy, they were given no respite until they reached the shelter of the Franciscan monastery on Mount Zion. There they were told by the monks that they were forbidden to walk alone, disfigure the holy places with graffiti; or profane by their presence the mosques.

The pilgrims to the Holy Land in the sixteenth century have not been the only ones to be disabused. In my turn, I was appalled by the Church of the Holy Sepulchre, a monument to human vulgarity, where the various Christian sects – with the Abyssinians hanging by the skin of their teeth on the roof – wrangle with each other over their altar territories, and draw lines to regulate whose brooms sweep whose floors. The edifice, winking like a pin-table with tourists' photo-flashes, denies prayer. The guides, like blowflies, wait to collect their own imposts. In the Holy Sepulchre itself, a bearded Orthodox priest collects gratuities.

The authenticity of so many of the shrines is dubious. The Way of the Cross, the Via Dolorosa, is now buried nine feet under the rubble of the centuries. It is only a guess where Pilate held court, just a pious tradition that the ancient olive trees in what may have been the Garden of Gethsemane were growing there in Christ's time. I tried, how I tried, to recapture the magic of the past – away from guides, picture postcards, officious priests, and packaged tours. I stayed in a Franciscan convent in the old city during Easter, a beautiful place – improbably named Casa Nova – in which, with other pilgrims, I was encompassed with holy hospitality.

I was told that I must see the old city in the moonlight. I walked through narrow unlit streets still mercifully clear of traffic. I moved in places in which the very stones seem to drip with blood. I almost persuaded myself, in the silver light, that I could hear the clank of the armour of the Roman legionaries.

In an alleyway, I saw a woman dressed as the Madonna might have been. As she passed me, she said 'Hello, darling'. I fled back to the good nuns. It had already befallen me that, in Bethlehem of all places, I had been inveigled into making a brief visit to a sleazy night club.

In the steps of the Master – and it seemed to me that H. V. Morton, in his gentle way, had arrived at much the same impression that I did – I felt closer to the story of the Gospel when Jerusalem, and the shrines of the Holy Places, were behind me. The emotive things were the shepherds leading their flocks of hair sheep, often with an orphan lamb in their arms, from one bit of miserable grazing to the next one; of an ox and an ass harnessed together in front of a primitive plough; of picking up a poor man, as the Samaritan did, in the barren country, where nothing seems to live but grasshoppers, on the way down to Jericho, and the Dead Sea; of watching farmers hand-sowing corn in the rock-strewn fields. I used to think that the sower in the parable must have been a rotten agriculturalist. After travelling the Holy Land I realise that he had no choice, in that unwelcoming terrain, but to chuck and chance it.

When the party of pilgrims reached Jerusalem in 1523, maybe Inigo alone was undismayed. Somehow he paid the Turks' taxes, probably out of the charity of his companions. The other pilgrims were looking forward to winning the indulgences of the Church which were awarded like trading stamps in the holy places visited by the devout. They aimed to make their way home with credit in Purgatory, the waiting room on the way to eternity. Not Inigo. He alone had no doubt what he was about to do. He meant to remain the rest of his mortal life preaching to the infidel in Jerusalem. When the others got ready to go he didn't even bother to assemble his meagre belongings. The Provincial of the Franciscans, with the authority which the Order exerts in the city up to the present time, told him that his mission was impracticable; that the Muslims wouldn't tolerate his personal crusade. Inigo was unconvinced until the Provincial showed him the papal bull giving him supreme authority over the Christians in the Holy City. He couldn't override the orders of the Pope. With a box of faded flowers, soil and stones he had collected from the holy ground – which, charmingly and characteristically, he planned to present to a pious woman in the convent of Las Jeronimas – he journeyed sadly back to Europe.

His brave mission had been a total failure. A proud man, and

a Spaniard to boot, he might well have committed himself to
oblivion in his cave at Manresa; indeed, he contemplated doing
just that. But, whatever it is that is genius – I am inclined to
think that it is often a matter of inspired timing – he pressed on
like a spider with a broken web. He concluded that he was
lacking in education, as he was. He was excited by the notion,
sung in popular terms hundreds of years later in the romantic
musical: 'Give me the men who are stout-hearted men, and I'll
soon give you ten thousand more'. He plodded on to immortality.

In the rotting timbers of ships about as seaworthy as walnut
shells, travelling on land at the speed of the pack-horses, people
at that time had something that we – cursing aircraft which
never take off when the airlines say they will, the hired car which
is never the one that has been ordered – have lost. They had
time to think. Inigo, at his own pace, came to nudge the pattern
of the world, ours as well as his.

It is memorable, considered in terms of a modern traveller,
that, after arriving back in Venice in the middle of January, 1524,
he tramped in February across the Lombardy Plains to Genoa.
Lombardy was at war with Spain. The Spaniards arrested him
as a spy and, after beating him, dismissed him as a harmless fool.
Times change, people don't. Unfortunate for anyone in Spain
today who has an incident with a car.

Inigo was picked up again by the Dons' opponents, the
French soldiers who, thanks to a meeting with a Basque friend
of his in that then small world, gave him safe conduct. He was
welcomed as a passenger aboard a prison galley rowing to
Barcelona. He was sick with colic; but after all he had done to
himself, and in the ghastly pattern of medical care in that age,
he clearly had a constitution of iron. He needed it. In the
pestiferous times in which he lived he was better without the
ministrations of the doctors, with their poisonous remedies,
their leeches, their blood-letting and their infected knives. It is
likely that he ultimately achieved almost his three score and ten
because he denied in sanctity almost all the fats of existence. His

ascetism made his belly moan; but his heart, with scarcely any work to do on his body, pumped as sweetly as a Rolls Royce. He was at last approaching to something like rhythm within himself. The gloom, the ghosts, the hysteria of Manresa were coming under his intellectual control. Aboard the prison galley – he was too young in social history to be horrified by the wretches in chains rowing him to Spain – it is possible that 'in a glass darkly' he saw his future.

He was still off-course. At just thirty-three years of age he went back to school in Barcelona to learn from the beginning. He insisted to his masters that, if he failed in his classical learning, he expected the same corporal punishment which was meted out to the schoolboys. No doubt he was a masochist. He was probably in the same extraordinary bent as Lawrence of Arabia, living in a fantasy world, inventing mysteries. He wasn't finished with his folly; but, step by step, he can be followed with the certainty of a balance glass, the bubble rolling here and there, until it finally settled on centre.

Another two years passed in the boys' school at Barcelona until, in the spring of 1526, two examiners declared him fit to follow lectures on philosophy in the University of Alcala in Castile. He was in two minds whether to study the humanities of the world, or devote himself exclusively to God. He wobbled about, first in Alcala, then in Salamanca, trying to organise a lay apostolate at the same time that he was pursuing his studies. He attracted, out of his early endeavours, disciples and supporters in the way that adolescent students are drawn to strong person-alities now. His command was emotional, rather than intellect-ual. Never a great scholar, his holiness, like an Indian Guru dominating a Beatle, brought domestic servants and prostitutes to his feet. It is a rather uncomfortable thing in Inigo's formative life that, giving religious instruction to illiterate nincompoops, he reduced them in the passion of confession to fainting, spasms and epileptic fits. In his piety he had forgotten it; but Inigo, the old Inigo, could seduce their minds.

His first handful of disciples adopted what we should call

today hippie dress. They came to be known as greycoats. Inevitably their activities, and his, roused the interest of officials of the Spanish Inquisition. It is popularly thought that the Inquisition was a Jesuit thing. It wasn't; it was a Dominican thing. And it was nothing like as evil as it is painted. Certainly the Inquisitors perpetrated horrors; but not in excess of what has happened in our own age, and not out of keeping with the rough custom of justice in its own period. It had a job to do in a time of heresy, religious decadence, and counter-reformation which was unpleasant, but not more unpleasant than some counter-revolutionary activities today.

Inigo was hauled in front of them twice. The second time he was imprisoned with irons on his legs, for forty-two days. But the Inquisitors could find no heretical fault in him. He was released on the understanding that he and his disciples were to stop preaching, wearing long hair and funny clothes. No more than might be said by a magistrate to the organiser of a demo today.

He made a brave attempt at Alcala, and subsequently at Salamanca, to start his army; but it was as callow as students' campaigns usually are. Mentally, he was still an adolescent. His recruits, enthusiastic at first, fell away. In disappointment, he left Spain. He loaded his books on a donkey. He paused, in the leisurely way of his times, for three months at Barcelona where 'pious ladies', who never deserted him, gave him twenty-five ducats for his further education. In the new year of 1528 he footed it a thousand kilometres to Paris. He arrived on February 2.

At the age of thirty-seven, he was determined to improve his knowledge of languages, to study Latin in which 'he had hurried too quickly from grammar to higher studies'; to take a course in philosophy at what was then the greatest university of the Western world, with four thousand students and over fifty colleges.

With sublime indifference he passed his twenty-five ducats, enough in the currency of the times to pay for a year's education, to a Spanish room-mate who squandered the lot. He became once again a beggar on the streets. In a then milling city of three hundred thousand people he at last began to realise that there was no future without earthly goods. He begged on the wealthy Spanish merchants in Flanders. Later, in 1531, he was to journey to London, 'from which he brought back more alms than all he had raised in these previous years'. Thenceforward, there was no more nonsense of throwing money away. Inigo had learnt its power, and he used it with discretion. He discarded beggar's rags, and adopted the students' black gown, which he wore for the rest of his life; and which is essentially the false-sleeved cassock which the Jesuits wear inside their houses to this day. With money in his pocket, he entered the Collège de St Barbe as a paying student.

He shared a room with two others; Pierre Favre, the gifted son of a French peasant, and a Spaniard with somewhat doubtful claim to noble rank. His name was Francisco de Jassu y Xavier; and he didn't let anybody forget it. From the start Inigo, with the eye of a spiritual sergeant-major, measured his companions for conversion and recruitment. Favre, a poor scholar grateful for the financial help Inigo was now able to offer, was an early disciple. Xavier regarded his fellow countrymen as an inter-fering crank. On his side there was the sort of antagonism which so often exists between room-fellows, especially in youth and in closed university life.

Xavier was a blade, as Inigo had been. He was riding high in the town, drinking them under the table, throwing the doxies into bed. He regarded the unctuous admonitions of Inigo with proud contempt. But, inevitably, there came a time when he was broke. Inigo helped him out. And there the story began.

It is possible that the fear of venereal disease, the new disease which had invaded a frightened Europe, gave Xavier first cause to consider the dangers of his excesses. Or it may be that he listened out of courtesy to his room-mate, who issued petty cash and, pursuing his indomitable mission, lectured him on spiritual exercise. However it was, Inigo unveiled uncertainties in his neophite's mind. For Xavier, learning came easily. But Inigo had the conviction which Xavier lacked. He drew the man to him, little by little, who was to become the most inspired missionary of the Roman church.

Xavier was volatile: and, although the lives of the saints are normally written in such solemn piety that you can scarcely believe that they were human at all, my guess is that he enjoyed a holy gaiety. Not Inigo. I suspect that he was without laughter. He clearly had the intensity, his whole life supports it, which attracts women. It is a generalisation, but there is a core of truth in it, that women resent men who are too quick to laugh. There are men, too, who can only fulfil themselves through the vale of tears. It is told of Inigo that, on an occasion when he was challenged to a billiards game, he accepted on the understanding that, if he won, he would subject the loser to a course of spiritual instruction. I doubt whether he said it with a smile. The people who in great causes and lesser ones, aim to improve us have seldom seen the joke. It may be blasphemous, but it has always disappointed me that there are no good laughs in the Gospels. Surely Jesus laughed? Or didn't he? If not, it's a rotten prospect in Paradise.

Nobody could have written that in Inigo's time. In the sixteenth and seventeenth centuries they were intolerant, to the degree of torture, of dissenters. They were intolerant because they passionately believed. We are tolerant because so many of us are doubters. In that period Heaven and Hell, however abstract the conceptions seem now, were accepted as concrete things which, in the words of the old Latin grammar, you could almost 'touch and see'. While the warring Christian sects devoutedly immolated their heretics, none doubted that their victims were going to a place where they either looked up or looked down.

It is the more remarkable that, in mediaeval Christian teaching, Heaven was only for the elect, the ascetics who found communion with God in ecstasy. It was predestined, it was said – Calvin, the brilliant Protestant, was one who believed it –

that only those who received a *donum extraordinarium* would receive the revelation of God. The doctrine didn't offer much hope for the ordinary fellow. St Teresa of Avila tried to help. Asked why she was so pious when quite ordinary people might well hope for some sort of reward in the next world, she replied: 'Your glass of happiness will be smaller than mine'. So the holy people were treated with unholy respect.

The man in bodily filth, hunger and inactivity, sitting in a cave with reason impotent, memory dead, every sensible perception dimmed, was able to behold the glory of God. It was called purification. It is told of St Francis of Assisi that, in his dedication to spirituality, he felt the sufferings of Christ so much that the stigmata of the Crucifixion showed on his body. It has happened to others since. No psychologist is surprised. Men and women can will outward physical symptoms.

In Mysore in Southern India, where mystics prevail today, I visited a holy man, made of skin and bone, lying on a shelf in a cave. He invited me to come again that night when he would pass into a trance. I found him as near dead as a hibernating reptile. Crouched on the stone of his cave, the pupils of his eyes had dropped in a sunset under the lower lids. His body temperature and heartbeat were negligible. When I anxiously returned the following morning, he was waiting brightly for baksheesh, and hanging out his washing.

Inigo, in his cave at Manresa, sought in the beginning a spiritual vacuum like a yogi in India. But, after the first emotional heat of his conversion, he woke to what amounted to the cold touch of a hotwater bottle after a deep night's sleep. What he passionately felt he had to preach is that the way to Christ is not for the few, and the very few – as Disraeli was to say later of privilege – but for all who, out of free will, bend their imaginations to the Godhead. He conceived, crudely at first, a disciplined mental order to achieve it.

The Spiritual Exercises, updated over the centuries, as their founder intended they should be, are difficult to read. They were never meant to be accepted as literature. In some respects they appear contradictory. But the work, small in length, is a drill book, in the army sense, which demands the practical application of the weapons of the intellect. It needs to be studied like poetry, lacking though it is in the felicity of its words. The wonder of great poetry is that so much of it can be only half-perceived. I doubt whether Shakespeare, relaxing over a glass of wine, could recall the Elysian inspiration in which he wrote; or, in after-thought, have told a fraction of what he meant.

It is a good comparison to think of the mystery of our minds as a series of moving concentric circles, black in the radial extremities, increasingly vague and grey towards the middle. In idleness, the circles scarcely move. In concentration, they draw in faster towards a hot centre. In genius, the circles all come together, however briefly, on a burning point of ultimate truth.

Since Inigo was trying to express the inexplicable, without the gifts of a Milton, a Dante, or a Goethe, the only way to understand his Exercises is to put action into his words.

Inigo instructs the exercitant to picture in his imagination the fear of hellfire, the smell of brimstone, the wails of the damned, the horrible majesty of Satan. He instructs his disciples, in deep retreat, to identify themselves with the Life and Passion of Jesus Christ, sharing His life in pictorial detail and not excluding what His world looked like from His birth at Bethlehem to His Crucifixion on Calvary. Eminent Catholics have subsequently challenged this way of thinking, arguing that it is no road to salvation to meditate on what the stable at Bethlehem might have looked like, how the Garden of Gethsemane was shaped, or the measurements of the road from Nazareth to Jerusalem. Opponents of all the Jesuits stand for have called the Exercises a brain-washing operation. So it is; but the phrase is unfortunately used in the current undertones of its meaning. In Inigo's Spiritual Exercises the individual, out of his own will, makes a voluntary choice.

The fact remains that the rough textbook which the Spanish soldier conceived in travail in Manresa, polished in the light of changing times, is probably the most remarkable testament of its kind ever written. The dedicated find that it lifts a man into a new dimension.*

The Exercises lifted Inigo's first companions into exaltation. There were soon nine of them, and they became fanatics. It is told that the first disciple, Favre, slept in the snow, and refused to eat for three days, 'For the Glory of God'. In due course they were all to adopt more reasonable attitudes. But the tradition of ascetism persisted. There was a theatrical aspect about their conduct, perhaps an unavoidable one, which was only later to be disciplined into dignified control.

In the spring of 1535, after two years' hard grind, Inigo received the parchment that, after passing searching examination, he merited the degree of 'Master in the world-famed Faculty of Arts of Paris with distinction and honour'. The degree referred to him as 'our dear and worthy Master Ignatius de Loyola from the diocese of Pamplona'. Paris changed his Christian name. He was to be known thenceforward as Master Ignatius for the remainder of his days. The change of name was the beginning of the third change in his life.

In the fall of the previous year, seven comrades had made vows of poverty and chastity. They went to the chapel of the Martyrs on Montmartre to confirm them. Fabre, recently ordained a priest, said mass. It was still the comrades' first aim to go to Jerusalem to convert the infidel. It was agreed that, once university studies were over, they would all meet, under the red cross on a white ground of the pilgrims' flag in Venice. The rendezvous was arranged for nearly two years later. Meanwhile, Inigo, troubled with his gall bladder and the protracted pain it caused him, agreed for his health's sake that he should return for a time to his home country of Loyola. His companions provided him with a small horse, and he marched again.

* I recommend students, who wish to tackle the Spiritual Exercises, to read the edition edited by Father Joseph Rickaby, S.J. It is never easy; but his commentary helps.

At home he was something of an embarrassment to his relations because he refused to accept such comforts as the house offered, and even drove out the women that one of his brothers was introducing through the back-door. He made penitence in the little town where he had sown his wild oats. He preached, fervently, to his native Basques. In a worldly way, I fancy that his family must all have been rather relieved to be finally rid of the pressures leading them to pie-in-the-sky. Inigo, with his little horse, pressed on to Venice.

Over the Apennines he had to crawl on all fours to mount the heights. At Bologna, he tumbled into the slimy moat, and then lay sick in the Spanish hospice. But he got to Venice in time to devote another year to study and prayer. In the sixteenth century it was customary to attribute accident to miracle. But it was a sort of miracle that, on January 8, 1537, Master Ignatius embraced his then 'nine friends in Our Lord'. Through thick and thin, after the passage of two years, they were united. They had made their way across Lorraine and northern Switzerland, crossed the Alps, and arrived, surprisingly, 'in good health and the happiest of spirits'. They were soon joined by another who made their number ten.

The pilgrim ships were not expected to sail to Jaffa until July. In the meantime in Venice Ignatius put his men to work among the destitutes and syphilitic 'incurables'. It was a self-effacing mission which he was later to regret. It was unorganised, and again over-theatrical. In the pursuit of 'Poverty and the Cross', his followers embraced sufferers of the foulest diseases, their senses revolted by the stench and the pus. After scraping out an abscess, Xavier put the stuff to his mouth to test his courage. Another companion took a leper to bed with him; and another, to punish himself for what he counted weakness, laid his body naked on a mattress, swarming with vermin, in which a man had died of some unspeakable dirt disease.

It was an unbalanced expression of spirituality; but it may well have been the essential preliminary to cooler thought. Ignatius sent two of his men to Rome to get the Papal permission for his company to preach in Jerusalem. The pope gave his blessing, but reminded the new crusaders that, militarily, the hour was ill-timed. The Turks were at war. In the event, Ignatius never got to Jerusalem again. It is interesting evidence of his change of thought that in after years he was pressing the authorities, not for a preaching mission but for an armed maritime invasion on Islam in which he would surely have liked to have been in the first boat.

Disappointed in their search for a crusade, the companions migrated to Rome. They were still unsure where they were going. It happened that Rome was in famine. The sick, the starving and the dead were uncared for. Venereal disease, the French disease as it was called, was affecting cardinals, bishops and priests. Scarlet gowns and velvet slippers were no defence against the insidious infection. The concubines of prelates, in what had been a permissive society, aroused a fear which grew into something like hysteria.

It is uncertain whether Ignatius and his men appreciated the whole squalid pattern from the start. They preached, emotion-ally waving their hats on street corners. At night, they cared for the horribly sick, found food from alms and buried the dead. Early on, in communal thought, they invented a then new thing in human society. They agreed that indiscriminate charity wasn't good enough; the sort of charity which was aimless, and perhaps only of spiritual merit to the individual who dispensed it. The followers of Ignatius wanted to get it organised. In a tentative way they invented the Welfare State.

They got hospitals and poor houses organised in the city. They decided that it was a waste of time to preach to simple people on street corners who were merely passingly amused. They agreed, too, that to be beggarly themselves was reducing their influence in high places. In future, they planned to live – as, indeed, they have ever after – in the style of 'poor nobility'.

There was another sect at the time called the Theatines which, in energy and sacrifice, was looking after the sick. Ignatius and his companions set themselves to beat them. With a devotion which was almost superhuman, they tended the prisoners, the diseased and the dying. In the sick Church, even cardinals came to see what the new sect was up to, watching them cleaning chamber pots, sweeping and scrubbing infested floors, digging graves, and serving the stricken.

In the sixteenth century the Roman Church had almost lost all contact with its people. In Southern Italy the peasants had reverted to paganism. In Rome itself, people could hardly recite the Lord's Prayer or the Ten Commandments. Of the Venerable Orders of the Church, the Franciscans, the Dominicans, and the Augustinians still preached. The Benedictines, as always, withdrew into their monasteries in the serenity of chant. Ignatius and his followers went out to the market places, threatened only by the appearance of an occasional miracle-maker, and brought the Church back on its heels.

Ignatius was ordained a priest in 1537, shortly after his companions had joined him. In 1540, the militant new order, after all the procrastinations which are the curse of the Vatican, was established. Solemn papal approval of the Society of Jesus came ten years later. Six years after that, in 1556, Ignatius died.

He had assembled over a thousand followers in a hundred houses. He had founded Jesuit Provinces in Italy, Sicily, Portugal, Aragon, Castile, Andalusia, Upper Germany, Lower Germany, France, India, Brazil and, briefly, Ethiopia. His life's work, to burgeon into something so much greater than he can possibly have imagined, was done.

From the time he founded the Order, still conscious enough of family pride to let his relations know in Loyola what he had achieved, he was the tidy administrator; a thorough, if pedantic man, who would copy out a letter again and again until he was satisfied with its content; wait for weeks while he contemplated a clause in the Constitutions of the Society; and engaged himself in seeing to the comfort of his men. He had long ago dismissed the asceticism of his own past. He required now that his brethren, as spiritual soldiers, must be well-clad, well-fed, and comfortably housed. He kept a paternal eye on catering, liking men about him who were fat.

Racked with gallstones, with none of the comforts of contemporary medicine, he at last lay down to die. He asked one of his companions to hasten to the pope for a last blessing. Officiously, his secretary insisted that the mail to his missionaries throughout the world had to be attended to first. So, like so many great men, he died alone. 'It was a tidy, ordinary death.' Perhaps he would have wished it that way.

He was beatified, with marked celerity for the Roman church, in 1609; sanctified together with the greatest of his companions, Francis Xavier, in 1622. Today his bones are enthroned, rather than interred, in the Jesuit Church in Rome called the Gesù – popularly pronounced in English 'Ger-zoo'. In a wealth of lapis lazuli and gilded bronze, displaying an idealistic silver statue – the whole conception 'a masterpiece of baroque art' – the pilgrims may wonder whether Master Ignatius would have wished it. The young Inigo would have loved it.

Throughout his life he refused to allow his portrait to be painted. After his death, looking at him as he was laid out for burial, an artist tried to recapture him. When the mourning members of the Community came to look at it they were all agreed that the picture had failed to evoke Master Ignatius. The death mask which was taken of him is a death mask. The peculiar radiance he seems to have had in life had left him. His true appearance, caricatured in pious images ever since, is lost to posterity.

III

The Black Pope

IN the entrance hall of the Jesuit Curia in Rome there is a
coloured plaster figure, an interpretation of Ignatius Loyola
which has a prominent place in Jesuit houses throughout
the world. Lost in ecstasy, ennobled with the familiar metal
halo, all reality has been smoothed out of his appearance. No
Jesuit was ever made of such sugary stuff. Ignatius's true spirit,
even his image, rests not in pious evocation but in his successors,
the flesh and blood Jesuits who carry on his mission.

The reigning General is carved in the veritable mould of
Ignatius. Meeting him, it is as if the death mask had warmed to
life. Pedro Arrupe, the twenty-eighth in the history of the
Society, is a Basque from Inigo's country. Light-weighted, with
broad shoulders, big nose and gentle eyes, he puts the silly statue
in the hall of the Curia into its proper perspective. The glory
and the guts of the Society of Loyola shine out of him. He wears
his responsibility with the compelling charm which I am
confident Ignatius had.

On first thought it would seem unlikely that a celibate body
of men can create hereditary genes. But the same family names
occur, generation after generation, before the initials 'S.J.'. In
crude woodcuts I recognise faces under birettas that I know
now. In drawings of Jesuit martyrs I am reminded of men of my
own time who would distinguish themselves with the same
noble sacrifice. Ignatius, in his holy image, is maligned. His
followers, like himself, are soldiers. Under my breath I cannot
forget a personable young woman who, after meeting some of
them, put her hands to her face and exclaimed: 'What a

wicked waste of manpower.' But it isn't; and it never was.

The global headquarters of the Jesuits is situated in quiet anonymity, as such buildings normally are, in a turning off the *Via della Conciliazione*, that ill-dressed street with its vulgar lighting and souvenir shops which Mussolini endowed to celebrate his *Pax Vaticana*. The dome of St Peter's rises graciously in the environs of the house to repair the balance of taste. Inside a brother of the Order stands guard over a formidable telephone switchboard to put the visitor in his place. It is a privilege, a privilege still largely denied to women, to pass beyond the bare hall into the sanctum beyond.

I have never visited the United Nations building in New York. I am not sure that I even want to. I have been welcomed into the Jesuit Curia where men of all the nations are truly united in a common creed and a common purpose. I was invited to luncheon. On the call of a bell the fathers assembled out of their rooms to collect their napkins from their appointed pigeon-holes and to take their place in the community refectory. They were men speaking in a dozen tongues, their Latin the only one they all shared. They came from provinces in Europe, Africa, Asia, Australasia and the Americas. They sat down as one. As one they sat in silence as a lector on the rostrum read them the martyrology of the day. White-aproned brothers of the Order, men who might have stepped out of a Rembrandt painting, served the meal. A quarter carafe of white chianti, from a Jesuit vineyard, was beside us all. Halfway through luncheon the Rector – a modest giant of an Englishman who had left the army to become a priest – gave a signal. The lector left the rostrum. The refectory swelled with conversation. Nobody was trying to prove that his racial demands were more significant than the other one's. In a disordered world an ordered one was joined together in undemonstrative agreement.

The constitution of the Jesuits was created handsomely earlier than democratic government in England; and, in the best sense of the word, it is communist. When they were first finding their way under Ignatius the disciples fluttered in disagreement like wild birds. But they soon recognised that their Society could have no solidarity if it was eroded by the promptings of individual conscience. They determined to accept the verdict of the majority. Once the rule was established the Jesuits found their collective character. Every house had its Rector, who was appointed by the Provincial who was appointed by the General on the advice of the Fathers in the various missions throughout the world. In office, the Superior spoke with the authority of Jesus Christ. In 'entire obedience' his community accepted what he decreed. The Superior exercised his authority with self-effacement. At the end of his term, usually about seven years, he was reduced to the ranks. The only man in the Constitution of the Order to hold his office for life was the General. He himself was elected and answerable to the Congregation of the Society as a whole. More powerful than a constitutional monarch he was still bound to accept the advice of the assembly of his brethren.

In days of greater religious intolerance the General of the Jesuits was nicknamed 'The Black Pope'. In his romances Alexandre Dumas could conceive of no darker fate for Aramis, one of 'The Three Musketeers', than that he should end in that office. It is ridiculous, but true, that until quite recently the works of Dumas – *père et fils* – were on the index of books which, under papal edict, Roman Catholics were not supposed to read. As a schoolboy I read them all in volumes from the libraries at Stonyhurst. So often the Church of Rome has pulled up its trousers too late. Belloc's characteristic comment is apt: 'The Church must be divinely inspired, or it wouldn't have survived two thousand years of such knavish imbecility.'

It is currently popular to suppose that ecclesiastics don't belong to the modern scene. Many of them undoubtedly don't. The Jesuits are the society which hasn't surrendered. Difficult to analyse until you see them in their houses. The hot potato voice of conventional clergymen is absent. The pious blessing isn't there unless it is asked for. The stranger is welcomed with sophisticated hospitality.

It was memorable to talk to the General in English while, over his shoulder, he was addressing his men in Spanish, French, Italian, German as well as Czech. It was no surprise to learn that he has written eight books in Japanese. He was master of the Jesuit novices when the atom bomb fell on Hiroshima. He turned the novitiate into a hospital. In 1940 he had tasted prison as a suspect spy.

He showed me his rooms; the office in which he conducts the business of the Order, his private chapel (his special privilege); and the bedroom where, like all Jesuits, he lives in simple iron-bedded comfort. It is an experience to meet a man with so much power, and yet so undemanding.

There is no question that the man designated to lead the Jesuits must be numbered among the portentous figures of the world. The Jesuits' whole history commands it. Their presence in almost every nation, the effective way in which a handful of them have constantly made an impression on affairs on the perimeter of western influence, cannot be dismissed. For hundreds of years in Europe they infiltrated the corridors of power. They had their fantastic successes and their bloody failures; but none could ignore them. They were better-educated, better-disciplined, better-led than missionaries had ever been before. Thirty-three thousand of them represent a force, more potent than many suspect, in this bothered world today.

In the outward composure of the Roman Curia, in the complexity of electronics which the Jesuits have adopted with the same casual ease that in the seventeenth century they taught the Chinese Emperor how to wind a clock, it is easy to believe that they have lost their Ignatian fire. It still glows; but just a little deeper under the surface. They have their problems; but problems of a kind on which they have always thrived. In the cobweb of world affairs there is no statesman who can rely so certainly on the men about him as the General of the Jesuits. As in any army there are defaulters. But they are relatively few. The Jesuits, contemporarily a little puzzled where to press their attack, are as formidable as ever.

I wonder whether they are still hated. In the past they certainly were. From the beginning the old orders of the Church were suspicious and, even while Ignatius lived, regarded his success with jealousy and increasing distaste. The Dominicans, the Benedictines, the Franciscans, all much more venerable than the Jesuits, believed that the way to salvation was through the cloisters, in the ritual chant of the office that the old orders made their way of life. Time-saving, the Jesuits read their daily office, saying their prayers as they found an interval for them in the crowded business of the day. Not for them the chant, the rope and the cowl. They dressed, not in penitential robes, but to suit the conditions in which they were working. They became quick change artists who adopted the disguise of the territory they invaded. They succeeded, where conventional missionaries had failed, by hiding the Cross behind their backs.

It is irrelevant now that, in the controversies of the Reform-ation and Counter-Reformation, they were involved in all manner of bitter theological argument. While none then doubted the reality of the Gateway of Heaven or the Portals of Hell, rivalling factions damned each other in useless and largely incomprehensible debate. One of the arguments was about the meaning of free will; whether all was predestined or, as the Jesuits argued, a man was the master of his own soul. A dispute over the meaning of free will actually developed out of the position of a comma in a papal bull. The debaters searched the precepts of the fathers of Christianity for argument. People were thrown into prison, even executed, for holding beliefs which they had formed from the writings of Aristotle, Aquinas, Jerome; and, latterly, Jansen. It became an issue whether 'the end justifies the means'. The Jesuits were accused of granting absolution to sinners too easily. It is a hangover of history that many of the myths which persist about the Jesuits today date from the time when their own brethren in the Church were determined to deflate them.

The history rests in the five libraries of the Curia in Rome. Jesuits, their faces lined in scholarship, explore little bits of it;

manuscripts in rusty ink on parchment, words set in wooden type, letters that travelled in ill-found sailing ships giving the account of lonely men in lonely missions to their General in Rome. Historians have never plumbed its depths.

It is a tradition of the Order that each one of them has the right to send letters, marked '*soli*', which may be read by the General alone. Most of them are composed over matters of conscience; some concerned with the world of human affairs. The General preserves his secrets. Alone, he represents them all.

The General is the leader of a vast international organisation which, although its aims are first and foremost spiritual, has never disregarded that the winning of human souls is best sought at the centres of political power; that, in preparation for a greater cause, nothing impresses men more than material achievement. The policy has cost the Jesuits a lot of trouble. How they gained their unsavoury reputation, how they suffered; and how they succeeded, often with spectacular success, always against odds in places where the temporal power of Europe had failed, spans the shaping of the modern world.

In the East, they explained the Solar system, created astronomical observatories, reformed the Chinese calendar, and produced maps of the countries lying beyond the Great Wall. They negotiated commercial treaties, initiated the Chinese into the art of casting iron cannon. In the New World, they opened up the interior, and were the first to explore it. It was said that, in Mississippi, 'not a cape was rounded, not a river discovered, without the Jesuits having found the way'. In the seventeenth century, in Paraguay, they founded the first ideal Communist Society, rather more successfully than Marx and Lenin.

It was Jesuits who sent to the Western world plants, spices and medicines such as the beneficent drug quinine (first known as Jesuits' bark), rhubarb, vanilla, and the secret of Chinese porcelain. A Jesuit in China introduced the umbrella to Europe. The camellia gets its name from Father Kamel who sent a specimen of the plant from the Philippines to the naturalist Linnaeus. The chinoiserie of the rococo period is derived directly from Jesuit drawings. They invented the magic lantern, which showed the way to motion pictures; and rediscovered the ancient principle of the burning-glass.

Not first on the moon, as they were in so many of the undiscovered places of the earth, the Jesuit astronomers, for hundreds of years, pointed the way. Many of the craters are named after them. I remember that, when the first lunar landing was made, a witty cartoonist in the *Catholic Herald* showed a Jesuit mildly approaching the astronauts on their great adventure with the enquiry: 'Can you give me a lift back to Farm Street?'

In the sciences, in the making of dictionaries and the definition of the grammar of languages, in the study of racial sociology, in the arts, the Jesuits made their formidable contribution. A Jesuit, Gerald Manley Hopkins, ranks among the noble poets; and the humble brother of the Order who painted the baroque ceiling of St Ignatius's in Rome created a work which is worthy of its place among the masterpieces of the City.

To learn the Jesuits in the large – as I first began to learn them in the miniature of Stonyhurst – it is good to live in the study of their manuscripts, their vast libraries, their scholarship; and, best of all, in their own magnificent and understanding intellects. They may often have been wrong in their impact on events. They may be wrong now. But so much is wrong now in the world that it is worth enquiring how far they have been right. So much of their renown is written in their missions. So much, like the causes of war, the results of elections, the consequences of encounters between blankets, happened by accident.

It is questionable whether Ignatius even conceived the apostolic mission which was to bring his society such worldwide fame. When he was frustrated in his ambition to evangelise Islam, it seems that he might have been content to serve as the superior of a nursing and welfare order in southern Europe. In his life there is little evidence of a planned campaign to stay protestantism in the Lutheran climate of the north. It was the notion of King John III of Portugal to ask the pope to send some of the enthusiasts of the newly-formed Society of Jesus to convert the heathens in the east where the outlook for Rome seemed more promising; and where there were easy pickings for the sovereigns of old Christendom as well.

When the Pope acceded to the request, it is said that it was fortuitous that the man chosen to be the first Jesuit missionary was Francis Xavier, the same who had shared rooms with Ignatius in the University of Paris. Another of the brethren, who was preferred, had fallen ill. Xavier, the second choice, stitched the holes in his worn cassock. With little more than his breviary in his luggage, he travelled with the Portuguese Ambassador to Lisbon.

Ignatius was by then a man of his past. Cradled in chivalry, his body racked in his mystical search for revelation, he was old and tired. Like a runner in a relay race he passed on the cross to Xavier. Xavier, the most successful missionary ever known, set the pace for all his successors. He conferred on Jesuitry its essential quality and flavour.

He set out, in his late twenties, in starry-eyed innocence, armed only with passionate faith and courage. He waited for a year in Lisbon before setting sail on the six months' voyage round the Cape of Good Hope to Goa, the then capital of the Portuguese territory in India. His first impressions were as shallow as a tourist's picture postcard. He reported that the sceptre of Rome had been carried triumphantly into the east; that the heathens were receiving baptism, that the pagan temples had been supplanted by Christian churches. He was much too percipient a man to be fooled for as long as it took his correspondence to reach Europe.

He soon discerned that the colonists were there, not in the name of Christ, but for what they could exploit out of the territory; that the native population, without a clue what Christianity was all about, accepted it in the name of peace and quiet. They were given baptismal Christian names in a language they couldn't understand on bits of paper they couldn't even read. In private they were still worshipping their elephant and ape gods, and their multi-armed idols.

For the next twenty years – Xavier never returned to Europe – he adopted a policy which has been the Jesuit way ever since. He assumed 'holy cunning and the mask of pride'. He showed, to the disgust of the monkish missionaries who swarmed in Goa to the number, it is said, of thirty thousand, that the way to win souls was to enter into the way of men's lives; that, for the greater glory of God, 'let the moneyed people see that you are just as well-versed in everyday affairs as they are'. 'Talk privately to the sinners about their faults, speaking always with a smile, without solemnity, and in a friendly tone.'

He learnt that a humble comportment is of no consequence in the east. He made himself a man for all men, adapting his social life to the people he was consorting with. With servants, near slaves, he wore their servility. In the company of their masters he showed, brilliant man that he was, that he was more knowledgeable, socially more polished than they were. He was everything that a fully-rounded man should be. He altered his clothes and his manner to suit his setting; fitting smoothly into the scene in a governor's mansion, in a gambling den, in a kitchen, and in open debate in the street with local bosses who tried to get the better of him. He wore luxurious clothes with the authority of breeding. He could make people follow him when he was wearing a ragged gown, and ringing a bell calling them to prayer.

Xavier far more than Ignatius, who was essentially a mediaeval man, was the first modern Jesuit. He recognised in his own time and in a remarkable way, that religion cannot be imposed by force; something which the old courts of Christendom could never comprehend. He believed in persuasion, the sort of persuasion which Ignatius exerted on him in his own rebellious youth. The Jesuits in Xavier's footsteps have recognised that to destroy a man's ancestral culture, to put him into trousers in the name of Western prejudice, is more likely to destroy him than enlighten him.

THE BLACK POPE

It is arguable that, by and large, Western missionaries have made more trouble than they have resolved. It is possible that the teaching of an alien religion has created even more. But the Jesuits' record, thanks in the first place to Xavier, has been immeasurably the most responsible, and in many ways the most important, in the introduction of other people to our way of life. The first interest of other men who exploded out of Europe was self-interest, and plunder. Xavier's brave and lonely mission was an assignment which, as a journalist, I can applaud as an achievement of history.

It may seem an insolence to compare one of the great saints in the canonical calendar with a mere journalist; but it is true. The message of the saints was in a higher cause, but the search for truth is what drives journalists as well. I see Xavier scarcely out of his twenties, making his way to India, a place he can hardly have conceived in the communications of his time, a place where he was expected, the way newspapermen are, to make a 'scoop'. One of my objections to the elevation of men to sainthood is that the devout are led to suppose that, in their lives, they were superhuman. Xavier was entirely a human person. I can imagine his foreboding at the prospect of the formidable journey he was making, the fear of failure in his mission; the premonition, only too justified, that he might never come back. He had the benefit of his faith and his prayers as journalists today have the benefit of telephone and a benevolent office. But, like a journalist, he was out on his own. I am sure that he struggled with his emotions as on lesser missions I have.

I remember when I was assigned to get to the Seychelles Islands in the Indian Ocean. In this age I thought that it was merely a matter of phoning up the travel agency. But there were no official sailings for boats, and no place aboard them for me. Nobody wanted to know – Xavier, I am sure, was in the same predicament – that my mission could be of any consequence. Mine was piddling; but the editor wanted me to move quick. I reckoned on the assumption that there is always somebody, within a few hundred yards of Piccadilly Circus, who knows the answer. I had the touch of luck which any adventurer needs.

In the logic of probabilities it had no business to happen the way it did. I had no knowledge of the place I was trying to get to, apparently no hope of thumbing a ride. It began over a drink in a London club. Without a notion of the scheme I had in my mind, a friend in the film business asked me if I could come to see the rushes of a documentary. Billy Bones, when he accepted the Black Spot from Blind Pew, can scarcely have been more certain of what was coming to him when I was told that the subject of the film was the Seychelles.

There was a group of people in the private theatre in Wardour Street where the film was shown. By way of introduction the director explained that the rushes were only roughly cut, that commentary would be dubbed at a later date. I knew what to expect. Nothing is so dull, and unrewarding, as a half-made film. I settled myself to watch a succession of colour sequences of steamships and coconut palms, surf and coral sands, turtles and tortoises, people in all shades of colour from jet black to burnt-white. There was a shot of two girls in bikinis bathing. Then, improbably, the sequence was repeated without the bikinis. As two bare bottoms bobbed over the too blue ocean, a man sitting behind me in the darkness said: 'My God, that's my secretary'. When the showing was over I asked him to have a drink.

It was in keeping with the element of the bizarre that the man I met, in the jargon of the Colonial Office, was the acting Colonial Secretary, in the absence of the Governor, administering the Seychelles. I bumped into him through the mere fluke that he happened to be in London at the tail-end of a home leave. I might have guessed, from the patient exasperation in his voice at the two girls sporting in the sea that he was a man who had been surprised too often by the idiosyncrasies of human nature to be surprised any more. I had the impression that he was one of those men who, if somebody brought him the news of bloody revolution, would unhurriedly finish his gin-and-tonic and restore order by way of an afterthought. He had the pallor which comes from long service in the tropics and, at first sight, deceptively lazy eyes. But, in wartime, he had been a naval intelligence expert in enemy-occupied territory. Talking to him, I was filled with the exhilaration which comes to a journalist when he chances on a man who knows the guts of a business and the snags. He belonged to a vanishing species in the faded scene of the British Empire. The world has lost something in the going of his kind.

He told me that, once I got to the Seychelles, everything would be laid on. And, in the event it was. But I had to get there. At that time, there wasn't as much as an airstrip on any of the islands, the only fast boats sailed once a month from Bombay and Mombasa; and I was likely to have difficulty in getting a booking on any one of them. It seemed that, in the twentieth century, I might have to wait for a passage, like Xavier, for a year.

I suppose that it was the Jesuit child in me that prompted me to ring the Admiralty; and ask them if they had a warship to spare. Reasonably enough, the navy said that at short notice it was a tall order. But, a few days later, I got a signal from a top brass with the splendid title 'Commander-in-Chief Persian Gulf and Arabian Seas' inviting me to join the frigate H.M.S. *Loch Insch*, which was making an official visit to show the flag in the Seychelles. If I reported aboard at Mombasa in East Africa, Captain Catlow would be happy to lift me on the last leg of my five thousand mile journey.

It can happen like that in this overcrowded over-trafficked twentieth century. Think of Xavier, with little else but his thumbed breviary, obeying his superiors' order to sail to the Orient. He had no guides, as I had, to brief him. He knew that it was a matter of mere luck whether his ship would make a safe landfall. At that time two out of three went to the bottom on the voyage. When he eventually got to the East he copied out his letters in triplicate, in the way of a war correspondent, in the hope that one of his dispatches, placed in three different vessels, would reach Rome. He was content that there was little chance that he would ever see Europe again. He died, twenty years later, at the age of forty-six years and eight months, on an island at the gateway of China – isolated and alone. The rebellious student who had known Paris, as worldlings know Paris; the hidalgo who had once laid claims to earthly nobility, laid down his life, and his splendid intellect, to a higher cause.

Inside the Curia in Rome Xavier's memory is green today. The quiet fathers, moving from their rooms to collect their napkins outside the refectory, are treading, in their various provinces throughout the world, in his footsteps. A stranger in their company feels immeasurably humble. It is relatively so easy to seize the good things of the world, so difficult to deny them. Xavier, like so many Jesuits now, could have been what, in material terms, is called 'a success story'. He chose to be a missionary, canonised in due course; but, in his middle and latter life, denying himself all the comforts that men enjoy.

The extraordinary thing about the Jesuits is that they have given so much to this world while they have concerned themselves with the next. From the first, they have industriously explored it, and passed on the information to posterity. About the next, they have been kinder to sinners than any other Order of the Church.

It is always difficult to define how a newspaper, a society, a club, a school, a nation, finds its individuality. The Jesuits found theirs through a succession of men of all the nations, creatively enlarging what had gone before. In the past, they struggled in unwavering purpose for a cause which the Church and the old orders of the Church had nearly forgotten. What they did then illuminates the spirit in which they may be expected to meet the challenge of new times.

IV

The Curtain of China

XAVIER died in the early morning of December 3, 1552, on a deserted island on the perimeter of the Middle Kingdom. Living in a squalid reed hut with one faithful servant, he sat day after day on the beach waiting in vain for a smuggler who, for twenty hundredweights of pepper, had undertaken to land him at Canton. Within seven miles of the coast of China, like a Crusader with his eyes on Jerusalem, he had a fever. In delirium he preached the Gospel in the languages of East and West until, at last, he lost the power of speech. He was buried in Malacca, and subsequently reinterred in a lavish tomb in Goa. His own circuit in the relay race was run.

Ignatius, his general, died in the serenity of belief that he had fulfilled his vocation. Xavier, I think, was a disappointed man. His achievement had been stupendous. His magnetism had impressed his personality on Southern India and, later, Japan. But Xavier, denied at the last his ambition to penetrate China, knew, none better, that his mission had been a paper victory. In Goa he recognised that the Portuguese colonists, parading to church under their palanquins, with their retinues behind them to lay their prayer rugs and bow them to their place, were there to serve themselves, not God. When the Paravas, a poor race of about thirty thousand people in the far south of India who made a pittance as pearl divers, appealed to the Portuguese to rescue them from Mohammedan marauders in exchange for the acceptance of Christianity, Xavier must have known that the conversion was a sorry farce. He mixed with them, ringing his bell, shouting in Tamil that he had good news for them. The children loved it. With Xavier's connivance, they enjoyed knocking down the heathen statues. Mass conversions to Christianity, in exchange for Portuguese military protection, became popular throughout India. Xavier did his best in Ceylon. Again he made use of the children of Kandy to purloin the sacred relic of Buddha's tooth, and to rub away the saint's footprint embedded in the rock.

It was imposition of Christianity by force. It evoked the same vandalism which has moved successive popes to nail their names and St Peter's keys to the monuments of ancient Rome. None of the pontiffs seemed to have remembered Christ's injunction 'to render unto Caesar the things that are Caesar's'.

Xavier knew that the mass conversions reported to Rome, conversions which were celebrated with rejoicing and the ringing of bells in the básilicas of the west, were meaningless. The native populations – glad no doubt to be told that they could forget their superstitious fears of their heathen gods – had no conception what the Christian God was all about. The important thing was that the presence of armed force enabled them to eke out their wretched existences without being in terror of their lives. The Portuguese were glad to give their protection for an extortionate price, the way gangsters always have.

Disillusioned, Xavier looked further east. At Malacca he came upon a Japanese murderer, by name Anjiro, who had fled the justice of his own country. Anjiro came to the holy man to implore him for absolution of his sin from the Christian God. Xavier had him baptised in the name of 'Paul of the Holy Faith'. He wanted to know more about Japan. Anjiro told him that in his country there was a religious system akin to Christianity; a religion of one God and celibate priests who spoke a language (Sanskrit) which was only understood by the initiates. They believed in a heaven, a hell and a purgatory; and honoured saints, not as idols, but as those who could intercede for them with the Supreme Being. Xavier, disenchanted with the corruption of Portuguese rule in India, the shell which passed for

Christianity, had a vision of a secret country, so far penetrated only by a few traders, which he could win for the true faith; a country which he supposed was spiritually half-won already.

With Anjiro's help, he eagerly set about studying Japanese. He had the most important articles of the Christian faith translated into the language, and learnt them by heart. He could leave India with an easy conscience because Jesuits were already behind him, 'four on the Moluccas, two in Malacca, six at Cape Comorin, two in Cochin, two in Bassein, and four in the island of Sokotra'. After the usual dangerous voyage, this time in a Chinese junk accompanied by three brethren, he made a landfall at Anjiro's native town, Kagoshima. The inhabitants were only too willing to forgive the murderer for bringing such exciting strangers into their midst.

For the strangers it must have been a daunting experience. Xavier and his companions, struggling with an unfamiliar language and a custom of life which was then almost unknown to Europeans, searched their way in a blind of paper sunshades and coloured silks. The Japanese were as curious about the world of the Southern Barbarians as Xavier was curious about the constitution of theirs. He knew how dangerously he was living.

Living, in the fullness of the word, is a dangerous business. I tasted a little bit of it when I penetrated the Jebel Druze country in the uplands of Syria. I met men with handlebar moustaches, women in beautiful silks with strings of gold coins decked about their foreheads, belonging to a way of life based on square black-stone houses with fuel made out of cakes of dung. The Soultane Selim Atrashe, hereditary chief of the warrior people, welcomed me into his peasant palace. He was convinced that I was a British secret agent. He couldn't believe that I could not speak Arabic. He waited for the gold which, in the manner of Lawrence of Arabia, he expected me to issue to rouse his men to occupy Damascus. In growing suspicion, when I didn't produce the gold, he had me arrested by the secret police. After the event I can laugh at the adventure. Admiration for Xavier is born out of the butterflies I have known in my own inside.

Inevitably Xavier attracted the attention of the local chieftain, the daimyo of the district. In faith and courage he welcomed the invitation. He can have been in no doubt that, at the nod of a head, his own would have been chopped off by a samurai katana. He faced him with Spanish pride. He made the courtesies and exchanged presents, asking nothing for himself but permission to preach. Permission was granted for the good reason that the missionary from the West might bring the trading ships with iron cannon for the defence of the daimyo's territory.

Xavier's standing in Japan rested on Portuguese traders. In his travels in the country he made sure that, when a ship came in, he himself was welcomed with a salute of guns and all the appurtenances of a V.I.P. The sailors threw down their cloaks so that he might walk over them. He played every trick to impress the native population. In his heart he had the blessing of humility. In outward appearance he recognised that oriental man has no respect for a humble aspect. He discarded his tattered gown and cowl for the lavish display of the east. He wore his silks with the authority of a knight of Castile.

It is probable that in his dedication Xavier, in his two-and-a-half years' mission in Japan, had higher hopes than he had ever had before. The Japanese were open to reason. They were troubled that the Christian God, who was all goodness, permitted evil, in the person of Satan, to flourish in the world. They wanted to know what form God took, what colour and shape, and were bewildered when Xavier explained that He was a Substance beyond human imagination. In the difficulty of mastering another new language the dialectic of a Master of the University of Paris must have been pressed to sleeplessness. It is remarkable that he is said to have converted a thousand Japanese to Christianity. But the daimyos tolerated him as little more than a commercial traveller for the Portuguese merchantmen. The shaven-headed priests, in defiance of his doctrine of

Son of God made man, viewed him with hostility. Xavier was disconcerted to discover that the Japanese religion, apparently so similar in so many ways to Christianity, excluded the vaguest concept of a Redeemer.

His early intention, the policy of so many latter Jesuits in other countries of the world, was that if he could win over 'the King of Japan' his subjects would follow the royal example. He travelled five hundred miles from the southern tip of the island, in drunken junks and on foot through knee-high snow, in search of him. When at last he reached the imperial city of Miyako, Kyoto today, he found a smoke blackened ruin. Told that it housed a university as great as Paris, he arrived at a capital ravaged by war and plunder. The great Voo, as he was called, was a nominal sovereign. A semi-divine figure, none could look on his face. The china used for his meals was broken as soon as it was used. But the poor wretch, celestially impotent, had to make a living copying out musical scores for rich patrons; and his women begged for food through the breaches in the palace wall. Xavier enquired who it was who exercised real authority in Japan. He was told that it was the shogun; but the present general-in-chief was a fifteen-year-old boy. The bosses were the daimyos, the local military upstarts.

Xavier looked for power where it resided. With the panache of a Spanish nobleman he equipped his own entourage with oriental ceremony and courtesy. He brought with him a train of obsequious servants. He presented clocks, as the chronicles record, 'which strike exactly twelve times a day and twelve times by night; a musical instrument which gives out wonderful sounds quite by itself and without being touched; glasses for the eyes, with the help of which an old man can see as well as a young man'. He dazzled the daimyos with showmanship.

Nearly four hundred years later Glubb Pasha, the dedicated British soldier then in command of the Arab Legion, impressed on me that I mustn't travel in the desert of Jordan without an escort. Otherwise the Bedouins would dismiss me with contempt. He seconded two cameliers of the Legion, with double bandoliers of highly-polished brass bullets, with silver-scabbered daggers across their groins, and a policeman with a spike on the top of his khaki topee. With their doubtful support I won through because I have a certain aptitude with a handgun. When, by sheer luck, I shot a sand grouse with a pistol from the back of an Arab stallion, my reputation was made with my escort, and my Bedouin hosts. In celebration I had to suffer the whole gamut of sheep's eyes, asses' milk and mint tea inside their open tents.

The incident is only worth the telling to emphasise the importance in the East of exercising a certain social superiority. Xavier, on his knees night after night in apology to Christ, hated the attitude that he had to adopt. He was playing a charade. But he knew that there was no other way of winning his hosts. The daimyos ordered it to be proclaimed that the stranger from the land of the Southern Barbarians had permission freely to speak his faith, and that all subjects were free to embrace Christianity.

It was an empty promise. For the Japanese Xavier was little more than an entertaining sideshow, the stranger billed like a circus act 'for the first time in this country', who indulged them with his knowledge of a foreign world; told stories and offered eternal rewards for the converted. It seems improbable that they even conceived what he was talking about; but they loved the discussion, the appeal to reason, and the personality of the missioner who had travelled so far to inform them.

Xavier, satisfying their insatiable curiosity about the universe and the lands of the barbarians, was disenchanted. He concluded that Japan, with its local chieftains, was a sort of provincial China. All oriental civilisation seemed to flower out of China. The Japanese had taken their language and culture from the world beyond the curtain of China. If he could penetrate it to preach Christendom he believed that he might convert the whole of the East. Strangers who entered China were liable to summary execution. Xavier was undeterred, defeated only by the fate that he died at the gateway of his desire.

He had achieved so little, and yet so much. His inspiration brought a succession of Jesuits to the Orient. They completed his mission. They crossed the curtain. Xavier's importance in history is not what he changed but what he began. A distinguished Jesuit historian has said to me that the conversion of the whole of China to Christianity rested, in the seventeenth century, on a mere razor's edge. I can nearly believe him. That it failed, with all the subsequent lack of communication between East and West, was the responsibility of Rome and the religious orders who persuaded the popes that the Jesuits were heretically encouraging ancestor worship, adopting pagan ways themselves in antagonism to the true faith. The Jesuits were in fact adapting themselves, chameleonwise, to local conditions which were scarcely conceived in the West beyond the doors of their own Curia.

The Society's Constitution was Ignatius's: Xavier created the Jesuits' style. The most important aspect of his own missionary work was not the converts he made but the dispatches he sent, like a special correspondent for posterity, to his superiors. He showed the way for all the Jesuits who followed him. In their turn, generation after generation, they preserved a continuity of information from the missions in which they were striving. Each man picked up the baton from his predecessor. Every Jesuit followed a consistent pattern of conduct, and wore the same face under fifty hats.

Father Barzaeus, ringing his own bell at Ormuz on the Indo-Persian border, dazzled Mohammedans, Jews and Brahmins by displaying that a Christian knew more of their various religious doctrines than they knew themselves. Robert de Nobili, the scion of a noble Italian family, appeared in Madura in Southern India in the saffron robes of a Brahmin, a turban on his head and wooden sandals on his feet. He insisted that he was one of the thrice-born, only different in the sense that he was a Christian Brahmin from the West. He strictly observed the Hindu discipline, adopted a vegetarian diet and never allowed the shadow of a pariah to cross his path. His superior scholarship persuaded the Brahmins to accept him as one of themselves. He, too, wore the mask of pride.

Xavier, it appears, had not recognised the caste system in India. He laboured among the beggars and the poor. Robert de Nobili saw the importance of winning the confidence of the priestly elite. Meanwhile, others of his brethren, in the penitential robes of yogis, were ministering to the pariahs.

The resourcefulness of the Jesuits was endless. When news reached them that the Grand Mogul, the Emperor Akbar in the north of India, was contemplating conversion to a purer religion than any he had found so far, the fathers arrived at his court to join in open debate with Brahmins, Mohammedans and Parsees. The method of debate that the Jesuits adopted was always the same. They began by praising all the other religions to the satisfaction of the various sects. They went on to preach that the Christian doctrine embodied the same truths, but expressed them more clearly. They nearly won over the Grand Mogul. When he had a war on his hands he took the Christian priests with him, talking to them far into the night in his tent. To the Jesuits it seemed that he might be another Constantine. But he died, unconverted, to extinguish their greatest hope of bringing Christianity to India.

The Jesuits, ever intrepid, were the first Europeans to reach Central Asia. Others joined caravans travelling north, and crossing the Himalayas, made the journey over the mountains to Western and Eastern Tibet. Their dispatches provided the first, and for a long time the last reliable information from that hidden world.

They were now firmly established in Japan. They had learnt all the finesse of polite ceremonial. In Japanese dress, they identified themselves with the elaborate funeral obsequies which were a sign of man's status in the east. They established schools and printing presses, and waved the stick of the advantages to be gained from trade with Portugal over the heads of recalcitrant daimyos. It is said that a quarter of a million Japanese accepted Christianity. The converts even pulled down

Buddhist temples, and expelled the bonzes, the white-robed priests.

The Jesuits hadn't forgotten Xavier's ambition to convert China. There came a time when one of the daimyos, Oda Nobunaga, attained to the position of ruler of all Japan. He restored the town of Miyako into capital splendour. In conference with the Jesuit fathers he even contemplated the conquest of the Middle Kingdom. They were only too happy to encourage him. All he lacked was a navy. The Jesuits proposed that a fleet should be built for him, at favourable terms, in Portugal. But Nobunaga was murdered before he could bring his plan to fruition. The fathers' hopes were dashed again, as they had been with the death of the Grand Mogul.

His successor, although taking kindly to them at first, changed his mind. The initial trouble was that girls baptised in the Christian faith repelled his amorous advances. Worse followed. A Spanish merchantman, beached on the Japanese coast, had its cargo confiscated. To intimidate the authorities, the Spaniards produced maps showing the extent and power of the Spanish crown. When asked how their King could subjugate so many territories they replied: 'Our rulers begin by sending priests to those countries they intend conquering. When the priests have conquered some of the people, our soldiers join them to bring the whole country into the power of Spain'. The inflammatory comment soon reached the daimyo. The Jesuits were forbidden to preach, the Christians were told to revert to the religion of their ancestors.

The tragic end of the brave mission came when Dutch merchantmen, who had lately discovered the sea route to the Far East, reached Japan, and made a bid to wrest the trade from Portugal. The Dutchmen assured the Japanese that they could supply everything that the Portuguese could. Soon after their ambassador arrived to propose the conclusion of a formal treaty. There was nothing for the Japanese to fear any more from the severance of the shipping link with the Portuguese. The Jesuits' insurance policy had run out. At the turn of the seventeenth century, forty of them were executed in a mass martyrdom. The Japanese crucified them, many of them, like St Peter, upside down. With terrible irony, it was a form of death that they had learnt from the Jesuits themselves. Long after, when Catholic missionaries were allowed into Japan again, the heroism in which the fathers died was remembered by descendants of witnesses who in secret had continued to profess Christianity.

But it is easier to forgive the daimyos, feudal men dyed in savagery, than the stab in the back plunged into the Jesuits by their own brethren in Rome at a time when they were on 'the razor's edge' of winning China for Christianity. In China they had performed even more brilliant tactics than those which had got their foot into the doorway of India and Japan. Three Portuguese merchants had been arrested for illegal entry into the Middle Kingdom. The Jesuits, never missing a trick, arranged that two of their fathers, with some knowledge of the language, should negotiate the price of their captives' ransom. They penetrated Canton as official negotiators.

They successfully arranged the release of the seamen. They succeeded in charming the Canton governor by presenting him with a watch, one of their few possessions, and they conquered his heart with their quiet charm, 'so pleasant, so tactful, and so learned'. Behind the pioneers' backs, in the college of Macao, a crash course was put into operation. Jesuits were trained so that they should have all the necessary knowledge of China, 'all the niceties of speech among the better class, as well as the dialect of the simple people'. They studied the difficult hieroglyphic writings, and acquired from a variety of books a knowledge of the history, the customs, the laws and the literature of the Kingdom.

The older fathers of the community in Macao thought that there was no future in the mission. The study was so difficult; the terrain it was hoped to bring to Christianity so closed to the outer world. A few Jesuits had penetrated into the Middle Kingdom, the Middle Flower, only to be kicked out when they had travelled more than a few hundred miles, nothing in China, into the interior. It seemed absurd that their best men were dedicating their scholarship to a forlorn hope. But, as happens again and again in the Jesuit story, a strong man, an Italian named Alessandro Valignano – one who had found his vocation, like Ignatius and Xavier, after tasting the world, wounding a courtesan and suffering banishment from Padua – determined that what couldn't be done could be done. Like a crammer and a commando leader he prepared his men for the impossible adventure.

Dr C. Northcote Parkinson writes in *East and West* that, in the ideographic script of the Chinese, a scholar needs to learn fifty thousand characters to attain mere literacy. With a need for classical learning, literary style and artistic calligraphy, the study could command a large lump of even an Oriental's lifetime. In fact the Jesuits were largely wasting their time. The common tongue spoken in Macao was not the language of the educated Chinese. To be accepted they needed the Mandarin dialect as well. Anyhow, it was work in a vacuum. Only the faith of Father Valignano drove his men on, to prepare for the invasion of the closed kingdom, an invasion which wise men thought was unattainable.

An impossible circumstance made it possible. A Jesuit, Father Roggieri, had achieved a brief encounter with the governor of Shiuhing in which he told him of one of his brethren who was a master of mathematics and astronomy; and who was also a maker of maps, clocks and spheres. The governor sent an emissary to Macao to invite the learned man to his province.

The man who answered the call was an intellectual giant. Father Matteo Ricci has good claim to be numbered amongst the greatest Jesuits of all time. His learning was devastating in its depth, his resourcefulness inspired. His dedication was so wonderful that he committed his life to the exotic world he entered. He was determined that he would never return to Europe, whether it ended in martyrdom, as it nearly did, or in lonely isolation. He struggled with the nuances of the Chinese languages until he became a master of them. He risked his life, again and again in solitary discomfort, in a cause which might have changed the history of the world if obstinate, narrow-minded and ignorant clerics in the West hadn't subsequently undone what he achieved. He was nearly bastinadoed, the punishment with a bamboo cane on the thighs, fore and back, which tortured a man for the rest of his days. He was subjected to all the contempt which the Chinese showed in their treatment of Southern Barbarians. Inside the closed Empire he made his way in. He made it, over the years, with such grace, that he changed the meaning of the word foreigner in China from contemptible barbarian to 'stranger worthy of special consideration'.

In his mission, he made few conversions to Christianity. What he achieved was a quiet conquest of the Chinese mind. They came to regard him as the wisest man who had ever come into their midst. On his first appearance in Canton he assumed the simple cowl of a Buddhist priest, patterning his way of life in accordance with that of the bonzes, begging alms like them in front of the temples, arguing the doctrines of Buddha. But he soon learnt that he was wasting his time. Impressed by his knowledge, a mandarin advised him to live like a man of learning, and he would everywhere be accepted with honour. Straightaway, Ricci discarded the cowl of a priest for the distinguished robes of a Chinese intellectual. He instituted an era of which a Jesuit father wrote: 'The fragrance of our faith began to be spread over the whole of China'.

How so many men of such brilliant attainment and courage were attracted to the Society of Jesus, in its then still early years, is something of a mystery. The present General calls it 'The Ignatian charisma'. It isn't quite enough of an explanation. Dr. Northcote Parkinson uses the simile, in his examination of the rhythmic rise and fall of power between East and West, of a piston. The power of the Western piston was on pressure when Father Ricci and his brethren adventured into China. All

At Montserrat, in the mountains outside Barcelona, Ignatius dedicated his sword to the Queen of Heaven. The contemporary woodcut suggests how it looked when he spurred his mule into the highland fastness

The Jesuit missionaries to Elizabethan and Jacobite England committed high treason. It was a period of dedicated courage, complex political purpose, and the summary butchery of Tyburn Tree. The first two Jesuits to penetrate the country were Father Robert Persons (*top left*) and Edmund Campion (*bottom left*). Persons escaped to live to old age, and to encourage Philip II of Spain in the launching of the Armada. Campion was caught, hanged, drawn and quartered. Father Garnet (*top right*) was accused and condemned for complicity in 'The Gunpowder Plot'. Titus Oates (*bottom right*), here in the pillory, was the notorious renegade spy who gave evidence against the Jesuits and their scholars

Qui Summi Pontificis primatum Reginæ in Anglia negant tribui posse,
tanquam Læsæ Maiestatis rei damnantur, et ad supplicij locum, Cratibus
impositi, ministris interim hæreticis ad fidem Catholicam deserendam
adhortantibus, per mediam Vrbem ignominiose raptantur. Sic Edmundus
Campianus cum socijs, alijque Catholici tum Sacerdotes tum laici ad
mortem tracti sunt. Anno Domini 1581. 1582. 1583.

32

Edmund Campion was dragged on a hurdle, in accordance with the custom of
the time, to Tyburn for execution. A triangular cutting in the stone at Marble
Arch in London now marks the site of the notorious tree. This contemporary
impression recalls martyrs other than Campion. It is Jesuit pride that they have
preserved Campion's 'brag', a declaration of his religious conviction which he
wrote in hiding before his arrest. A reliquary at Stonyhurst contains a length
of the rope in which he was bound to the scaffold. Evelyn Waugh, amongst
many, has written of this heroic and holy man who, before he left the Continent, seems to have anticipated the dread fate which was destined for him

Romantic pictures convey the impact that the Jesuits made on every court in the known world. They penetrated them all. They almost converted the Grand Mogul in northern India into accepting Christianity. They campaigned with him in his wars. He died a little too soon for them to achieve their object

In the name of the popes, Jesuits became the professional diplomats of Christendom. Father Possevino, at the court of Stefan Bathory (*above*) makes peace between Poland and Russia. Catherine the Great (*below*) welcomed them when they were suppressed by the pope. In Russia, they kept their identity

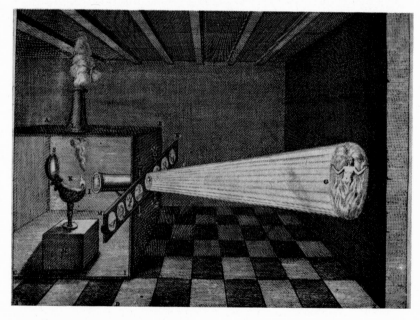

The Jesuits (*above*) were the first to discover the medicinal value of quinine. It was originally known as Jesuits' bark. They developed the magic lantern (*below*), the forerunner of motion pictures. They sent the camellia to Europe.

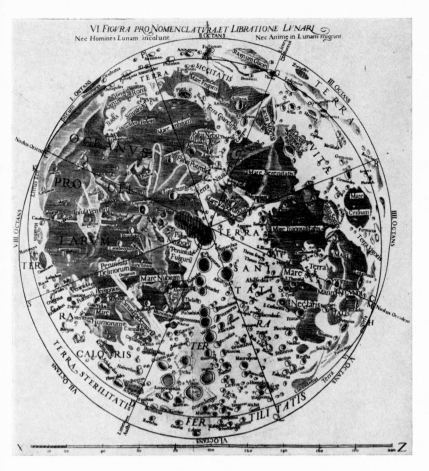

The Jesuits were the first to map the moon. Many of the craters are named after their astronomers. The Jesuits, in opposition to Rome, realised that the earth circles the sun. Their number includes the first inventive scientists

Father Matteo Ricci S.J.

The portrait of Matteo Ricci, one of the greatest Jesuits, was painted, as he was laid out on his deathbed, by a gifted brother of the Order. To win the confidence of the Chinese Emperors he had entirely adopted Chinese dress and ways. He was the first 'barbarian' to bring the wisdom of the West to the East cylinders were firing when the West exploded across the Continents. It is perhaps not surprising that the best men were happy to serve for the advance of Western civilisation and 'For the Greater Glory of God'.

Ricci, in the disguise of a Chinese learned man, established his mission in a small house in Canton. He knew that the Chinese were inordinately proud of their advanced culture and intellectual development. On their maps, the rest of the world outside China was marked with a few fly-blows designated as 'Barbarian Countries'. They were convinced that they had nothing to learn from any other race of people. It is probably true that they still feel the same way today. Ricci determined not to disabuse them. In Xavier's style he professed the greatest respect for the profound wisdom of the East, humbly apologising for his own lack of knowledge. He didn't preach. Instead, he allowed the high class Chinese who now besieged the house of 'the Holy Doctor LiMa-t'ou', as he was then generally called, to look at the collection in his laboratory, artifacts used in the study of mathematics, physics and astronomy, glass prisms through which all the colours of the spectrum could be seen, horological instruments, gauges, compasses, musical instruments, books, pictures and maps. As his fame spread he listened in humble composure, only making a comment when the excited curiosity of his guests demanded it. Of a map on his wall he told them that it was the world drawn to scale. It showed what a relatively small part of it China represented. 'A belief which had prevailed for three thousand years in China was shaken: on that day began a new epoch in the history of Chinese civilisation.'

His reputation as a learned man grew with every revelation that he made, always insisting what a lesser man he was within the greater culture of China. It was only later, when he had convinced them that the Europeans might have a culture the equal of their own that, with great circumspection, he introduced in his house pictures of the Virgin Mary and other religious subjects. He explained that Western beliefs were only

little different from their own. They were puzzled, but respect-
fully interested in the words of a learned man who could teach
them astronomy, geography, gnomics and arithmetic.

His fame travelled. He was invited to the province of Kiang-si
to debate with some of the most prominent mathematicians of
China. They were good. But Ricci had served under the great
Jesuit astronomer Father Clavius in Rome – the same who had
helped to create the Gregorian Calendar and who now has a
crater of the moon named after him – and the Chinese mathematicians couldn't confound him. He found some errors and
omissions in their teaching. He compiled in the Chinese language
a geometry, based on Euclid, a subject on which they had only
fragmentary knowledge. He showed the professors how to
construct sundials, explained to them the principles of acoustics,
and the nature of astronomical calculation. He was welcomed
'as one of the greatest and most learned of teachers'. He had
scarcely exposed his hand as a Christian missionary. He was
more anxious to persuade the Chinese that he knew as much
about Confucianism as they did; and, apologetically, that he
knew more about the natural sciences than they had ever conceived. They gave him full marks.

Under his Chinese hat, Father Ricci never lost his Jesuit
identity, or his determination to reach his ultimate objective.
It was none less than to beard 'The Son of Heaven', the Chinese
Emperor, in his own formidable palace of marble, jade and
bronze. His subjects were not allowed to look upon him. He
was protected by a ring of mighty walls, thirty miles long and
thirty feet high, so thick that twelve horsemen could ride
abreast on them. The walls were defended day and night by
lancers and cannon. Only a Jesuit could have looked at them,
and felt undismayed.

He had made a journey which extended three years from
Rome to Canton. He landed in China in the autumn of 1552,
passed fifteen years in Shiuhing and five in Nanking. It took
him altogether about twenty years to reach the forbidden city
of Peking. For most of the time he was out of all contact with

Europe. The replies to some of his letters, about fifty survive, did not reach him for nine years. He was in constant danger of his life from the ten thousand eunuchs who dominated the corrupt Imperial court. He was imprisoned, nearly drowned in the Yangtsze, and subjected to every form of Oriental contempt. By sheer intellectual brilliance, he won a sort of acceptance. He knew things the Orientals didn't know.

In retrospect, Ricci may be said to have failed. In his mission he converted only two thousand Chinese out of one hundred and ninety million. He never set eyes on one of the last of the Ming Emperors, Wan Li, who had never himself looked on other than his concubines and his eunuchs. Perhaps it was as well. The emperor, at thirty-eight years of age, was a fatted monster of whom it is said that his voice wouldn't carry more than ten feet. There came a time in Peking when Ricci was invited to a royal audience. He polished the kow-tow and, in company with merchants in search of jade, bowed at the dawn of morning to an empty Dragon Throne. The Emperor didn't appear.

But, earlier, he had introduced his own Trojan Horse. It didn't bring him face to face with the emperor. But the man from the Land of the Southern Barbarians aroused the Celestial Being's intense curiosity. Ricci's gifts from the world of the Far West were holy pictures, drawn in perspective which the Chinese had not mastered, books, prisms (they used parchment for windows, and knew nothing of glass); and above all, clocks. Ricci brought two, a pendulum clock which couldn't be mounted in the low ceilinged palace, and which was subsequently erected in a Jesuit-built tower in the garden, and a small spring clock. The small clock, which ticked enchantingly, won the emperor's heart. It had not been without difficulty that Ricci had circumvented the suspicions, traitorous and effeminate eunuchs about the forbidden palace, the walls within which he was the first European ever to be admitted. He wondered if his clock, his present to the emperor, would ever pass up the official hierarchy. But the marvellous thing, which seemed to have a life of its own, actually reached the Son of Heaven.

In due course the clock ran down. None of the mandarins, or the eunuchs, knew how to wind it. Father Ricci was summoned to the gates and, with a few deft twists, had it working again. The clock became the emperor's dearest possession. The College of Mathematicians, under his instruction, had to learn at the peril of their lives how to handle it. The Son of Heaven, in remote splendour, now ordered that the men from the West should teach the court how to play the clavichord. The Jesuits knew it all. He became interested enough to enquire who these men were; what did they eat, what clothes their people wore, what were their marriage customs, and how great were their kings. He was even sufficiently interested to require that the strangers should be painted, for his personal interest, by the court artists. Chinese art, with no sense of perspective, was empty. Father Ricci, and his brethren, looked at each other in surprise at what passed for a representation of their features. The great Jesuit is better represented in the posthumous portrait of him painted by a brother of the Order in 1610. It is fair to say that the Chinese didn't understand. What is notable is that the Jesuits at last established themselves within 'the rose-coloured walls'. The emperor made them a monthly allowance of rice and silver. When Father Ricci offered his presents to the emperor, 'religious paintings and a reliquary set with precious stones', he explained himself as a humble subject, 'an ignorant and unworthy man, asking to turn to account his unworthy talents'. It is remarkable that the reliquary and the holy paintings which the Master of Ceremonies had proclaimed in Peking would bring ill-luck were displayed in one of the most important reception rooms with incense burning in front of them. Such was the honour in which Dr Li and his brethren were now held. He was entrusted with the duty of instructing the Emperor's favourite son in ethics and the mathematical sciences. By the time Dr Li died the bells of over three hundred Christian churches were sounding in the Chinese Empire. The Emperor provided a large plot of land for his ceremonial burial, and proclaimed to the disaffected among his subjects: 'Be persuaded that in the hearts of these learned men from the West there is neither lust for fame, nor lust for worldly gain. Nine times ten thousand miles have they travelled in their journey to our country, defying monsters and cannibals that they might save us from eternal damnation. Was there ever such nobleness of spirit . . . take up the books of the wise men from the West and study them profoundly. From them you will receive enlightenment, and thereafter tremble with dismay at your former errors!'

The death of Father Ricci, a quiet death in 1610, might have been calamitous; but another, a German Jesuit named Father Adam von Schall, was there to inherit his mission. The Jesuits, in the German sense of the word, were as *formidable* as ever. In the chaos that was the Chinese Empire, order such as it was was represented by a law of the Universe known as the *Tao*. In Western terms it might be called a sort of 'Old Moore's Almanack', a mad mathematical horoscope which, with the blessing of the Son of Heaven, was presented to the people, with appropriate ceremony, each year. Following it was supposed to be a sure guide when to plant crops, when to get married, when to go to war, and almost when to cross the road. But for years the omens had been ominously inadequate. Harvests had failed, the empire was in ferment, and there was a general feeling that the mathematicians had got their sums wrong.

Inevitably, the Emperor turned to the Jesuits. With their usual zeal the fathers demonstrated that the mathematical tribunal had made grave errors. None, including the mandarins of the old school who resented the newcomers, might have believed them. But it happened that an eclipse of the sun, a phenomenon which the Chinese regarded with mystical gravity, was imminent. The Chinese mathematicians were unable to anticipate it. The Jesuits timed it to the day, and the hour. The emperor ordered that, henceforward, the Mahommedan system was out of date. In future, the European system of calculation must be adopted. Father von Schall, 'a second Confucius', was appointed to take charge. He took charge of so much that one winces at his responsibility. When the Tartars first descended from the North, threatening the Ming dynasty, it was again Father Schall who undertook to teach the Chinese how to cast cannon, to show them how to establish an arsenal on European lines. How the holy man, bending over the Mass and his breviary, came to know such worldly things passes normal human achievement. But he did it. He trained the gun crews, and gave the Chinese the wherewithal to drive the Tartans beyond the Great Wall.

China has never been conquered even by the Chinese; just as it is said that Russia has never been conquered, even by the Russians. The Jesuit missionaries struggled in a muddled world in which there was no central authority. In the vast provinces the most the emperor could command was a certain religious respect. During their stay in Peking, the last of the dynasty of Ming committed suicide. The last prince of his line died in exile in the south, after he and his mother had submitted to baptism, and accepted the Christian name of Constantine. Imperturbably, the Jesuits accepted the new regime. The new Manchu rulers also believed in the Tao. They were reluctant to throw out the men who understood the mathematical pattern better than they did. Father Schall was appointed director of the mathematical tribunal, and given the rank of 'Mandarin of the First Class'.

In the early decades of the Manchu dynasty, the young Emperor, Shun-ci, lost his favourite wife and only child. He abdicated and retired into a Buddhist monastery. The next emperor, K'ang-Hi, was a minor whose affairs were managed by a council of Regents. Earlier the Jesuits had been given full freedom and the power to preach. Eunuchs in the court had embraced Christendom. There was a Christian church in Peking. But under the Regency, with the conspiracies that such form of Government always involves, in the civil disturbances within the Empire, they looked for a scapegoat. Who better than the alien Father Schall? His authority as a master gunner, his position as president of the mathematical tribunal, his lowly

.status as a foreign dog, demanded it. He was arrested, tried and condemned to death. The Jesuit books were burnt. A Chinese mathematician was appointed chief of the tribunal of the calendar.

An eclipse of the sun came to the Jesuits rescue again. Father Schall didn't have his head chopped off because the Chinese hadn't got the date right. The Jesuits had. They were given permission to erect an observatory, equipped with the necessary instruments 'with an armillary sphere for determining the position of the stars, an astrolobe for calculating the length and breadth of the celestial bodies, instruments for determining altitudes and azimuths and a telescope'. The Jesuits had won again. When Father Verbiest, their champion when Father Schall was under sentence of death himself, died, distinguished mandarins, including the emperor's brother-in-law, the officer in charge of the emperor's bodyguard and the commandant of the palace, were required to accompany the bier on horseback. The Christians from the capital and neighbouring districts, bearing candles and banners, led the procession, being followed by the missionaries in white robes, whilst fifty horsemen of the Imperial Guard closed the procession.

In recollection of all the Jesuits of that period, Father Schall stands large. He had proved to the Chinese that his mathematical calculations were superior to theirs; he had taught them how to make cannon, and he had suffered the horrors of incarceration with little hope that it would end other than with the executioner's sword. He returned to freedom to pursue the education of the young emperor, K'ang-Hi. He himself had not long to live but he imparted to the young man, who had a lively curiosity, a love of learning. He died in the knowledge that the new Son of Heaven would continue to seek the wisdom of his brethren. He was right. The emperor sedulously devoted himself to their scientific teachings. The poor fathers had to stir themselves at four in the morning to explain geometrical construction, chemical and medical problems, optics and acoustics, and philosophical speculation.

Others were expected to lay themselves on their faces in the presence of the emperor. The Jesuits were allowed to stand. He gave them complete freedom to practise Christianity. He himself contributed the money to provide a Christian church and composed the inscription to be placed over the door. It ended 'The true Creator of all things without beginning and without end'. Truly the Jesuits, admitting more and more Chinese to the Christian faith, had reason to suppose that with the emperor on their side, the miracle that Xavier conceived was about to happen.

In the halcyon days the emperor, having heard so much about the power and dignity of the Christian pope, came to think that a marriage relationship with the Prince of Christendom would confirm the link between East and West. With the most worthy intentions he composed a letter to Rome. As one who has always considered that one of the funniest letters ever written was Evelyn Waugh's fictional one from 'Seth, Tyrant of the Seas, Bachelor of the Arts of Oxford University, to Messrs Mappin and Webb, Greetings, Peace be upon your house', I withdraw. The real letter which the Emperor of China sent to the pope is better. The original is preserved in the archives of the French Ministry of Foreign Affairs. I present it as a mere diversion:

'To you, Clement, most blessed of all popes, blessed and great Emperor of all Popes and Christian Churches, Lord of the Kings of Europe and Friend of God. The most powerful of all powers on earth who is greater than all who are great under the sun and the moon; who sits on the emerald throne of the Chinese Empire, raised upon a hundred golden steps, in order to expound the word of God to all faithful subjects; who exercises the power of life and death over a hundred and fifteen kingdoms and a hundred and seventy isles, writes this epistle with the virgin feather of an ostrich. All hail and long life!

'The time has come when the bloom of Our Imperial Youth shall bring to maturity the fruit of our age, so that at the same time the desire of our true subjects may be fulfilled and a successor to the throne given *to them for their protection. We have resolved, therefore, to unite ourselves with a beautiful and distinguished maiden, who has been nurtured on the milk of a courageous lioness and of a tender doe. Since the Roman people have always had the reputation of progenitors of brave, chaste and unsurpassable women, we would stretch forth our unsurpassable hand, and take one of them to wife. We hope that it may be your niece or that of another great priest on whom God looks with favour ... We wish her to have the eyes of a dove contemplating heaven and earth, and the lips of a mussel feeding upon the dawn. Her age shall not exceed two hundred moons. She shall not have grown taller than a blade of green wheat, and her girth shall be as a handful of dried corn ...*

'In gratifying our desire, Father and Friend, you will create an alliance and eternal friendship between your kingdom and our powerful land. Our laws will be combined as a creeper clings to a tree. We shall ourselves disseminate our royal blood through many provinces, and shall warm the beds of our princes with our daughters, whose portraits the mandarins as our ambassadors will bring to you ... In the meantime we rise from our throne to embrace you. We declare to you that this letter is sealed with the Seal of our Empire, in our Capital of the World, on the third day of the Eighth Moon in the fourth year of our reign.'

Although the proposition, not surprisingly, was never realised, it is an interesting speculation what might have been changed through the sort of marriage of convenience which was then the custom throughout the monarchies of Europe. The Jesuits at that time were confident that they could manage China in celibacy on their own. With the patronage of the Emperor, who instructed them to make new maps of his territory, they travelled in every province. With an impressive entourage, they kept the local chieftains in their place, arranged the building of new churches, and raised the morale of the Christians wherever they went. It is said that, under the benevolent K'ang-Hi they baptised nine thousand Christians. It is questionable what sort of religion the Chinese thought that they had adopted. It was one of the criticisms aimed against the

Jesuits by the ecclesiastical authorities in Rome that Christ on the Cross, a conception of God which was offensive to the Eastern mind, had been tactfully suppressed. The emphasis was put rather on Christ in glory with his Mother at his side. It is more likely that the Chinese converts, like fans at a football match, played with a prevailing fashion. In the upper echelons of the Middle Kingdom the Jesuits were admired, even by the emperor K'ang-Hi, for the scientific knowledge that could be squeezed out of them. The Chinese mind couldn't comprehend the Western one, and the Western one could only impress them by tailoring worldly affairs to their advantage.

The Jesuits were masters at that. Unpaid, too. Asking only permission to preach they served the Son of Heaven with skilled devotion. When there was trouble on the Sino-Russian border, and some of the more warlike Tartars threatened to side with the invaders against Peking, the Manchus hadn't a clue what to do about it. The Jesuit Father Gerbillon went to the Russian camp and explained how advantageous it would be for them, in exchange for certain disputed territories, to make a profitable treaty. To the satisfaction of both sides he made the first commercial treaty which the Chinese had ever concluded with a European power.

As universal providers they were called in when the Emperor, 'aged, weary, sick and tormented with pain', looked like dying. They pulled him round with a box of little balls of dough which they assured him had cured the mighty Dauphin of France. In hindsight, it may be regarded as faith medicine; but it worked. Latterly they hauled him on to his feet again, after an intermittent fever, in which four princes 'had to act as guinea-pigs before the emperor would try the cure, with doses of 'Jesuits' bark'. Again, it worked. The emperor made a public appearance to record his satisfaction. In the end, when he returned from hunting, with severe inflammation of the lungs, the Jesuits could do no more than ease his passing with some of the altar wine which they received every year from Manila. He died in peace, protesting a love for the Christian God who had enabled him to pass the last hours of his life in serenity. Subsequently, people throughout China came to the missionaries for medical attention. Grateful patients accepted baptism. Réné Fülop-Miller, to whose book *The Power and Secret of the Jesuits* I am indebted for so much valuable scholarship, adds: 'Thus many souls were gained for the Kingdom of Christ with the aid of French pills, Indian powders and Spanish wine.'

The son of K'ang-Hi, the way sons so often shape, had no sympathy with the respect his father had shown to the foreign priests. On his ascension to the throne, he ordered three hundred thousand Christian Chinese to recant. In the fear that foreign magic would ultimately overrun his Empire, he destroyed churches, and suppressed by force communities which the Jesuits had so patiently cherished. Irrepressibly, the Fathers bided their time. It happened, soon after the accession of Yung-cheng, that a Russian mission arrived to arrange a second important commercial treaty. The Chinese couldn't manage it any more than they could time an eclipse of the sun. Inevitably the Jesuits were called in. Inevitably, they arranged the affair to better advantage than the Chinese thought possible. The emperor in more friendly mood relaxed the persecution of the Christians. The fathers could take breath again.

The fourth ruler of the Manchu dynasty was a megalomaniac who believed himself to be God. No mortal might gaze upon him and, when he issued out of his palace, mounted soldiers were sent before to clear the streets, shut the shops, and blind the windows and doors of the houses. So that he might have some knowledge how mortals lived he built a town inside the palace walls in which, when he was in the mood, his harem and his eunuchs acted the parts of ordinary people. They busied themselves in a bogus market. They hung out the washing, attended to the domestic animals, and gossiped in the streets. The Jesuits, who would have been happy to act with the others, had no part in it. They survived because the fathers still held the presidency of the Mathematical Tribunal, the making of the annual calendar which none but themselves knew exactly how to compute. But, in their audiences with the emperor, they had to address him extended on their faces on the ground.

The emperor was a contemptible wretch. Any but the Jesuits might have conceived that their cause was hopeless. But it came to their knowledge that in his godliness he believed that his surroundings in his palace and his summer residence were unworthy of him. Painters, gardeners, artists and mechanics were called in to make all more worthy of his presence. The only people who had any communication with him were those who contributed to his greater glory. Proved mathematicians, astronomers, and philosophers, the Jesuits changed, almost over-night, into landscape gardeners, makers of mechanical toys, portraitists, engravers, and experts in hydraulics.

It is a wonder why they thought it all worth while. For the pleasure of a mad emperor, they patiently found out how to master the ways of fountains, mechanical animals, and engrave copper plates to reproduce the glory of the Manchu Son of Heaven. I have an impression that, in that mad frustrating period the Jesuits had a certain exuberance. They must have, or they would have chucked in their hands. Men are never so holy that they can carry on when no one believes in them. I sense in them at that time a frivolous, almost boyish enjoyment in creating hydraulics, mechanical lions, theatres for the idiot who thought he was God.

The latter Jesuits in China had no choice but to dedicate themselves to playroom trifles. All that Ricci and his successors had struggled for had been elaborately denied in Rome. As missionaries they had made a tremendous impression. By saving the life of the emperor, K'ang-Hi, by arranging a treaty with Russia, they had brought western culture to the east, and given east to west. As a consequence chinoiserie, as it was called, influenced the eighteenth century.

They were defeated by their own kind. 'As the Chinese Mission grew, Franciscans and Dominicans entered the country. Their method of evangelising was direct, uncompromising, and took little account of the different psychology of the people to whom it was addressed. The mendicants walked through the streets holding up crucifixes and, when a crowd gathered, preached that all the long line of Chinese Emperors were burning in hell.'

Nine Italian cardinals, conducting their conference in Latin, none of them with any knowledge of the East, decided unanimously that the veneration of ancestors, the nice way that the Chinese ceremonially honoured their dead, was in opposition to Christian doctrine. A Frenchman, Charles de Tournon, cursed with tactlessness and personal overbearance, was sent to Peking to enforce the claim. He chose as his interpreter a French Bishop named Maigrot who had lived twenty years in China, and apparently learnt nothing of its ways. The enlightened Manchu Emperor, K'ang-hi, faced with the papal legate, remarked angrily: 'How can the pope judge of things which he has never seen, and with which he is not acquainted? So far as I am concerned, I would never presume to pass judgement on customs in Europe of which I know nothing.' A Chinese judge said of a Dominican who was a prisoner in his hands: 'I know the Jesuits well; they are true preachers and brave men who have brought us books, clocks, telescopes and similar useful objects. You others, however, are false preachers, for you neither know the high science of mathematics or astronomy, nor have you brought us clocks or books.'

The Holy See destroyed a mission which might have changed the order of the world.

V

The Awakening of North America

IN 1926 my great aunt Emily, Sister Philippine de la Croix, then in her eighties, wrote a letter, in a steady copperplate hand, to my own father, recalling her memories of the American Civil War. 'I remember every incident of the action at Harper's Ferry', she wrote, 'as it happened on my eighteenth birthday.'

'I had a few friends to celebrate it. After their departure my parents and I were sitting talking about the strange behaviour of the Northern Troops who then occupied the Ferry. We had noticed that all the day they had been carrying beds from the barracks to the Arsenal which was nearly opposite to our house on the other side of the canal. About 10 or 10.30 a loud knock came to the door. A gentleman was outside who said "For God's sake, Mr Hastings, take your wife and children to the mountains, for we shall be blown up in five minutes". It seems these beds were filled with gunpowder. The soldiers had set fire to them, and then ran across the bridge into Maryland as they were expecting an attack from the Southerners (Brave men ! !). I rushed upstairs and dragged my brother and sister out of bed. My brother was so sleepy he could not understand the danger and kept getting back into bed, so there was no time to dress the children. I gathered up all their clothes and took them out of the bedroom on to the mountain where I met my Father and Mother and lots of the residents all going as far as possible from the Arsenal. Your own father then dressed and I dressed my sister. We never expected to see our home again. All the young men hastened to the Arsenal and, at the risk of their lives, pulled out the ticks filled with gunpowder, and threw them into the canal. There were some small explosions, but only one workshop was destroyed. The young men directed their attention to the armoury, now in flames. It was some little distance from the Arsenal. All the men could do was to rush in and save as many rifles as possible, and take them to their houses. A friend of ours got one for himself and one for your Father who was only eleven. The armoury which supplied the whole of U.S. was utterly destroyed. About 2 o'clock in the morning, word was sent to the fugitives that all was safe, and we returned home to find everything just as we left it, though all the doors were left open. My brother and sister were made to lie down on their beds in their clothes for fear of some further disaster. My parents and I remained up and sat on the porch which was high up above the road. About 3 or 4 o'clock we saw troops of cavalry passing noiselessly below. The horses' hooves were muffled. The men wore large cloaks and soft felt hats. They didn't see us, and I don't think anyone saw them enter but we three. The next morning the inhabitants were much surprised and pleased to see the Stars and Stripes had been hauled down from the flag-staff, and the Confederate flag floated in its place. All the people gave their sympathies to the Southerners after the dastardly behaviour of the Northern Soldiers.'

In her letter she promises my father, on their next meeting, to tell the use his own father made 'of his beautiful new Minié rifle'; 'of the splendid behaviour of the Confederate Army'; and of 'our departure from Virginia'. The departure is easily explained. Such little fortune that my great-grandfather had was invested in the Confederate cause. As a child I was told of the bonds in the attic, variously signed by Lee and Jackson, 'to be paid in Washington after the War'. Papa's children had used them to raise steam in a toy locomotive. My uncle Lewis remembered the Minié rifle acquired as a boy by his father; my own grandfather who, for the rest of his life, had three pictures in an ivory frame on the mantelpiece of his study, underlined with the injunction: 'Pray each night for Papa and Mama, and "Stonewall" Jackson.'

I have quoted a family link with the past because so much that we know of early American history is based on memories like that. None more than the letters of the pioneer Jesuit missionaries, letters written under duress with small hope of reaching their destination, sent by pious and cultivated men to inform the old world about the new one. Before newspapers, their dispatches made the news. The martyrology, read in Jesuit refectories now, dates from a time when the Fathers were informing not only their brethren but the world. The letters have come to be generally known as the 'Relations'. Inspired by Xavier in India and Japan, they are some of the most important and trustworthy documents left to history. Edna Kenton, in her abbreviation of Jesuit Relations in America, puts it succinctly: 'Jesuits, trained in all the arts that make for intelligence, were endlessly curious and for ever alert in their quest after knowledge. Having come to North America to know the aborigine, they took a strangely royal road to that end. They deliberately went with him into his wilderness, paddled for him on his waterways, foraged with him for food, endured his filth, sickened with his diseases and, although amazingly seldom, died his death. They learned his languages, spelled his so-far unspelled words, delved into the mysteries of his syntax, and put them into grammars and dictionaries. Sitting with him in his Councils, they listened to his oratory, noted his native trends, collected his extravagant metaphors, took over his symbols, his logic and form of reasoning, and later, in his Councils, matched harangue with harangue. They fraternised with his Sorcerers and his Jugglers and his Medicine Men, and with a daredevilry that gave all to win all, staked miracle against "miracle", magic against "magic", wit against wit.'

Whether it was worthwhile to go through so much to gain so little, as Dickens wrote of the Charity boy when he got to the end of the alphabet, is a matter for doubt. It is fashionable now to say *mea culpa* for the crimes committed, in the cause of material gain and in the name of Western civilisation, against 'the noble savage'. But there was little that was noble in him. The aboriginal Indian was sadistic, dirty, treacherous, idle, cannibalistic, and unfit to settle in an advanced society. The baddies of the Westerns, flogging firewater to him in exchange for pelts, were fulfilling the destiny of history more surely than the missionaries who laboured for the salvation of their souls. The American Indians were a human relic left behind, like the remnant of primitive bushmen in Africa, by more vigorous races. I once encountered a bushman family group in the arid waste of the Kalahari. I couldn't even interest the children in the ticking of a watch. Utterly lacking in intellectual curiosity they only cared for the meat which I could bring down with the miracle of my gun.

Races who cannot keep up with the rest of the human kind will always vanish. It is a paradox that the Jesuits, primarily dedicated to winning the American aboriginals to the True Faith, largely failed in their first purpose; but, through their explorations and observations, their cartography and illustrations, their mathematics and astronomy, their agronomy and immense correspondence, have fair claim to be numbered amongst the founders of modern America. That their savage children have been all but extinguished in the process is a contributory factor that they cannot have anticipated; nor, indeed, stayed.

The first Jesuits were sent to America only thirty-four years after the first foundation of the Society. In 1568, fourteen of them travelled from Spain to Florida. They wrote the first textbooks of any kind printed in North America (1570). They compiled a grammar of the native Guale tongue which was spoken in what is now the coast of Georgia and South Carolina. One of the brothers made a catechism in the Indian dialect. It was a waste of scholarship. The Seminole Indians were unapproachable, unpredictable and unreliable. With six other Jesuits the Superior confessed failure, and founded a new mission on the shores of Chesapeake Bay. Within a few months of their arrival the entire Jesuit community was massacred, with what indignities we shall never know. They were the first Jesuit martyrs in the United States. Florida was abandoned for Mexico where the natives were said to be more civilised. A succession of Jesuits tried again.

In the course of the next one hundred and fifty years over three hundred members of the Society came from France to North America. The missionaries at that time were mostly Frenchmen; but, such is the supranational constitution of the Great Society that it is inappropriate to identify any of its self-sacrificing missionaries with a particular country. None of the priests or brothers of the Order would have wished it. Essentially, nationality was unimportant to them. As Gertrude Stein might have written: 'A Jesuit is a Jesuit is a Jesuit.' Frenchmen, Irishmen, Italians, Spaniards, Portuguese, Germans, Belgians, Englishmen forgot their racial quarrels in the higher cause of 'the Greater Glory of God'. How wonderful it would be if, in a lesser cause, the whole world was united like them.

Again and again, greed, envy and suspicion – all the vices of the jury in *Pilgrim's Progress* – denied them the just reward of their labours. They lost the East, from an Italian poniard in their backs, when the Middle Kingdom seemed almost within their grasp. Later, a handful of them so nearly changed the shape of South America that it must rank amongst the most glorious failures in human history. The mental development of the North American aborigines was too retarded to meet the broad shoulder of the West. But the Jesuits tried with implacable determination; and, in the pursuit of a lost crusade, they were among the first to enlighten the West about the vast unknown country which was still called 'New Spain'. It is perhaps untrue that, in the exploration of the Mississippi, 'not a cape was rounded, not a river discovered, without the Jesuits having found the way'. Fur traders may certainly have gone before them; but without culture, curiosity or care. The Jesuits made the maps, studied the ecology of the region and its inhabitants, and reported in educated detail what they learnt.

It is a pity that, in the American story, so much emphasis is placed on ruffians of the Frontier whose only merit was how quickly they could draw a gun. I wonder why Hollywood has not honoured one of the fathers of California, Father Eusebio Francisco Kino, S.J., whose achievements put the gunmen into their proper perspective. Father Kino, an Italian, born Quino, near the City of Trent, that city known to history as the seat of the Great Council of the Church, is one of the most formidable figures in early American history.

He could have been a distinguished professor of mathematics at Ingolstadt, one of the great universities of Europe. He was a cosmographer, surveyor and map maker. He chose, in dedication to Ignatius's injunction to Xavier, 'What doth it profit a man if he gain the whole world, and suffer the loss of his own soul?' to exert the rest of his life (1683 to 1711) in the service of the primitive Indians's living among them in humble authority, poverty, and lonely piety.

So lonely that, for a hundred and fifty years, history forgot him. He was rediscovered by Professor Bolton, of the University of California. With scholarly pertinacity he uncovered forgotten archives. In a book called *A Padre on Horseback*, which James J. Walsh describes as 'that precious little volume', Father Kino rides again.

His endurance in the saddle, confirmed by contemporaries, was so remarkable that 'southwestern cowboys stand aghast'. Dick Turpin's legendary ride from London to York was something that Father Kino regularly carried out on a tour of his parishioners. He normally rode a hundred miles a week, looking after Church business, baptising his converts, and finding hours a day for personal prayer. In fifty-three days, in the fall of 1695, he rode when he was past fifty, fifteen hundred miles. When he was fifty-six he made eleven hundred miles in thirty-five days, contacting his Indians (the Pimas), preaching to them and baptising them in their villages on his way. On an errand of mercy he is reputed on one occasion to have ridden seventy-five miles in twenty-four hours. One wonders what sort of ponies he had to stand it. He disdained a bed. At night he slept on the hard ground covered only with his horse-blanket. In his saddlebags he carried maize for Indians he met on his way. The children followed him out of their villages, the little ones seeking a ride behind his saddle. The Indians could understand, and admire a man like that. They were even prepared to undertake desultory work for the Santa Claus in their midst.

No portrait, no description of him by any of his contemporaries, exists. A seventeenth century Italian, it is unlikely that he had any of the physical characteristics of a rangy long-legged Texan. My own guess is that he was a slight man, with the body of a steeplechase jockey, and muscles like bands of iron. It is said, I am not surprised, that he was completely fearless. He needed to be, unarmed and alone for twenty-five years among savages who, at any moment and without a twinge of conscience, might have split his scalp with a tomahawk. In fact he died in his bed – no, he couldn't agree to accept the comfort of bed. He died lying on the ground. He was in his seventieth year.

That he succeeded so long, in unexplored territory, in bringing his Indians to believe in 'The Great White Father', was a triumph. What he brought to California, now that the Indians he loved have been overwhelmed, ought to be remembered in our own generation.

When he began his labours at the end of the seventeeth century, none knew whether Lower California was an island or a peninsula. Father Kino, who was a keen conchologist, noticed that some of his Indians, who had never been to sea in a boat, had shells which were only found in Lower California. He concluded that it was a tongue of land joined to the mainland.

He recognised, in the then virgin south west, the immense potential of wealth in its soil. 'The stock raising industry at nearly twenty places on the modern map owes its beginnings on a considerable scale to this indefatigable man.' He planted fruit, the beginnings of the vast output of the territory. He persuaded his lazy Indians to harvest what they grew. Above all, in his brave churches, with steeple bells from Spain, he sounded the future; but a rather different one from what he anticipated.

It is sad, but I believe that it was inevitable, that so many of the early efforts of the missionaries – some of the latter ones, too – ended in disaster. Rome, its eyes veiled, couldn't conceive that the spread of Christianity through love without the sword was an empty endeavour. Backed by the sword, conversion had no validity. The early Jesuits went, with zealous purpose, to achieve the impossible. They nearly won the orient with their clocks and calendars; but how far they brought an understanding of the Christian God to Eastern minds is an inscrutable question. In America they suffered and died in martyrdom to bring the Indians into the compass of a religion which was beyond their neophytes' comprehension. Backward children, the aboriginals hadn't even arrived at the use of reason. With a vocation daunting in its nobility, the black robes laboured in squalor and, thanking God for it, embraced the crown of martyrdom.

They starved in winter with the savages; they existed on their nauseous food when they had any; they slept with their curs, they endured the spectacle of their lascivious orgies and drunkenness, and looked on in horrified silence when the braves tortured one of their enemies to a prolonged and ex-cruciating death. The missionaries knew that any time, any day, the same fate could be theirs. The Indians were fickle as well as feckless. They regarded all strangers in their midst as omens of ill luck. A famine, a pestilence, a reverse in their interminable tribal wars was enough for the elders to sentence the black robe in expiation to fortune. They had a horrific custom of inviting the victim they had decided to sacrifice to a banquet before leading him to the stake. They then tried to keep him alive under torture as long as possible; meanwhile, as one of the Jesuits reported, endearing themselves to him as if he was a loved one. It is terrible to have to recall that Lutherans among the white colonists actually encouraged the Indians in their superstitions. They wanted to reduce Jesuit influence among the aboriginals. They can't have wished to subject them to a slow death – indeed they rescued missionaries from the Indians more than once – but they must have been aware of the consequences of their evil council.

The Dutch Calvinists at Fort Orange rescued one of the most redoubtable of the French missionaries, Isaac Jogues, from the Mohawks. The burghers hid him and put him, in a mutilated condition, in a sailing vessel of 50-tons burden bound for Europe. He had been ambushed by the Iroquois, one of the most hostile Indian tribes. After torture, they had kept him in slavery for fourteen months. Father Jogues, a fastidiously cultivated scholar, had been born in Orlèans in 1607, joined the Jesuit novitiate at seventeen and, in 1642, in answer to his fervent prayer, was ordered to the Jesuit mission in Quebec.

Know what happened to him, a frail man in physique who, in his explorations, was fascinated by the dream that Lake Superior might be the legendary road to China. But he sacrificed the golden years of his life to people who had no inquisitiveness at all. I myself believe that they weren't worth the saving; unless you are convinced, as he was, that all souls are worth saving. He succoured the sick, he endured, like his brethren, incredible privation; and he lived, worst of all for a man of learning, in an intellectual vacuum. His comfort was prayer, the discipline of the Spiritual Exercises which have enabled the Jesuits over the centuries to show valour which has surpassed normal human endurance.

In the summer of 1542, then in his thirty-fifth year, Father Jogues was ordered to Quebec. The mission in Huronia was destitute. The Iroquois were on the warpath. It was a matter of survival to get back supplies. He started homeward, if one may call it homeward, with forty in his company, four of them Frenchmen, in canoes heavily laden with goods for the mission. The Iroquois intercepted them. Many of the Indians in the company fled into the woods. Father Jogues stood firm beside the twelve to fourteen who were taken prisoner. Surrendering himself voluntarily, some of his native Christians showed equal bravery, he made his peace with his God. The courage of his companions, in face of the horrors that the savages perpetrated, was transcendent.

What they did to Father Jogues makes its own comment. They battered him to the ground and, a little later, tore off his nails, and bit with their teeth his two forefingers to the bone. His own wounds and the wounds of the captives were so terrible that they putrified, so that worms dropped from them. The Iroquois tore out their pubic hairs and their beards (the Red Indians have little of either themselves) and wounded their victims with their nails. They marched them amid hunger, heat and blows. On the way they made a show of their prisoners, burning one of Father Jogues' fingers, and crushing another with their teeth. One of them only relented, at the last unforgiving moment, from cutting off his nose. In due course, the savages whipping out the flesh with it, drew the father's last two nails, taunting him as they did it. They beat him, passing under the yoke in the ancient Roman style, with iron bars. A squaw cut off his thumb. He let it fall in case, according to their custom, they made him eat it. They took away his clothes, and the skin was burnt from his neck, shoulders and arms. They beat him on the bones of his legs. They chained him, and threw coals and live ashes on his bare flesh. He was sure that he was to be burned.

I have told enough, although there is much more horror to it. Father Jogues had to look on the anguished passing of so many of his companions. Constantly ready for death himself, he was enslaved among families in the Mohawk tribe who had a habit of naming their slaves as a sort of reincarnation of dead relations. He was 'aunt'. With his mutilated hands he was called to the most onerous and menial tasks, carrying weights, travelling distances, reduced to an animal of burden. He sought comfort by carving crosses in birch trees; made himself an oratory, and even recovered a few pious books. The Mohawk family to which he was attached ultimately gave him more friendly freedom. He made contact at last with a Dutch fort.

At first he wouldn't even run away, although there was a ship which could have taken him. He felt that he couldn't desert his responsibility to the Frenchmen who were prisoners with him. At last, when he accepted a passage on a miserable boat to Europe, in which he lived and slept on coils of rope on the deck, he only agreed in the conviction that he must soon return. He did.

Writing to his Provincial in France he blessed Providence that the Indians had not taken his right thumb so that he was still able to report to his superiors. In detail, with never a trace of self-pity, only loving pity for the brethren who suffered with him, he reported like a correspondent of the London *Times*. Back in France, with his mauled hands, he had to ask special permission of the Pope to offer mass which he could no longer do without help. Pope Urban VIII remarked that 'it would be unjust that a martyr for Christ should not drink the Blood of Christ'.

Early in 1644, with incredible dedication, he sailed for Canada again, making a landing in the new-found city of Montreal. That year the Iroquois sued for peace. It was a characteristically treacherous treaty they wanted. They excluded their hereditary enemies, the Hurons and the Algonquins. In treating with the French, Father Jogues noticed that their chief captains were missing. But, with his knowledge of the native language, he was sent as ambassador into the Iroquois country. On his return he left a box of his property, vestments and holy vessels behind. He wanted to avoid the tiresome business of carrying his meague belongings twice over the watery trail. The Indians, discovering it, counted it the cause of one of their misfortunes.

They intercepted Father Jogues, waylaying him two days before his arrival on his third missionary visit to their villages, stripped and ill-treated him, with his companion, another Jesuit

John Lalande, and tomahawked them both. Typically, they killed Jogues after inviting him to a meal in one of their cabins. They palisaded his head facing the route from which he had come. Naively, they brought to the Dutch some of his simple possessions, his missal, ritual and cassock.

In 1649, Father Jean de Brebeuf, one of Father Jogues' closest brethren, was tortured to death by the Iroquois with Father Gabriel Lalement. The butchery they inflicted on the two men was unthinkable; burning out their eyes, cutting off noses, tearing off lips, and, finally, eating their flesh and hearts. Father de Brebeuf, who was a portly man, had the luck to die of his torments within a few hours. Father Lalement lived under torture from six o'clock in the evening till about nine o'clock the next morning.

The savages who perpetrated the horrors they did may be forgiven, as one good father after another, in his death agony, prayed that they should be. In the violence in which the United States was born nothing is more shameful than that the English should have shared in it. So determined was Lord Bellomont, the Governor of New England, to destroy the influence of the Jesuits over the redskins that he placed a price on every priest's head. In 1699 the Governor even went himself to the cruel Iroquois to tell them that 'for every Papist priest or Jesuit, you shall receive as your reward one hundred pieces-of-eight (in those days a small fortune) for we have in this province a law which entitles us to arrest such disturbers of the peace'. Such was the bigotry of the times that it was suggested that French Jesuits were paying their Indians for the scalps of white men.

For an English writer it is shameful to record that, in 1727, a venerable old French missioner, Father Sebastian Rasle, who had been the pastor for over thirty years of the peaceful Abnaki Indians in their home country along the Kennebec river in Central Maine, was murdered by the muskets of the English soldiery. They did it with cries of 'Death to the Babylonish dog, down with the beast of Rome'. The old man, who had passed the larger part of his life in an untamed wilderness, in which he largely subsisted on pounded maize, fell when he offered his body to protect his flock. His only crime was that his Indians occupied a disputed territory between the British colonies and French Canada. 'When, after the departure of the troops', writes James J. Walsh, 'his Indians were able to return to the village to bury the dead and attend to the wounded, they found the body of their dearly beloved pastor pierced by numerous wounds, scalped, the skull split by blows of a hatchet, mouth and eyes filled with mud, the bones of the legs broken and all the limbs mutilated.' At least, he died quickly.

In the undertones of history, it is remarkable how much the formation of America was brought about by religious and fratricidal quarrels in Europe. The Puritan fathers were only the first to make a new home in a virgin country. In 1634, led by the Papist nobleman Sir George Calvert, later Lord Baltimore, a small band of Catholic colonists, fugitives from Protestant intolerance in England, made a landfall to the north of Virginia. They named their new colony – Maryland. Jesuit fathers adventured with them.

'Near the mouth of the Potomac,' wrote Father White, one of the pioneers, 'we came to a small river in the north as large as the Thames. On one bank we have laid out our plantations, and built the town of St Mary; on the other bank lives King Chitomachon.'

There is an ominous ring in the name. King Chitomachon was worshipped by his people as an Emperor, 'a chief of all chiefs'. He distrusted the white men with good reason. They had taken possession of his forests and his prairies. In 1570, his people had mercilessly massacred the first Christian missionaries who preached the hostile demon of a new God. In retaliation, the early settlers shot any redskin within range. Both were frightened of each other. With their customary aplomb the Jesuit fathers set out to repair the rift. After learning the native dialect they armed themselves with just fishing-hooks, needles and confectionery. They crossed the river, and mildly presented themselves before the terrible Chitomachon's wigwam. In his own language they explained the use of the needles and the fish-hooks. Chitomachon ruminated over the confectionery, which he found good. He made friends with the fathers who carried such useful presents. He allowed them to explain their religion. Such was their persuasion that he separated from all but one of his numerous wives, and proceeded in ceremonial procession into Maryland where he took communion, and was married in the Christian rite. An enormous cross was set up in celebration. Other tribes accepted Christianity in exchange for fish-hooks, needles and confectionery. The colonial authorities, who had hitherto only trusted firearms, agreed that 'the natives, when treated in a friendly and just manner, show themselves to be quite peaceful'.

It might have been the beginning of a new harmony between white and red men. But, as new immigrants arrived, they cast greedy eyes on the land over the river. Protestants soon dominated the original Catholic community. The Jesuits were exiled from Maryland. They tried again in New York. The Duke of York, after whom the city had been renamed, was openly sympathetic with the Order; one of the fathers was his personal chaplain. As James the Second, he allowed the Jesuits of his times to acquire power and influence in the court of Whitehall. It all came to an end, once again, with the accession of William and Mary. The Jesuits fled back to Maryland. They held their ground by establishing schools, an art in which they were masters, for whites and Indians. In Georgetown, where my grandfather went to school, and my great-grandfather taught for a time as a classical professor, they founded the first Catholic educational institution in America; and, arguably, a university as old as Harvard. From there, they extended their activities to Virginia, Delaware, New Jersey and Pennsylvania.

The Jesuits' educational net stretched from the new world to Europe, and back again. The Carrolls of Carrollton, one of the richest of the old Papist families, sent their boys on the long journey from Maryland to the Jesuits' academy at St Omers where I began this story. One of them, John Carroll, a friend of Benjamin Franklin, became a Jesuit. On Franklin's special recommendation, he was appointed prefect apostolic, and afterwards became the first Catholic bishop of the United States.

His cousin Charles Carroll, friend of Washington, is an immortal in American history. He was the last survivor of those who signed the Declaration of Independence. To him is generally attributed the clause that the newly-formed United States included in its Constitution the principle of religious freedom.

VI

'A Vanished Arcadia'

FOR more than a hundred and fifty years, centred on the seventeenth century, a handful of Jesuits, never more than three hundred, administered on behalf of the King of Spain the settled areas of a territory which covered almost half of the southern continent of America. It extended from Central Bolivia in the north almost to the Straits of Magellan in the south, from the Andes to the Atlantic seaboard. Politically it was one of the bravest, most successful and certainly one of the most self-denying social experiments in human history.

I have never visited South America. In this, largely a pilgrimage based on personal reflection, I can only write of what others have written before me. For that reason I have titled this chapter after the classic work by R. B. Cunninghame Graham. I might have left it out, my own authority is so slight; but no one can write of the story of the Jesuits without reference to what are called 'The Paraguay Reductions'. The state of Paraguay today is not much larger than Great Britain. In the seventeenth century its capital Asuncion discharged, so far as the communications of the time allowed, the responsibilities of an Empire.

Until a few years ago I only had the sort of knowledge of the country which is conferred on a reader of Graham Greene's novels. Then, out of the vast archives of the B.B.C. – surely the Alexandrian library of our own times – I saw photographs of the ruins of jungle-tangled *estancias;* the snake-haunted remains, somewhere in the forest swamps south of the Amazon, of churches which had sounded the call to prayer with Spanish bells; the left-overs of a civilisation wreathed in a wilderness of

173

exotic flowers; the cenotaphs of Indian races which have been largely wiped off the face of the earth. As the skeletons in the filing cabinets were revealed, I was reminded of the last pages of Gibbon, his description of the stones of ancient Rome as he saw them in the eighteenth century, as Piranesi beheld them in his sad engravings. I have said elsewhere in this book that I believe that there was a certain inevitability in the decline and fall of the indigenous Indians. The advancing and ruthless world of the West couldn't stop its own clockwork progress to preserve Arcadias. It is a grim comment that in our own times, in a polluted environment, we are wondering desperately how to go into reverse.

A mere forty-five years after the Jesuits were founded, the Dominican bishop of Tucuman appealed to Philip II of Spain and Father Aquaviva, the General of the Society and great successor of Ignatius, for help in the thinly-garrisoned mission-ary field. Three Jesuits arrived in 1585. As others followed they founded over the years a chain of academies, up to a university level of education, which stretched from Mexico to Buenos Aires. The fathers in the Jesuit way began to penetrate into unexplored Indian territory. They might have been content to pursue their apostolic mission in uncontroversial devotion. But, disconcertingly, they began to direct their attention to the welfare of the savages – negroes brought in by the slaver ships as well as the Indians who, in nominal freedom, were subjected to the control of colonists who, excusing themselves on the grounds that they were proselytising them in the Christian faith, made serfs out of them.

For a long time the government had awarded to any well-to-do Spaniard who had rendered the colony some kind of service a number of Indians, *encomendados*, under his special protection. It was such a lucrative way of getting free labour that the white settlers went on, without much chance that they would be interfered with, organising slave-hunts and auctioning the captive Indians in the market at Rio de Janeiro. A ploy that produced rewarding results was to incite the various tribes to make war on each other, something that they were only too ready to do. The white colonists bought the prisoners from the victors, in exchange for pocket knives, tobacco and needles; and sold them at a substantial profit on the stock market.

Waxing rich on the slave trade, they viewed with suspicion and growing hostility the activity of the fathers on their slaves' behalf. One Jesuit, Petrus Claver, even made a practice of meeting the slaver ships, bringing aboard biscuits, fruit and sweetstuffs for the fettered negroes. He doctored them, as best he could in the filth between decks, stepping over the dead to help the half-living in their chains. When they were landed he housed them in clean huts, baptising them in a chapel in which negroes over the altarpiece were represented as the happy children of God. To the white settlers, it verged on the blasphemous.

In an attempt to subvert the interfering priests, colonists, by way of alms, presented Indian serfs to the Jesuits themselves. The fathers freed them, paid them money, settled fixed hours of weekly work, and only kept them if they voluntarily agreed to stay in their service. They quoted the words of St Augustine: 'Man should not have dominion over man, but only over the animal world.' Endlessly, the Jesuits agitated at the court of Madrid, and ultimately secured a royal order that the Indians were henceforth to work 'solely by the sword of the Divine word'. Authority from three to six months' journey away made small impression on the Paraguayan subjects of the sovereign of Spain. They accused the Jesuits of making common cause against them with the savages. They insisted that the missionaries were striving for nothing less than the establishment of an independent Indian Kingdom under their personal authority. In certain respects the white settlers were quite right.

The missionaries, disgusted as Xavier had been with the corruption which passed for Christianity in Southern India, disabused that there was any charity in the colonists in Southern America, certain of the necessity of preventing the slave-traders from exploiting their Indian children, sought the patronage of the far-distant sovereign in Spain. They had by then got a footing among the Indians in the wild. They were confident that they could found village settlements – reductions as they came to be called – which could be self-supporting. They undertook to pay an annual poll-tax to the crown. The king, then Philip III, who was short of money, was only too pleased to accept. The missionaries were determined that, henceforward, the bagmen, the sly traders, the outlaws and the slavers, would be kept out. They extracted a patent from Madrid, reaffirmed by Philip IV, that, henceforward, no white man would be allowed into their territories, except the governor, without the missionaries' permission. In extraordinary circumstances they won a lot, lost a little, gained a triumph; and, after a hundred and fifty years in a primitive Arcadia, were destroyed by a stab in the back; as usual, from Europe. In the wake of their martyrs – thirty-seven in South America, many of them victims of their fellow white men – they created a social system which was a wonder of the world. Alas, a world which the power of Christendom willed to pass.

Cunninghame Graham conceived the Reductions as an Arcadian society. Other writers have referred to the great experiment as 'a benevolent dictatorship' and 'the ideal communist state'. It has been suggested that the ordering of it took its structure from St Thomas More's island of Utopia; and the imaginative concept of Campanella, the Dominican who, in *City of the Sun*, wrote of a classless republic ruled by a priest. The Jesuits themselves are reluctant to have any of it. For them it was the expression of 'the Ignatian charisma', a form of administration individualistically theirs; or, to put it in the endearing way that they always refer to their own people, 'Ours'.

The older orders of the Church, the Dominicans and the Franciscans, were in Paraguay long before 'Ours' arrived. It is not difficult to imagine that they were a little surprised by the enthusiasm, even brashness, in which the new order of the

Church started on its brave mission. All about the European
settlements, in vast regions wholly or partly unexplored, tribes
of vagrant Indians wandered through the forests. Those who
had seen a white man recognised him as an enemy who, if he
could catch them, plunged a branding-iron into their shoulders
and sent them to slavery in his plantations.

The first Jesuit *conquistadores* into the South American wilds
were six missionaries who, in pairs – according to the rule of
the order – set out on what we should call today 'a mystery
tour'. The poet Southey evokes the courage in which they
went:

> Behold him on his way, his breviary
> Which from his girdle hangs, his only shield.
> The well-known habit is his panoply,
> That cross the only weapon he will wield. . .

At first, as they canoed the rivers, made their camps on the
banks, the Indians with good reason made themselves timidly
scarce. I want to believe Fülop-Miller's anecdote that, to keep
up their own spirits, two of the first fathers paddling on the
Parana, joined in hymn. They observed that Indians with long
oily-black hair, flat noses pierced with bones and coloured
feathers, were peering at them from their forest haunts – and
giving signs of extraordinary pleasure. The Jesuit sirens, never
missing a trick, made a practice of taking musical instruments
on their future voyages, singing their hearts out to call the
Indians to their spiritual net. Chateaubriand in his *Spirit of
Christianity* writes that 'they (the Indians) descended from their
hills to the river banks in order the better to hear the enchanting
notes, while many cast themselves into the water and swam
after the boats. Bows and arrows fell unheeded from the hands
of the savages, and their souls received the first impressions of
a higher kind of existence and of the primitive delights of
humanity'. When the Indians approached, and discovered that
the missionaries could actually speak their strange dialects, 'the
sounds resembling sneezing, stuttering and coughing rather

than human speech, they invited them to their homes in the forests and plains, there to sing to the old people, and explain what they sang'. The foundations of the Jesuit Reductions were laid.

At their peak in the middle of the seventeenth century there were thirty settlements with a total population of not much short of one hundred and forty thousand Indians. Not without bloody tribulation, not without calumny, not without the unrelenting hostility of most of the white colonists, not without plots behind their backs from Asuncion to Rome, the Jesuits triumphed.

Their Reductions, drawing in the roving Indians from the forest, were laid out with the precision of Roman legionary camps. The centre was the church, often a well-found stone building flanked on one side by a hospital for the sick and infirm, and on the other by the simple house of the missionary fathers, in which they preserved what privacy they could find. Beyond were storehouses and workshops and around them the single-storeyed houses of the Indian families in groups of about ten lined with a continuous verandah. There was a large *piazza* in the middle of the settlement, in the centre of which was a crucifix or perhaps a column surmounted with an image of the Virgin Mary. The village was enclosed by a palisade and a ditch. Outside the boundary there was a hostel for visiting Spaniards who, under strict supervision, and for limited periods, were given hospitality for purposes of trade. There were also manufactories, tile kilns, corn mills and tanneries.

Beyond the palisades, in prosperous times, the Reductions ranched tens of thousands of head of cattle. The missioners introduced plantations of *verba mate*, a plant of which the infusion of the leaves made a mildly stimulating drink. Hitherto, the Indians had been accustomed to travel miles to collect it. It became, in due course, a valuable export of the Reductions to Buenos Aires and Sante Fé. The mission grew maize, fruit, cassava and sweet potatoes. But above all, they developed an economy, and also a full and simple way of life, which has never been matched in an untamed land; and, to a large extent, not even in a tamed one.

The discovery that the primitive Indians were enchanted by music, much better that they had a natural gift for learning it, led the fathers to create a musical kingdom. They found that they could teach their Indians to play sophisticated European instruments. They could hold them together, without a false note, in community singing. Their simple children, indolent by nature, could be roused to work and prayer by a band. They marched them into the wilderness, making music as they went, to fell the trees, plough the land, and enrich the earth. The forest sang, from dawn to sunset, in simple tune.

In their green jungle world the missionaries recognised that their savages needed colour to distinguish themselves; for the same reason that, in modern cities, young people like to show off in unusual garments. So they dressed their parochial officials, in the pleasant bureaucracy they had created, like parrots. In gorgeously coloured raiment their Indians paraded their authority. Long-haired and bare-footed, they happily carried their wands of office under the authority of self-effacing, cultured men in patched black soutanes and worn shoes.

The missionaries taught the Indians, so far as they could, to manage their own affairs. Officials, elected in the manner of a rural district council, administered the Reduction. Civil cases were decided by neutral officials brought from other settlements. Wrongdoers were punished in public court with lashes to which they submitted, usually with apology to the presiding father, in atonement. In serious crime the missionaries refused to administer capital punishment. They passed the culprit to the authorities of the King of Spain.

To the outsider it was a dream world. The Tyrolese missioner, Sepp, has left a description of the welcome he received at one of the Reductions: 'We landed at sunrise, and were greeted from the bank by the Indians with the joyous cry of "Yopean! Yopean!" They all hastened from their huts, some half-naked, some clad in garments of skin; one mounted his black horse, another his grey; one seized his bows and arrows, another his slings and stones, and one and all ran, as only they could, to the river bank . . .

'There now appeared in the middle of the stream two splendid craft, like armed galleys, filled with drummers, reed-pipe players, trumpeters and musketeers. The bands played, the trumpets sounded and the guns were fired, and a sham fight took place between the two vessels. The Indians leapt into the river and fought, partly below and partly above water, a pleasant sight to behold. Finally, they all swam round our boat, greeting us joyfully.

'On the bank stood the father superior with two troops of cavalry and two companies of infantry, all of them Indians, but all splendidly accoutred with Spanish equipment. They were armed with sabres, muskets, bows and arrows, slings and cudgels; they staged a very fine sham fight. While this was in progress, four standard-bearers waved their flags, four trumpeters rallied the people, the cornets, bassoons and reed-pipes sounded the alarm, while we gradually appeared from our verdant leaf-coloured huts, embraced, and, to the sound of joyous pealing of bells, entered the church under green triumphal arches, accompanied by some thousands of Indians. . . .'

Masters of spectacle, the fathers made a spectacle of every great occasion and feast day. Perhaps they had learned it from their brethren in the Chinese Imperial Court. On *Corpus Christi* day living birds of all the exotic hues of South America were tied, poor things, to triumphal arches of flowers and foliage. 'Chained lions and tigers' were placed beside basins of water containing wonderful fishes, all nature rendering homage to the Body of Christ. In the Easter procession the ground was strewn with herbs and flowers, and perfumed water. Clockwork statues of the saints, with movable eyes and limbs, excited the savages' enjoyment of the fiestas. They were not without mechanical skills themselves. Never creators or inventors, they had the ability of copying almost anything that the fathers showed them. Fülop-Miller writes: 'If a crucifix, a candlestick or some similar object were shown to an Indian with a request that he should reproduce it, he immediately made a copy which was hardly distinguishable from the original. The women could reproduce very closely the most costly Brabant lace, while a number of Indian workpeople even constructed a remarkable organ based upon a European model. They engraved metal figures and made copies of missals in such a way that no one could tell which was the printed and which the written copy. The trumpets made by the Indians were fully equal to the products of the Nuremberg instrument-makers, and their watches were in no way inferior to those made in the most famous Augsburg workshops.'

The Jesuits' dearest wish was that they could leave their Indians to prosper on their own. They had lifted them out of savagery – waywardness, cannibalism, drunkenness, and polygamy in its most destructive form. They had got them out of their nomadic life into civilised settlements, made them into smiths, joiners, weavers, tailors, shoemakers, tanners, turners, pewterers, watchmakers, sculptors, bellfounders and instrument makers. They had brought them into the ambience of Western civilisation. Their mission, in their constitution, was never intended to be a permanent one. In the event, they never escaped. In the end what they created was destroyed.

The essential incapacity of their Indians was that they couldn't count much beyond the numbers of their toes. They lacked completely the squirrel's anticipation of hard times. They lived for the day, even eating the beasts, unless they were watched, which the missionaries supplied them to till their fields. Perforce the fathers had to be there to discipline them. They conserved the corn, only issuing it in rations at the appropriate times. In spite of all their careful husbandry, destitution in their Reductions, hundreds of miles away from the European centres, was a constant threat. The missionaries themselves lived on little more than a hominy of maize. It had been agreed that two missionaries should be supported by the Government on the stipend of one secular priest. In their vow of poverty they wouldn't exceed it. Least of all would they presume to help themselves to the produce of their Indians. But they were forced, against all inclination, to manage the financial affairs of the Reductions. The taxes had to be paid to Spain. The Indians needed protection from the white traders who would have robbed them, in exchange for a few gimcracks, of their produce.

The Europeans, cheated of what they counted the perquisites of colonisation, regarded the missionaries with increasing enmity. They murmured that the Jesuits built fences and ditches about their Reductions to keep their Indians from getting out. In fact they were there to prevent the slave traders from getting in. Any Indian could leave a Reduction at any time at his choice. It was put about, so successful were the Jesuits in meeting their taxes, handling their exports, and generally conducting their financial affairs, that they had secret gold and silver mines, a vast treasure which they were concealing from the outside world. Throughout their history it has been the most recurring accusation against them; that the Jesuits have hidden untold stores of secret wealth. As late as the Spanish Civil War, the Communists were digging for it. Nobody has ever found it, because it has never existed. Like Oxfam in our own time, the Jesuits deploy large sums of money. They have never kept it for themselves. But, again and again, their success has aroused the avarice and envy of lesser men who couldn't imagine how it was done without skulduggery. So it was in South America, where the Jesuits' greatest treasure was their Indians, red ivory for the European plantations.

In the early seventeenth century, San Paulo was one of the most notorious towns in the Americas. It swarmed with half-breeds, *mamelucos* of Portuguese, Spanish, Italian and Dutch extraction. The Jesuits were depriving them of their chief industry, the slave trade. In well-armed bands, they infested the country about the settlements, robbing, plundering, seizing any stray Indian they could find. They were the precursors of the Paulistas who between 1611 and 1627, allied with fierce pagan Indians named the Tupies, ravaged mission after mission, often with the connivance of the Spanish Governors and secular priests as well. 'The number of Indians lost to the missions during the three years 1629 to 1631 by death, enslavement, or flight without return were estimated at 200,000.'

The Jesuit Provincial of Paraguay came to a momentous decision. It was none less than to migrate with all the convert Indians in the north east territory of the country, down to the southern lands watered by the Parana, hundreds of miles from the predatory settlement of San Paulo. Abandoning their Reductions, an exodus of men, women and children, loaded their meagre possessions on seven hundred frail rafts, and sailed downstream. It must be numbered among the most remarkable migrations of all time. Smooth in its beginning, the Great Cataract stood between them and their promised land. They had to abandon the rafts. Bandits gathered to cut off stray Indians. The migrants were reduced to eating reptiles, toads, snakes and lizards, and chewing every leather object they could find. How the missionaries held them together, how they prevented them eating the seeds which were to provide their next year's food, is a wonder. But new Reductions rose and lived. It is said that, in the folklore of wandering Indians to this day, they have a faint tradition of the great trek carried out by a chief called Montoya – Padre Ruiz de Montoya, another of the great Jesuits who have inscribed their names on history.

The successful migration of the Guayrá tribe, under the command of the Jesuits, only made the missionaries more accursed by the Paulistas. In the old territory, three fathers were martyred, one by pagan marauders when he was driving sheep from Santa Fé; one by witch-doctors who counted the mission-aries their professional enemies; and one by the Paulistas themselves. In 1637, it was said that 25,000 Indians were carried into slavery. Governor after governor sided with the irregular outlaw bands. One, when the Jesuits begged for his help, retorted: 'May the devil take all the Indians! Write that to your missioners!'

The Jesuits, ever realists decided that they could never carry, on at the whim of corrupt officials and at the mercy of the scum of San Paulo. The answer was to create an Indian defence force. To that end two of the fathers – one of them the same Father Montoya who had led the great trek to the lower Parana – sailed to Rome and Madrid to supplicate arms for their Indians. They arrived in 1638. After eighteen months Father Montoya received much sympathy, but nothing more than royal decrees. In Rome his colleagues could only win papal edicts. On the other side of the world, they would have used them to wad their muskets. What Father Montoya wanted was permission for his Indians to carry guns themselves. He had to wait for three more years in Madrid, until 1646, before he persuaded the authorities that the entrusting of arms to the Indians would not imperil the crowns of Spain and Portugal.

He returned to organise an army. He returned also to face the proclamation of Portuguese independence of Spain, which reduced the Reductions. A lay brother of the Jesuits, an ex-soldier named Domingo Torres, seems to have been the first arms' instructor and regimental sergeant major. The armed forces of the Jesuit Republic were tested soon after. The enemy came down the Uruguay – '450 Portuguese and 2,700 Tupies in 300 canoes'. The Jesuit army was 4,200 strong, 'armed with native weapons, with 250 arquebuses, and, most unpleasant surprise of all, a piece of artillery. Brother Torres poured out the powder, rammed home the round shot, and laid the gun. With his shot he sank three canoes. The Paulistas abandoned their boats to try their luck on land. For three days, a running guerrilla-type battle went on in the forest. Torrential rain, as it so often did in primitive warfare, induced both sides to abandon hostilities. The invaders decided to withdraw upstream as quickly and quietly as possible. Under the command of the redoubtable Brother Torres, his Indian braves ambushed and routed them. The insolent attacks of the Paulistas were lastingly subdued. The Christianised Indians became useful soldiers of the realm of Spain. The new Reductions began to flourish in peace.

At last the extraordinary Republic of Paraguay became a real state. The fathers established cannon foundries and small arms factories. Each Reduction had its military garrison. A troop of cavalry constantly patrolled the surrounding area. The passes giving access to the country were closely guarded. A missionary wrote: 'In case of emergency, we could at once raise a force of 30,000 mounted Indians who are well-acquainted with the use of sabre and musket, who can form squadrons and carry out their manoeuvres correctly. They are all paraded and drilled by the fathers.' In due course, King Philip V was to describe them as 'the military bulwark of Spain'. In due course, regular Spanish and Portuguese forces, attacking the Jesuit Republic, were thrown back. The Jesuits fortified their Indians' positions so well that it was believed that they must have skilled military engineers at their disposal. They defeated aggression, in the carve-up of the territory between Portugal and Spain, on every front. It was too good to last.

The Jesuits brought peace and industry to their settlements. They even founded a printing press. With their Indian army they could hold off the warring interests of Portugal and Spain. In the play *The Strong are Lonely*, by Fritz Hochwälder, the theme is that they commanded enough military power in the eighteenth century to run both Spain and Portugal out of all the Latin colonies in South America. Their mission, as so often before, was destroyed in cupidity and ignorance behind their backs. They were suppressed by their own commander-in-chief.

In humble obedience, they accepted the decree of the Papal Legate disbanding their mission. They used their influence over the Indians to prevent bloodshed. In 1767, two hundred and twenty-four Jesuits of the Paraguay were shipped like cattle to Spain. Some of the older ones died on the way. After a five months' voyage, Spain didn't want them. They passed them to the Papal states which didn't want them either. Refugees on the move, they sought shelter anywhere they could find it in an unwelcoming Europe.

With the expulsion of the Society from South America, all order went with them. Portugal seized Spanish territory. The Indians scattered again. Neither Portugal nor Spain now possesses a single foot in the area. The indigenous Indians, whose country it was, colour the blood of the present population; but, as a pure race, they have virtually disappeared. The *ileana* flowers, clutching at the stones of the ruined churches, are all that is left of beauty in a little lost civilisation.

To learn how the tragedy came about, it is unnecessary to look to grasping officials, scheming politicians, shameless prelates, slave-dealers, and Paulistas – there were plenty of all of them – in the excitable heat of the South Americas. It was plotted in boudoirs, gilded salons, the smelly corners of palaces, and in the whispers of secrecy behind velvet curtains and great doors. It was in the old courts of Europe that the Jesuits were betrayed.

In his book *Golden Years on the Paraguay*, Father George O'Neill, S.J., attributes the origins of the conspiracy, although he agrees that it was much more complex than the affair in South America, to persuade the Spanish King, then Charles III, that the Jesuits – not only of Spain but the whole world – had determined to oust him from the throne and set up in his place his younger brother, Don Luis. The plot was to pretend that Charles was an illegitimate child, whose mother had confessed to the Jesuits; and, as a consequence he ought to be set aside in favour of the legitimate prince, Don Luis; and even assassinated. They brought the bemused king sham coins of the 'Emperor Nicholas I', supposed to have been struck by the Jesuits in Paraguay. For a period which extended from 1767 to 1773, evil-minded courtiers encouraged the Spanish king to end, as he supposed, the deadly plotting of the Jesuits. The wretched Hapsburg fell for the whispers in his ear. His advisers, guided by their own material interests, smiled as they thought they saw the Jesuits into final dissolution.

The deed was done with the thoroughness of despotism. It was assumed, correctly, that the missionaries would offer no resistance; although, at a voice of command to their Indian braves, the soldiery of Spain could have done nothing to displace them. The fathers accepted the authority of the Crown; the indignities, and worse, which were imposed upon them. Nothing but the personal influence of the missioners prevented Paraguay going up in flames. Their meekness brought them no kindness. Their achievement was smothered in the tropical forest. Their Indians were doomed. The Hapsburgs were doomed. Only the Jesuits were destined to rise again.

VII

The Tangle of Europe

T O celebrate November the Fifth, in the early twenties, my father wrote a light essay which he called *The Truth about Guy Fawkes*. It appeared in the London newspaper, *The Evening Standard*. What was remarkable, in those days, was that it was given space in a popular print. It exploded a folk tradition, nurtured for over three hundred years, that the 'Guy' the English were bonfiring that night, with a salute of fireworks, was a foreign anarchist who, in 1605, attempted to blow up King and Parliament.

In truth Guy Fawkes (or Faukes) was a Yorkshire yeoman, almost certainly guiltless of what he was accused of; and perhaps one of the most maligned figures arraigned in the misjudgements of history. After the publication of the article Matheson Lang, a distinguished actor manager of the period, commissioned my father to write a romantic play about the soldier, 'tall, with brown hair and auburn beard', who has become England's fall-guy. The play was never staged. At the point of production, Lang felt that the theatregoing public would not stomach Fawkes as a hero. In his generation he was probably right.

There are historians who accept the traditional account of the Gunpowder Plot today. They are in a minority.* In brief the amount of gunpowder, over three tons, which 'the conspirators'

---

* Fr John Gerard, S.J. had first exposed its essential improbabilities in a book, *What Was the Gunpowder Plot?*, at the turn of the century. Hugh Ross Williamson and Fr Francis Edwards, S.J., in scholarly examination and latter knowledge, have subsequently each blown the legend to pieces.

were said to have assembled under Parliament was a feat which defies reasonable belief. How they could possibly have introduced such a load of explosives without anybody learning a wink of the business, in the crowded narrow streets of early seventeenth century London, would have been marvellous enough. How they could have laid hands on such a quantity of powder – the making of it was a government monopoly and three tons represented one twelfth of the annual national production of the period – would have been a staggering achievement. Even with foreign connivance, they could never have shipped such an enormous cargo from the Continent, and horse-drawn it to the eye of London, without government agents, who swarmed at every point of entry, getting the wind of it. Anyhow, its value, in modern terms, was about £10,000. The accused, all Catholics who under the penal laws had been fined into penury, could not have paid for the stuff. But, if they indeed contrived it, the blow-up could scarcely have amounted to an explosion great enough to destroy the whole of Parliament, and all inside it. The powder of the times was ill-milled. In kegs as the authorities said it was, without compression to increase its force, it is unlikely that it would have done much more than disintegrate a few walls and ceilings. But, assuming that it might have been more effective than that, there is not an iota of contemporary evidence that the cellar in which it was said to have been placed even existed in the old Parliament buildings. All the documentary evidence which survives is suspect; much is demonstrably forged. The Gunpowder Plot was bogus, as politically motivated as Goering's Reichstag fire.

Then who stood to benefit from its invention? Without much doubt, the true plot was contrived by Robert Cecil, James the First's Minister of State. He overestimated the strength of Papist resistance to the Anglican church. He miscalculated the extent of the underground movement of the Jesuits; just as the police agents of Elizabeth's reign had been conned into thinking that they were confronted with an army of priests because a handful of men used so many aliases and disguises that they seemed to spring like dragons' teeth. Cecil's plan was to subdue the recusants, once and for all. If I am right, it was one of the ugliest and most impressive public relations operations of all time. It aroused popular hate against Rome so successfully that it has lasted to an age when even English Catholics let off fireworks on November the Fifth to celebrate the anniversary.

Naturally, the Jesuits were said to have engineered the whole business. Four of them, Garnet, Owen, Oldcorne and Ashley, in the barbarous manner of the times, were put to death. It is questionable whether they knew that such a plot even existed; if it indeed existed. Of course they associated with the recusants. Of course, they ministered, at the risk of their lives, in the cause of the old faith. It is sure that there were many of their secret communion nursing all sort of madcap schemes for the overthrow of the regime. But, if I know the Jesuits, they would have been the first to advise against precipitate action, much as some of them may have wished to have seen James follow Henry the Eighth and Elizabeth to what they believed was eternal perdition.

Cecil, one supposes on false information, overplayed his hand. In their turn, the Jesuits blundered in their belief that the disaffection of England was a monarchical thing which had its beginnings in the six wives of Henry the Eighth. That was only the immediate cause of the rift with Rome. The real cause was lodged much deeper in European history. The first Jesuit missionaries came to England in the mistaken hope that just a nudge among the nobility would bring the country back to the old Faith. They were disillusioned on the scaffold. The first, Jesuit superior of the English mission, Father Robert Persons was convinced that Philip the Second of Spain, of Great Armada fame, had a greater right to the throne of England by legitimate descent than the illegitimate daughter, in the eyes of Rome, of Henry the Eighth.

What he failed to perceive, what the Vatican failed to perceive long after it ceased to wield any temporal power in Europe, was the growth of nationalism. England was no longer in a mood to be bossed about by what future generations came to call 'wops' and 'frogs'. Even in Good Queen Bess's time, the recusants rallied to fight in her service. Cecil need never have bothered to cook his Gunpowder Plot. The English, from the grass roots to the flower of the aristocracy, were already determined to stay out on their own.

All the greater tragedy that so many brave men laid down their lives in the teeth of one of the inevitabilities of history. It is only fair to say that, from the start, Jesuits on the Continent had reservations about the advisability of an English mission. It may be true to say that the politicians among them advocated the adventure and the saints lost. Edmund Campion, one of the most admired of the Jesuit martyrs, seems to have sensed, long before he arrived in England, his end on Tyburn Tree. He carried out his mission, which he conceived as no more than the bringing of spiritual comfort to his deprived co-religionists, with glorious nobility in obedience to the Order to which he had dedicated his life. I cannot blame the English authorities of the time for what they did to Campion. I blame his superiors for sending him, and his successors, on a forlorn hope.

The enigma in the sorry story of the Jesuit invasion of England in Tudor and Stuart time is Father Persons, a North Somerset man born in a sleepy village called Nether Stowey, a last place one might have expected to spawn one of the controversial characters of European history. He was swept into Jesuitry on the Continent. But his heart remained in England. He was convinced that he could recall his own country to Rome. He was the man who founded the prestigious academy of St Omers for exiled English scholars. He has been condemned by many writers. Modern historians among the Jesuits try, as I think too hard, to argue that he could never have wished to upset 'the divine right of Kings'. But his friendship with Philip the Second of Spain, at a time when the Dons' hostility to England was at its greatest, cannot be disregarded. Unlike Campion, he must be accounted one of the Jesuit politicians.

There is no question of Persons' bravery and power of presence. He was the first Jesuit missionary to arrive in Protestant England. Swaggering in the uniform of a Continental army officer, he fooled the officials, who all had information that Jesuits were on their way (they even had their names), into admitting him personally and promising to facilitate the way of Campion, in the guise of a merchant, following on a ship in his wake. He was ingenious enough to found a printing press, to evade the informers, and make his return to the mainland of the Continent. He lived to a ripe old age. Enough that Campion has recently been canonised. Father Persons has not yet joined the saintly company. A remarkable man, perhaps a great one, Rome has not yet numbered him among her elect.

In the peace of Huddington, a black-and-white timbered house still lost in a byway of the English Midlands, its moat paddled by rafts of duck, I stood for a while in the past. The house is scarcely changed, not even the lock on the front door, since police officials hammered against it; since Thomas Winter, its ancestral owner, was condemned for his alleged part in the Gunpowder Plot; since Nicholas Owen, the Jesuit lay brother who was tortured to death, carpentered ingenious hiding-places for the hunted priests in the walls. It is a macabre thought that, in secret places in English houses now, the bones may lie of priests who were never discovered, and never escaped. The Jesuits made their headquarters in recusant houses in the heart of the Midlands. Huddington is only one of the hides which sheltered a lost cause.

In the seventeenth century, the Jesuits in the Catholic mainland of the Continent became born losers, too. Their story, again and again, is the same. They pressed into areas of the outer world where nobody in Western civilisation had ever penetrated before. They enlightened an awakening world, East and West, with astronomical knowledge, cartography, dictionaries, botanical specimens, and expert dispatches. Society in West and East ultimately dismissed them in hatred and a blind disdain. The English persecuted them because the English hated Rome.

On the mainland of Europe, where they enjoyed a passing command, they were cursed in due course with such calumnies that there is no finding the truth of them. I suspect that their own sin was the arrogance of culture. They got themselves into the trouble they did, as confessors of the old courts of Europe, because they expected kings and queens to obey unwelcome moralities.

It has been said that the suppression of the Jesuits by the pope in the eighteenth century was largely brought about by Madame de Pompadour, the mistress of Louis the Fifteenth of France, whose Jesuit confessor would not grant his absolution unless she returned to her husband. The story is a likely one. Women, in their way, have had their way throughout history. But the story is an older one, even than that. It is difficult to define when the Jesuits were first named 'the hated society'; but the seventeenth century is as good a time as any to date it. It was the period, and not only in England, in which a growing national consciousness was increasingly resenting interference from the popes and the popes' men. The black robes, the forward troops of the Papal States, were endeavouring to impose the mediaeval will of the Church on people who were increasingly disregarding it. How they fought, from fixed positions, with nothing but their own guile to support them, was surpassing.

To unravel the Jesuits' rise and fall in the courts of Europe it is essential to define their aims. Ignatius, with impetuous and characteristic enthusiasm, had laid his spiritual sword at the toe of the successors of St Peter, however unwise or fallible individual pontiffs might be. The policy of the popes, all of them, was to establish the dominance of Rome, the only begetter of the true faith, throughout western Christendom; and, hopefully, the world. The Jesuits, dedicated to their founder's vow, endeavoured to implement the popes' wishes by infiltrating the corridors of power; and, in their schools, educating the youth who could be expected to inherit power in the future. Rome, purblind then as now to the march of time, lost in theological concepts, dragged on the wings of their gowns. Crimson-robed cardinals, comfortably enthroned in the Curia, sent the Jesuits to do their work for them.

At the Council of Trent, a meeting point in the affairs of the Church, the Jesuit General Laynez had briefed the order of spiritual battle. Sovereign power, he declared in one of his discourses, was originally vested in the people, and had been voluntarily designated by them to the monarch. If the sovereign failed to govern in accordance with the wishes of his subjects, then they were free to reassert their prerogatives and depose the sovereign. This applies, he insisted, more particularly in the case where a ruler of a Catholic country falls away from the faith which alone can procure salvation, and so brings about the damnation of all his subjects. It was a militant statement which clearly animated all the fathers who followed him. Kings were disposable; priests, in the name of the sovereign church, were entitled, even called to assist in the removal of royal heretics.

In England, the activities of the Jesuit missionaries were in the plain black and white of the half-timbered houses in which they earthed. They were hunted like the fox, with no outlet for manoeuvre except to run. In Catholic France, the antipathy that they brought on themselves from university professors and supreme court judges was even more hostile; more deadly in its opposition than the English informers and police agents who, with no thought for foreign niceties, followed a scent with the blind enthusiasm of hounds.

It has been said that the Jesuits aroused the ideological justification for the dreadful religious wars in the sixteenth century against the Huguenots in France, and thus spurred the revolution in the eighteenth. It is so difficult to find truth in the complex of tribal history that it is best to accept that the Jesuits' part, if they had a part, was a small one. Anyhow the story of the times is such a cat's cradle that historians will never cease fighting about the truth of it. The important thing in this context is that from their foundation, in the untidy cobweb of the then nations of Europe, the Jesuits were always there; and at the centre.

In recollection, no doubt, of the exhortation of their general,

Laynez, they associated themselves with the armed uprising in Paris, in the late sixteenth century, against the homosexual, Henry the Third. A revolutionary mob, encouraged from every pulpit to exert 'the sovereignty of the people', rose against the heretic who had associated himself with the Huguenots, and Henry of Navarre. When Henry, with his cousin of Navarre, invested the capital, the Jesuits inspired the crowds, and even organised the military defence of the city. A Dominican monk, Clermont, stole into the camp of the French King, and assassinated him. Henry of Navarre, when he ascended the throne as Henry the Fourth, survived two more assassination attempts. The Parliament and University of Paris, anxious to salve their own consciences, found it convenient to have Jesuits on whom to put the whole blame.

It happened that a Jesuit had spoken too loud. One Mariana, who had been in the court of Madrid as tutor to the future King Philip the Third of Spain, had written of the abuse of power by despotic sovereigns. He spoke favourably of Clermont, the assassin of Henry the Third. 'The majority of people,' he wrote, 'look upon him as having done due honour to France.' It was not long before the Parlement of Paris had used it as a pretext to make the Jesuits primarily responsible for the murder of Henry the Third, and for the two attempts on the life of Henry the Fourth. Two Jesuit fathers were pronounced guilty of high treason, and hanged. The rest of the black robes were run out of town. Considering the interminable quarrelsome mess of Europe throughout so many centuries, the incarnadine *vendettas* between sect and sect, I cannot find it in my heart to say that the Jesuits were always guiltless. They were committed, in the most dedicated way, to causes which, often enough, must have seemed hopeless. However spiritually disciplined they were within themselves, they must have thought, in the thin communications of the time, how often Rome was mad. They were subjected to diplomatic and moral absurdities. But they were bound by a vow of utter obedience.

There were so many paradoxes. As early as 1407, the French

National Church had asserted its Gallican individuality which, while not breaking with Rome, deprived the pope of all direct authority in the disposal of ecclesiastical offices and revenues in France. It was in direct opposition of the bull, *Unam Sanctam*, proclaiming the subordination of temporal power to spiritual power. When Henry the Fourth of France, who had been excommunicated, made his rapport with the pope, the Curia was delighted to dissolve his marriage with Marguerite de Valois, to marry again the zealous Catholic, Marie de' Medici. The dialecticians have a thousand good reasons why the divorce was theologically correct. In material terms the writer was nearer the truth who said 'the union seemed to offer a guarantee that France would remain true to the cause of Rome'. Henry the Eighth of England seems to have missed a trick or two.

The Jesuits never missed any in their mission to bring a revolting world back to Rome. They were at their best when they counter-attacked in the Lutheran stronghold of Sweden. The king, John the Third, had married an ardent Catholic who, between the blankets, persuaded him that he ought to enter into negotiations with the Papal See. As his people were not in the mood for it he agreed on the understanding that the emissaries of the pope should in no circumstances disclose that they were Catholics. The Jesuits were wise to the problem. Although I am sure that they were innocent of the Gunpowder Plot, they were plotters. In 1574, on the invitation of King John of Sweden, a cunning Polish Jesuit, in the guise of an elegant courtier, danced and bowed his way into the salons of Stockholm. None, except the King, knew his identity. Father Stanislaus Warcewicz let none, except the King, know that he was there to introduce the Catholic liturgy into the Swedish church.

Soon after his arrival, there appeared in Stockholm a Protestant professor of theology named Lorenz Nicolai, who expressed himself in the unequivocal voice of Luther. The King appointed him lecturer at the newly established seminary in Stockholm; and all came to hear the learned theologian. The King himself argued with him; and, in debate the King admitted himself beaten. Nicolai was a disguised Jesuit. After selling Lutheranism, he proceeded, in the gentlest language of debate, to destroy it. It seemed that the Papacy had won an apostate country. The King had his private chapel. Newly converted students were sent to the German College of the Society of Jesus in Rome.

John's Catholic wife died. He married again a Lutheran who was equally devoted to her own religion. For peace and quiet, one may suppose, he ended his honeymoon with Rome. The Jesuits, before John's second marriage, had sent a new man to confirm the conversion of the Swedes. John had advised the pope of his readiness, in principle, to accept the Catholic faith if the rules about celibacy were relaxed, if the administration of both forms of the sacrament was sanctioned, and divine worship could be celebrated in the national tongue. Philip the Second of Spain offered a fat tribute to encourage King John to accept. John refused because he feared for his own crown.

The Jesuit who was appointed by the Papal See to negotiate with him was Father Antonio Possevino, the greatest diplomatist of the Order, and one of the most astute negotiators of the seventeenth century. He appeared in Stockholm as a nobleman, with a dagger at his waist and a two-cornered hat under his arm. He called himself an ambassador of the German emperor; and no one, except the king, knew that he was a priest of the formidable Society of Jesus.

In the end both lost, both won. John's first wife had given him an heir who, in due course, pretended to both the Swedish and Polish thrones; who was educated by the Jesuits, married to an Austrian princess, and never forsook the Roman Church. But the king's second wife ensured that Sweden remained, with only an occasional challenge, an essentially Protestant country.

In Sweden, the Jesuits' ploy, when they seemed so near to victory, was brought to nothing, as such matters so often are, in the marriage bed. Possevino looked over his shoulder with only mild disappointment as he passed on his way to unpick the bird's nest of his lines in other countries of Europe. 'He enjoyed the confidence of the pope as well as of the Hapsburg monarch, of the Archdukes of Graz and Vienna, and the Great Council of Venice. He was acquainted with all the innermost aspirations of all the chancelleries of Europe; he was fully informed of the financial situation of every government; he knew the military strength of every country, and, accordingly, was able to pursue diplomacy in the grand style, and to excel all his lay colleagues in such matters.'* He was sure that, in the fullness of time, Sweden could be angled into the arms of the mother church again.

In a world of instant communication it is easy to forget that, until the early nineteenth century, months went by before messages passed between one power and another. Europe was divided into a jigsaw of sovereignties which today it is difficult to place on the map. Where was Transylvania, Styria, Staritsa on the Volga?† The diplomats of the time, trundling in springless coaches over unmade roads, riding post-horse, sleeping in crude inns, had no contact with their governments. Revolutions came and ended. Sovereigns rose and fell. Emissaries, plugging along on desolate bridle-paths, could know nothing about it. The pace of world affairs was happily slow.

Now that most of the kings and queens, the archdukes and electors, have vanished from Europe; now that international crises can blow up in minutes on a hot line, one may envy an age, brutal as it was, in which local difficulties remained local difficulties. Diplomacy was a leisurely albeit uncomfortable profession. Even as late as Palmerston's time, the Prime Minister of England could send a gunboat to a trouble spot, and forget the matter until it had possibly resolved itself. Wasn't it Canning who sidestepped tricky decisions by saying 'leave it alone'? Time was on the side of statecraft.

In afterthought it seems incredible that a Jesuit priest, out on his own, could influence the great affairs of Europe. Father Possevino did just that. Soon after his return from Stockholm,

* Réné Fülop-Miller.
† See endpapers.

a messenger arrived at the Vatican from Ivan the Terrible, the tsar of Russia. He brought a portentous missive. The tsar entreated the pope to initiate peace negotiations with the Polish Empire. The Ruler of all the Russias was then hard-pressed by the victorious troops of Stefan Bathory, the Polish King. In return he offered to join in a combined crusade with all the Christian princes against Islam. He could not have suggested a more attractive proposition to Rome. Since Ignatius's time, and long before, the Papal See had cherished its plan of destroying Islam. A bargain with the tsar, which might bring the Byzantine Church back to Rome as well, was overwhelmingly attractive. Today, a vast diplomatic mission would have been sent on its way. Father Possevino travelled, virtually alone.

He went first to Venice, then the greatest maritime power in the Mediterranean. Although the Council of Ten were in a pacific mood he was able to persuade the doge and his advisors of the immense commercial advantages of business with Russia. The Venetians, traders all, became quite enthusiastic. He went on to Graz to bribe the Archduke Charles of Styria, with a rose of gold for his wife and the promise of financial support from the Papacy, to put down Protestantism in his land. In Vienna he got the Archduke Ernest of Austria, who had been recommended by Ivan the Terrible as candidate for the Polish throne, to give him a warm recommendation to the tsar. He had worse luck with the Emperor Rudolf the Second in Prague who had dedicated himself to alchemy, and was *incommunicado*. His most important assignment was with Stefan Bathory at Vilna, the headquarters of the kings of Poland. King Stefan was quite sure that he could drive the Russians into Asia. Father Possevino, his brief to make a treaty between Russia and Poland, played on the king's vanity.

Stefan Bathory fancied his scholarship. Possevino, with a display of Latin, discussed the works of Aristotle, and the doctrines of Catholic asceticism. Soon, he won the arrogant and warlike man into walking with him arm in arm. Possevino told him that his people were war-weary; that financially he could not support the continuation of a campaign in the cause of an empty conquest. King Stefan accepted his advice. 'The papal legate was furnished with a guard of honour consisting of Polish cavalrymen, and set out accompanied by numerous interpreters and officials on his journey.'

Possevino left Rome for Russia on March 27, 1581. Four and a half months later, in August, he reached Staritsa on the Volga, the then headquarters of the tsar. He was welcomed at the gates of the fortress with a splendid black stallion, a gift from the emperor. The priest, surrounded by magnificently arrayed dignitaries, rode through the gates 'to gaze into the clear eye of the Ruler of All the Russias'. There was nothing clear about it. The tsar was a trembling madman with a Byzantine crown on his head and a cudgel in his hand with which he crushed the skulls of people he disapproved of. The little father would have been less than human if, in the barbarous court, he did not feel dismay. Proudly, among the cowering courtiers, he spoke for Rome: 'Our most Holy Father, Pope Gregory the Thirteenth, Lord Bishop of the All-embracing Church, the Vicar of Jesus Christ on earth, the successor of St Peter, ruler of many states and provinces, servant of the servants of God, greets your Majesty, and extends to you his blessing!' He brought the mad tsar to his feet in courtesy.

To the nimble-witted Jesuit, the procrastinations, the circum-locutions, the obscurities of the suspicious Russian mind, were as exasperating then as they are now. But he had won the tsar's respect. He dared to tell Ivan, only sane at intervals, that in theological matters, the pope was the representative of God on earth. Ivan chose to say that the pope was a wolf. The *boyars* in the retinue expected murder. Possevino, with a gentle smile, enquired why if such was the case, the tsar had asked a 'wolf' to negotiate peace with Poland. He had found what Winston Churchill in a latter context was to call 'the soft underbelly'. Loaded with gifts, Father Possevino went on his way from the Kremlin with the Russian envoy who was to carry on future negotiations. It was perhaps the most fantastic diplomatic success that the Jesuits ever achieved. The quiet priest brought Russia and Poland together. He was named the arbitrator between the two great powers. From a peasant's hut, in a miserable hamlet called Jam Zapolski in the snowy steppes, he stood between the tents of the two sides, praying over a portable altar for peace. Hopeless as ever, the Russians tried his patience to the limit of his endurance. But, at last, the Russo-Polish war was settled in treaty.

In his hour of triumph, the papal legate went on, like a wise uncle in a world of quarrelling relations, to settle affairs in countries which have long ago been lost to the map. Father Possevino, the greatest of the Jesuit statesmen, was the last. After his death, in the twilight of Rome's temporal power, others who followed him, and not less gifted, were struggling against the grain of a new order. In Russia, the Jesuits backed a usurper who claimed to be a son of Ivan the Terrible, and who was probably an Orthodox monk. The 'false Demetrius', who dedicated himself to the Jesuits, became tsar. He sanctioned the establishment of Jesuit colleges, seminaries and churches throughout the realm. His reign was brief. The patriarchs of the Orthodox Church regarded him with increasing suspicion. The protegé and devoted servant of the Jesuits was assassinated. It was said that 'he had let himself be used as a tool for the devilish machinations of the pope, the Jesuits, and the King of Poland. It was a mercy that true Russians had brought this shame and infamy to an end in good time!'

The Jesuits weren't beaten, not yet. It is remarkable that, in the middle of the seventeenth century, a Jesuit child, a member of the Society, ascended the throne of Poland. John Casimir, by first accepting cardinal's rank, then marrying his brother's widow, had opted out. But he remained a Jesuit at heart. He mismanaged affairs so badly on the throne of Poland that the power of the Jesuits in Eastern Europe was never recaptured. In 1668, he was forced to abdicate.

In England, the short ascendancy of the Jesuits was as adventurous as in Russia and Poland. After the persecutions of

Tudor and early Stuart times, they saw full hope under James the Second. James had told his confessor that he was 'a son of the Society of Jesus'. The queen added, 'and I am their daughter!' James made the Jesuit, Father Petre, scion of one of the great families of the Old Faith, a member of his Privy Council. The Jesuits occupied the buildings which stood on the site of what is now London's Savoy Hotel. The worry was that the Catholic King had no male heir. A Jesuit of the time, Father Ruga, wrote desperately that 'nobody can tell what will happen after his death, and how the Catholics will continue to exist in the midst of so large a number of heretics; there are, indeed, about twenty heretics to one Catholic. Oh, how necessary it is to beseech Our Lord to provide what is needful!'

In the end, James had a son, from his second wife. It was gossiped throughout London that the Jesuits had got a nun with child, and introduced it into the royal apartments. The English believed it, because they wanted to believe it. They had no patience with Papistry. They welcomed the 'glorious revolution' which cost King James and, in effect, the Stuart dynasty, the crown of England. The Jesuits lost, once again, in support of a cause which the new Europe did not want.

England was done with Rome. In the German and Scandinavian states, Lutheranism and Calvinism were taking an increasingly stronger hold. The consciences of Catholic kings were worthless. Admitting all in the confessional box, it was only in impotent old age, and fear of death, that they even showed any piety. None could then conceive that the sovereigns of Christendom were creatures of the past. But they were. They hung on for a few more generations; but debilitated in a sleep as deep as Rip van Winkle's.

While Ignatius was still alive he sent missionaries to launch the counter-reformation in the German principalities. Ninetenths of the population, it is said, had gone over to Protestantism. Pierre Favre, one of the first disciples who, in 1540, had gone to the religious conference at Worms, reported: 'Pray God that in this city there are even two or three priests who have not

formed illicit liaisons or are not living in other known sins!'
The Jesuits' first task was not to fight the counter-reformation,
but to reform the Catholic priesthood. They modestly set an
example by caring for the poor, administering alms, and nursing
in the hospitals. At first they deliberately refrained from attacking Lutheranism. On Ignatius's order they began by 'meeting
heresy with gentleness and kindness'. But Germans were
Germans. Their language alone was a barrier to a union with the
Latin culture of the Roman hierarchy.

It was one of Favre's Jesuit successors, Peter Canisius, one who
was to become the founder of the Jesuit Colleges at Vienna,
Ingolstadt, Prague and Freiburg, who recognised that the
printing press was the best counter-weapon to Lutheranism. 'A
writer is accounted of more worth in Germany than ten professors.' It all started in a friendly tone. The General Aquaviva
administered a stern rebuke to one of his brethren who had
written a spiteful tract against Luther. But that was the way to
make the Teutonic mind interested. Before long the pam-
phleteers of both sides were hurling abuse at each other in the
language of the 'yellow press'.

The Lutherans described the Jesuits as 'the most arch and
arrant betrayers and persecutors of Christ, the very spawn of
hell which the dragon of hell spues out; papal asses, wolves and
miserable devils'. To their intellectual discredit, the Jesuits were
goaded into replying that the Protestants were 'at once cats and
wolves, tearing each other to pieces like cats and wolves, and
must be loaded with every ignominy, coming as they do from
hell'. The dialectic used was strangely reminiscent of what came
out of the climate of Germany within living memory. On
Goebbels' principle of the greater the lie the greater the impact,
it was mooted about that the saintly Jesuit theologian, Cardinal
Bellarmine, 'always had in the stable four goats which he used
for his pleasure, and had them brought to him adorned with the
most costly jewels, precious stones, silver and gold'. An Ingolstadt Jesuit, Mayrhofer, wrote in his *Mirror for Preachers* that the
putting to death of Protestants was 'no more unreasonable than

to say that thieves, counterfeiters, murderers and rebels can and should be punished with death'.

The invective steamed a head of hysteria which, inevitably, drove Europe into armed conflict. The overwhelming ambition of kings, the zeal of proselytising clerics, boiled, at the beginning of the seventeenth century, into the Thirty Years War. It was as barbarous as religious wars always are. It was fanned by princelings, professing devotion to Rome, who had no scruples about getting together with their Protestant subjects to find finance and manpower to extend their territorial possessions. Rome teetered impotently on the sidelines. The soldiery fought on because they were bent on pillage and rape.

The holocaust began, in the usual manner of war, when Bohemian nobles, exasperated by restrictions on Protestantism instituted by their Catholic King, Ferdinand, threw two of his ministers, and a private secretary, out of the palace windows of Hradshin into the castle ditch. 'The Defenestration of Prague', as it came to be called, like the assassination of the Archduke Ferdinand at Serrajevo in 1914, provided the traditional excuse that was waited for.

H. A. L. Fisher, no friend of the Jesuits, writes in his monumental *History of Europe:* 'The *primum movens* was a crowned Jesuit . . .* He hated Protestants and determined to uproot them from his dominions by a resolute course of persecution begun in Styria (1598), continued in Bohemia, and carried throughout the length and breadth of his Austrian dominions he succeeded in his object of "liquidating" the heretics and bringing all the religious and intellectual life of his realm under the iron rule of the Jesuit Order.'

I doubt it. To a man of a past generation, with some inherited prejudices as hidebound as Macaulay's and Carlyle's, a Jesuit was something as unpalatable as the appearance of ullaged port would have been on the high table of New College. Like the great historian, the Jesuits may have been prone to the excesses

* He wasn't a Jesuit, but a Jesuit child; educated by them as most cultivated young men in the courts of Europe at that time were.

and misjudgements of their period. Wrongheaded they certainly became in the pamphlet war which led to the thirty years one. They were among the first protest marchers; but they embarked on their missions with a greater sincerity, and a clearer notion of their cause, than any protester in the troubled society of today. Of course, they must take a certain responsibility for the excesses of the Thirty Years War. In Middle Europe, as Fisher says, 'it left a country barren of literature and art, burdened by an almost unmanageable language, and in its social manners and customs sunk to a Muscovite barbarity'. He comforts himself that, at the wretched end of it, the Peace of Westphalia (1648) ensured enclaves of Lutheranism and Calvinism in Central Europe. His enemies, the Jesuits, were not the only bigots.

Ignatius, in his first little company which he supposed would never extend beyond sixty disciples, liked to think that his Jesuits' place was in suffering with the drop-outs of society, sharing the pus of their diseases, humbling themselves to disgust in eager dedication to a Christlike cause. As his Society of Jesus grew much bigger than he had ever imagined, he had reservations at the hint of the prospect that his brethren might become the confessors of kings. But his men were the best educated men in Europe. At the end of his own time he saw them syphoned into other causes. Although the continuing record of the Jesuits in poverty, chastity and obedience has never been seriously challenged, although the grey robes startled the decadent courts of Europe with their withdrawn sanctity, not without a frightening authority in which they spoke the word of Christ, their presence was demanded in gilded palaces where kings and queens, with guilty consciences, hoped for the blessing of God and Rome before it was too late. It was incidental that, inside the confessional, admissions of heresy led the Jesuits to become a powerful influence in affairs of state.

A new sort of Jesuit emerged who combined unworldly piety with worldly wisdom; too much worldly wisdom for the comfort of the temporal authorities. One such was Father

William Lamormaini who became confessor to the Emperor Ferdinand. As early as 1626 the papal nuncio at Vienna reported to Cardinal Barberini: 'It is certain that the Jesuits, through the favour of the emperor which cannot be overestimated, have attained to overwhelming power . . . They have the upper hand over everything, even over the most prominent ministers of state, and domineer over them, if they do not carry out their will . . . Their influence has always been considerable, but it has reached its zenith since Father Lamormaini has been confessor to the emperor.'

Ferdinand's confessor in Vienna was so enthusiastic in state affairs that he even incurred the hostility of his rival Jesuit confessor in Munich. He was such a busybody that his work-room, lined from floor to ceiling with meticulously labelled correspondence, in cabinets marked 'Internal Affairs', 'Spanish', 'Italian' and the rest, turned a priest's home into a chancellery. He needed the restraint which my grandfather, who was something of a busybody himself, printed at the head of each folio of his account books; Thomas à Kempis's admonition that 'a man should not be over eager in his affairs'. Father Lamor-maini's general in Rome felt obliged to order him to be more secret in his business.

But the rise of the Jesuits in the statecraft of Germany was overtaken in the prestige they enjoyed for a hundred and fifty years in France. At the end of the sixteenth century, they had been driven out like cattle, slaughtered like cattle, for their alleged complicity in the assassination of Henry the Third. They came back, under Henry the Fourth, after negotiating the repeal of his excommunication and arranging a second marriage with a daughter of the Church. It settled a tiresome war with Spain. Such was the diplomacy of Europe at that time.

The Parlement of Paris and the Sorbonne remained the Jesuits' enemies. But the court relied on them. In the reign of Louis the Thirteenth, they could do little in face of the absolute power of Cardinal Richelieu, himself Jesuit-educated, and wise to their ways. But while the great cardinal would tolerate no interference from them in his conduct of France's foreign affairs, he encouraged them in their mission of education. Under his patronage the Jesuits created seats of learning which were the wonders of civilised Europe.

After Richelieu and his pupil Mazarin – who live today more fully in Dumas's romances than in the history books – the Jesuit confessors served Louis the Fourteenth, the sun king who also lives more fleshily now in the writing of Nancy Mitford. Even in his divine autocracy, Louis liked to have the Jesuits with him as a sort of insurance policy against damnation. Even though he paraded in the queen's carriage, with two of his mistresses in attendance, even though the Jesuits had to refuse him Easter communion because he was in mortal sin, he gave them a bone or two in the right to recommend vacant church benefices.

Forgiving in so many matters, the Jesuits were adamant in their opposition to his amours. While he was young and potent, they paused. There came a confessor, Father La Chaise, who, trusting in God, decided to wait until the volcano of Bourbon desire had quietened. History has criticised La Chaise for his 'laxity'. It is difficult to know what else he could have done. There came a time when, interspersing his conversation with the discussion of numismatics, a subject in which the King was interested, he talked of 'carnal sin'. He brought the King to marry the ageing Madame de Maintenon. In penitence, and old age, the court of Louis the Sun became a worldly bore. Unfortunately, Louis ordered the suppression of the Protestants in his realm as well. To secure her entrance into heaven, Madame de Maintenon put the Huguenots under pressure again.

It is easy to admire so many of the Jesuits. Just once in a while, a sour man steals the scene. After Father La Chaise's death, Father le Tellier, a man of no background and one suspects of surprisingly little liberal education, assumed the office of king's confessor. A wood engraving of the time reveals the man, a shrivelled lemon who exacerbated opposition to the Jesuits by an unscrupulous persecution of the Jansenists. The first thing that Philip, Duke of Orlèans, did on his accession as regent after the death of Louis the Sun was to banish the wretched man from the court. His religious opponents, who had been thrown into prison, were released. The University of Paris declared that in future, it would not grant degrees to students of the great Jesuit College of Clermont. Le Tellier did lasting harm to the cause of the Society of Jesus. He sowed the seed of latter persecution.

For the Jesuits, the ambience of the French court was never the same again. In political matters, Louis the Fifteenth was willing enough to listen to the advice of the fathers. In his private life he was as promiscuous as all the Bourbons, sexual gymnasts, who secreted semen at a rate which was even alarming to their mistresses. But the Marquise of Pompadour, who is said to have been naturally frigid, found it less difficult to submit to the king than to the requirements of the confessor who instructed her that, unless she desisted, she risked eternal damnation. The whisper of her waspish disapproval passed out of her salon to the courts of Europe. By then there were many looking only for the merest excuse to cut the Jesuits down to size.

It began in Portugal where the Society had also attained considerable influence over a number of unusually weak-minded kings. The Portuguese prime minister, the Marquis of Pombal, was restless for an opportunity to get rid of them. He got it in comical form. Joseph, then King of Portugal, was making secret visits to the Marchioness of Tavora, a beauty of the court. Her husband, who would not put up with it, even from the King, waylaid him on one of his nocturnal expeditions, and put a bullet in his arm. The King panicked. Pombal had little difficulty in persuading him that he was a victim of the machinations of the Jesuits. Their houses were surrounded by soldiers, the confessors arrested for a plot against the King. Nothing could be proved except that the Jesuits had also been confessors to the Tavora family. Charges of heresy were produced as a basis for a trial by the Inquisition. One father, Malagrida, was pronounced guilty and burnt at a solemn *auto-da-fe*. The King signed a decree by which the Jesuits were

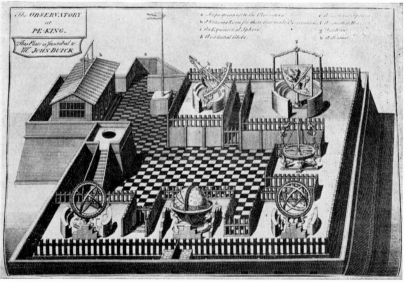

A succession of gifted Jesuits entered the closed world of China. Adopting local customs and dress, they were accepted as wise men who brought maps, astronomical instruments, and calendars; and preached a doctrine which the Chinese learnt to respect. It is notable that the observatory they constructed in Peking (*below*) is still there. They were stabbed in the back, not by the Chinese, but conformists in Rome who thought they were not indoctrinating Christianity according to the strict rule of the Church. Posterity was the loser

As confessors to kings and queens, the Jesuits made their influence felt throughout Europe. They occupied dangerously high places. They believed, wrongly that influence was best wielded at the centres of monarchical power

In the eighteenth century they were thrown out of France (*above*), Spain (*below*), Portugal and Naples. They were suppressed by the pope. The old monarchies, although they didn't know it, were themselves on the edge of extinction

Paul III approved the Society of Jesus

Clement XIV suppressed it

Pius VII re-established the Society in 1814

Jesuit children today. The Jesuits remain one of the great educational forces of the world. In the five continents their schools are famous. Stonyhurst, in which the author was photographed in the church, is a bigger school now than it ever was. Throughout the Americas and Africa, Jesuits are pursuing their historic mission. But they are doing it with ever fewer men to point the way. They have a crisis, not in the work that the modern world calls them to do, but in manpower. The Jesuits are desperately short of recruits. The crisis in traditional world institutions, not merely religious ones, is also their own

They were all Jesuit children, except one, at a time when, in a thousand academies, the Jesuits were the chief educators of the civilised world. Rousseau, Molière and Voltaire were just three of the men of genius who were pupils of the Order. Pascal identified himself with the dictatorial opposition to them denounced as 'traitors, rebels and enemies to the realm'. They were expelled from Portugal.

To justify his actions, Pombal flooded Europe with propaganda from the new printing-presses. He didn't have immediate success. Voltaire's cynical comment was that there was found together 'a superfluity of the laughable with a superfluity of the horrible'. But there was enough antagonism to the Jesuits in France for their opponents to wait for the opportunity to follow Portugal's lead. It came when the superior of a Jesuit settlement in Martinique, anxious to put it on a firm financial footing, engaged in extensive trading enterprises. One day, some of the ships carrying valuable cargoes were taken by the English. He couldn't meet his obligations. Commercial firms, who had financed the operation, demanded that their loss should be made good by the general in Rome. The general said that the Jesuit superior in Martinique had broken the rule of the Society by indulging in a commercial operation. The matter was taken to court in Marseilles, and the plaintiffs won.

In the mistaken belief that the Parlement in Paris, their sworn enemies for so many years, were more likely to afford them justice, the fathers foolishly appealed. Parlement demanded to see the secret constitutions of the Order on which the appeal was based. They did not merely dismiss the appeal, they eagerly seized on the opportunity to declare that the Jesuit Order was immoral and a danger to the State. The evil of gossip, the devil of half-truth, mutterings of scandals in the past, completed the dirty work. In August, 1762, the Parlement decreed that the Society of Jesus, being incompatible with the welfare of the state, should be expelled from France.

The circumstances in which the Jesuits were thrown out of Spain was even more ludicrous. Charles the Third was an autocrat cursed with the Spanish pride which has cost the Peninsular so much misery and humiliation. He was easily persuaded by his aristocratic entourage that the fathers were dedicating, as the police reported, too much of their time to the welfare of the common people; an offence, in the eyes of a

Spanish nobleman, comparable with the encouragement of civil strife.

I am afraid that it is valid even today. A personal anecdote will emphasise it. A few years ago I was a guest on a partridge shoot in the *meseta* about Toledo. The Spaniards conduct their sport quite differently from the English, who never count an individual's score, only the total bag. In Spain, a 'secretary' is appointed to each gun to mark the game which has fallen to him. During the day, after I had shot a number of head, my secretary asked if he might have a hare. When I agreed, I was surprised to see that he hid it under a bush. He thanked me so profusely that I assumed it was because one hare would be lost to the score on my game card. When I mentioned the matter to the grandee who was my host, he raised his eyebrows. 'Of course the man was delighted', he said. 'He is a poor man. That hare will provide a banquet for his family. Afterwards it will make stew and soup.' Thin-lipped, he added: 'You shouldn't have given it to him.'

Thus, Spain invites social disaster. Thus, Charles the Third looked at the common people who, in opposition to his stern decree, dared to appear outside his palace in wide-brimmed hats and cloaks, a fashion which he had condemned as defiance of his sovereign rights. It looked to him like the uniform of revolution. His Walloon guards could not control the wide-hat mob. From his palace window, Charles was terrified by the swelling movement of 'the mutiny of hats'. He made a speech, promising this and that. And then the Jesuits appeared. Quietly, they told the mob to disperse. The demonstrators obeyed. Peace reigned again in Madrid.

In safety, the Spanish king raged against the Society which had held the rabble in such restraint. It was put in his ear that the Jesuits had organised the whole demonstration to prove how indispensable they were. Immediately, it was decided to expel from Spain the Order which had perpetrated such a thing. It was done in secret, and the usual brutality. On the night of April 3, 1767, the Jesuit houses were surrounded by the soldiery.

The fathers were thrown on the doubtful hospitality of the Papal States. Very soon, the Bourbon states of Naples and Parma followed like spaniels on the heels of the great powers. Charles the Third, not content with the mischief he had already made, demanded of the Pope Clement XIII that the Society should be suppressed.

Clement XIII died in time to prevent that coffin nail becoming his own. Clement XIV prevaricated. Maria Theresa held out as long as she could; but the pressures were on. The remaining Catholic princes joined the conspiracy. The vacillating pope was at last forced to close the Order's seminary in Rome in 1772; soon after, all the Jesuit colleges in the Papal States. Finally, on July 21, 1773, Clement published the breve *Dominus ac Redemptor*, which pronounced the complete suppression of the Society.

It is a shameful document which admits of nothing but contempt for the prelates who, for their own peace and quiet, betrayed the most dedicated soldiers of the Church.

VIII

Twilight

DENIED by Rome, ousted from their great colleges and seminaries, their communal property confiscated and looted, homeless and penniless, the Jesuits flighted like pigeons who had lost their cotes. They never ceased to exist. They found havens, uncongenial enough, where in anonymous feathers they tenaciously existed in strict accordance with the constitutions of the Society of Loyola. They even found support where they might least have expected it.

The heretic, Frederick the Great, informed the pope that, at the annexation of the Silesian provinces he had conquered during the Seven Years War, he had promised religious toleration; and he was therefore unable to agree to the dissolution of the order. The schismatic, Catherine the Great of Russia, told the papal nuncio that she had promised to recognise the Jesuits. Both had the same good reasons; the importance of promoting national education and the advantage that, with straitened revenues, the Jesuits were teachers who charged nothing for their services. In 1801, Pope Pius VII, trimming his sails to the wind, authorised the Jesuits domiciled in Russia to style themselves again the 'Society of Jesus'. A general was appointed, 'duly charged and entrusted with the requisite and necessary authority to follow and maintain the rule of St Ignatius Loyola'.

In Catholic countries, the order pursued its mission under various aliases: 'Brothers of the Faith of Jesus', 'Society of the Faith of Jesus', 'Society of the Heart of Jesus', 'Confraternity of the Holy Sacrament'. From an affiliated sisterhood of pious women there emerged the nuns of the Sacred Heart. Cells, they were just that, were established throughout Europe. The hard core of the Jesuits, desperately short of new recruits, remained. In any country they hardly had more than a few years of peace. Predictably, Robespierre, during the reign of terror, guillotined a number of them. Napoleon, Metternich, Garibaldi, Bismarck, even ex-President John Adams of the U.S.A. shared a distaste of them. 'I do not like the reappearance of the Jesuits,' Adams wrote to his successor Jefferson in 1816. 'Shall we not have regular swarms of them here, in as many disguises as only a king of the gipsies can assume dressed as printers, writers, publishers and school masters? If ever there was a body of men who merited eternal damnation on earth and in hell, it is this Society of Loyola. Nevertheless, we are compelled by our system of religious toleration to offer them an asylum...' Jefferson replied: 'Like you, I disapprove of the restoration of the Jesuits, for it means a step backward from light into darkness.'

Napoleon wrote to his minister of police, Fouché, that in no circumstances would he allow the Jesuits to settle in France again. 'No matter what guise they may assume, I will tolerate neither "Heart of Jesus" nor "A Confraternity of the Holy Sacrament" nor any body resembling a military religious organisation.' Bismarck, with characteristic nationalism, declared in the Reichstag that the Jesuits were dangerous not so much by their Catholicism as on account of 'their whole international organisation, their abjuration and absolution from all national bonds, and their disintegration and destruction of all national bonds and national movements...' The invective is endless. The significant fact is that the Jesuits have survived it all, including the large number of the regimes who invented it.

In 1814, a few months after Napoleon's abdication and temporary exile in Elba, Pope Pius VII in his bull *Sollicitudo omnium Ecclesiarum*, sanctioned the reinstatement of the Society of Jesus in all its former rights and privileges. In 1829, the passing of the Catholic Emancipation Act in England theoretically restored complete religious freedom although, as Cardinal

Newman said, the word Catholic still sounded unpleasantly like superstition. The Jesuits built their church in London in a slum-place where it was unlikely to attract too much attention. Their mission, they felt, was again primarily to minister to the poor. They little guessed that, within a lifetime, what had been a slum would become the enclave of the very rich. The Jesuit church in Farm Street is now in the shop window of Mayfair.

Even after the Napoleonic wars, in the *Pax Britannica* which settled for a hundred years, the Jesuits had no cause for quiet. In 1847, they were thrown out of Switzerland. In the following year, they were banished from Austria. The same fate, under Cavour, befell them in Sardinia; and, under Garibaldi, in Sicily and Naples. There were three ejections from Spain. Determined opposition came from Prussia which at the dissolution of the Society had given them security. In France, Portugal and Russia, in uncertain times, the Jesuits were always the first victims. In civil strife it seemed that they were provided by providence to accept meekly the first anger of any revolutionary who tasted power.

Over the years they slipped back into India, Japan, China and South America to pick up what traces they could of their early missionaries' work. Apart from Mao's China (perhaps not apart from Mao's China), they are still there; under the rose they are certainly in Russia. In all the old missions and in the relatively new ones like Africa, the fathers are dedicating themselves with the same self-sacrificing energy of their forebears. But their world has changed. All the old courts of Christendom except one, the court of the popes in Rome, have been dissipated or made impotent in the passage of history. The Jesuits no longer wield any public influence in affairs of state; although, in private, it would be precipitate to assume that an international society, with a foothold all over the world, isn't consulted by official-dom. But the pattern, like a Victorian kaleidoscope, has been in change for a hundred and fifty years.

From Ignatius's time until they were suppressed, the Jesuits' course, tough as it was, was as plain as a jump jockey's. In obedience to their owners, the popes, their job was to win, even if they couldn't beat Islam, against Lutheranism and Calvinism; to defeat the dirty practices of all the European monarchs in the game. To pursue the analogy, the popes weren't above pulling a horse; and ultimately disqualified the best jockeys they had. It may be a cheap way of reading what happened; but it is effectively the truth.

The Jesuits, on their reinstatement in 1814, sought their way in a new world. Within a year the old order in Europe, dominated by France, ended at Waterloo. There was no longer any call to keep up diplomatic relations between Rome and fading monarchies. There was scarcely any Catholic nobility, with hope of power, to educate. The Jesuit system hung on in Maryland in America and in isolated enclaves of Europe like Stonyhurst in wildest England. The great centuries in which the fathers had played their hand on the table of European diplomacy; the period in which, surprisingly, it may be argued that they invented modern theatre, opera and ballet, had passed. Frivolity was never their calling; but they recognised, long before the Church got round to it, at the Council of 1962-–65 that secular things are not secondary to spiritual things. Nothing much revolutionary in that to a layman. In theory, if not in practice, the notion was a faltering step forward for the fathers of the Church. The Jesuits, attacked in the seventeenth century for their worldly laxity, have seen their judgement confirmed. In a detail like that lies much of the hope of what they can contribute in the future.

They are still in a twilight, after the sunshine of their mission in world history. So is the Church. Malachi Martin, formerly a Jesuit priest and formerly a professor in the Pontifical Biblical Institute in Rome, expresses his own opinion neatly*: 'It (Christianity) claimed absolute authority, just as it claimed absolute authenticity, in proposing man's way to salvation. It claimed that all other ways to salvation either were abrogated by its arrival on the scene, or could be justified only by virtue of

* *The Encounter: Religions in Crisis* (1970).

its exalted function. It claimed further to be the only religion to which God had made inner revelations about His own nature. Finally, it was unique in that it claimed that each and every member of its body could be in living mystical communion with God – in a way neither described, nor possible, nor suspected, in any other religion. Christianity, in a word, made the most demanding requests on its adherents. In return it promised the ultimate of ultimates in religious surety, moral perfection, and after death, eternal happiness of the most elevated kind.'

It is a reckoning from a mind moulded by the Jesuits themselves. Malachi Martin's proposition is that the three religions of the world – Christianity, Islam and Judaism – are in decline. Christendom, united, created the wonder of the cathedrals of Europe. In disunity, worse than in indifference, the edifice is tumbling. '*Hush, hush, nobody cares, Christopher Robin has fallen downstairs.*'

Martin concludes that none of the three religions is able to intervene effectively to control the present development of man. 'The end . . . could only come if the religions set about ridding their individual beliefs of all that is not essential, of all that has been acquired by historical accident and by regionalisms of various sorts.' He quotes an American rabbi who says simply: 'God is where we come from, and God is where we go.'

In a scene in which dedicated Jesuit priests, especially in the United States and Holland, are making statements which, only a generation ago, would have outraged their brethren, the words of the failed Jesuit have, in fact, aroused little more than a ripple. The book reviewers, those instant judges of what is contemporarily surprising, have scarcely noticed it. Presumably, Martin's scholarly work has no shock force among thinking people any more. They agree with him.

Religious prejudice, except in a few backward corners, has died. Forward looking Christians, those who are still Christians in a crisis in which the sheer existence of organised religion is in doubt, are looking hopefully to what is called ecumenism;

Protestants and Catholics arm in arm in a common cause. Jesuits ask themselves what Ignatius would have said if he had lived today; more important, what the Man Christ would have spoken. Issues, unchanged for two thousand years, have been brought into ferment within fifty years, forty, thirty, twenty, ten. In the next five years who can guess what will happen. The 'futurist' is the thinker today, the philosopher who succeeds the men who only knew how to search for wisdom by studying the texts of the past.

I myself am a fan of that pioneer of futurism, Marshal McLuhan. Of course he says a lot which is arguable; so did Aristotle, Thomas Aquinas, and most of the Fathers of the Church. But, in his personal struggle for truth, he has got his essentials right. The American Jesuit, Father John Culkin,* tells how when he met Marshal McLuhan for the first time, the new seer made the comment: 'I think the Jesuits must be in real trouble these days.' He pointed out that the Society had been founded on literacy, the inspired use that they had made of the invention of printing, the power of movable type. It counted more, in the early mission of the Jesuits, than the spoken word. In Marshal McLuhan's vernacular it doesn't belong any more in the audio-tactile world today. The new Jesuits are not un-aware of it. Electronics are high on their list of priorities. Communication has always been the Jesuits' business.

They are an old Society, deep-rooted in their beginnings like Kipling's cat who walked by himself – 'Oh my friend, and oh my enemy' – but they have come to terms with the hostilities of the past. After four-hundred years of conflict – a splendid old Jesuit said to me that 'what we want is another good persecu-tion' – they are moving, whatever the cost to their tradition, into a meeting with the bewildered society which is ours – a world so far removed from the old one in which they fought, the old world in which the Church could solemnly declare that the sun circled the earth; and damned Galileo on doctrinal grounds for suggesting otherwise.

* Quoted from *The New Jesuits* by George Reimer.

There is a promise for the future that a great Jesuit astronomer, Father Clavius, dared even then to confirm Galileo's findings. Of course he made no impression on hidebound clerics in Rome whose successors, in the third quarter of the twentieth century, live so much in the past that they believe that the pope can put the world into reverse with an encyclical.

3

THE JESUITS
TODAY

I

The Making of a Jesuit

IN a stern house in the misty environs of Edinburgh – the
sort of place you can only find after reversing the car up and
down farm tracks, consulting likely-looking characters on
tractors, and releasing reluctant five-barred gates lashed with
rusty wire – I sat in a room so sparsely furnished that it seemed
that the removing men had just gone out or were shortly
expected to move the furniture in. It was the guests' parlour in
the then Jesuit novitiate of the English Province. By comparison
with the rest of the gloomy pile it was luxurious, with a tin
ashtray or two and the sort of armchairs you can acquire on
two years' hire purchase without deposit.

I was entertained by the superior, a gentle old priest who told
me that he had been recalled from parish work to take over the
rectorship of the house. It seemed anomalous that a pastor in
his mid-seventies should have been called to preside over a
proving-ground for Jesuits of the future; the more so when he
confided to me, in effect, that the Society was going to the dogs.

Did I know that, nowadays, novices are permitted to read the
newspapers, write letters and use the telephone; that, under a
new rule, they speak more English than Latin; that, throughout
hours of the day, the discipline of silence has been relaxed? It
is even allowed that there are occasions when they may be
granted the extremity of working on a factory floor and wearing
a collar with a tie. Loyal Jesuit that he was it was evident that
the new order was almost more than he could stomach.

In a kind of outrage over the leniences tolerated since he was
a novice himself, he took me over the house. Not the least of his

regrets were that on my first visit the novices, in his reckoning, were on parole. It was something which never happened in his own day. Some were nursing the mentally sick, some were on university courses, some were actually associating with their own families. 'This new generation, they're too gregarious, we have to make them learn to live alone.' We clattered through passages littered with lurid prints from the Ignatian Exercises. We looked into chapels, bare as cells, in which the novices prayed; the open cubicles in which they slept, almost their only possessions a crucifix, razor and toothbrush, and the bare minimum of clothes. In what passed as a recreation room there was a table tennis table and a television set – the rector snorted at that – and the sort of outdated magazines associated wih dentists' waiting rooms. Sybaritic it may have seemed to the old Jesuit, it was Spartan enough for me.

In the echoing house I ventured to ask who it was who did the domestic chores. With the snap of a regimental sergeant major I got the reply: 'There are no servants here.' Sure enough, on a later visit, I found the novices scrubbing the floors, weeding the garden, peeling potatoes and cooking the dinner. I wondered how they found time to pursue their higher vocation. When I asked some of them they made enigmatic grimaces. I oughtn't to have asked the question. They were dedicating their lives to the answer.

The priest in active command was not the rector, but the novice master. He clearly shared none of the regrets of his superior for the past. With quiet authority he was concerned with his responsibilities in the field, the task of moulding a modern army. He talked of tactics rather than tradition. He was concerned with new styles of spiritual weaponry. I was reminded of military attitudes which emerged after the disaster of Dunkirk when regimental officers of the old sort were bowler-hatted because they had 'too many grey hairs'. I suspected that the old rector was there only because the ranks are now so thin.

The recruits the Jesuits need to inherit their wings are dwindling alarmingly. Postulants are increasingly failing to stay the course. Unless they can arrest the trend the sheer validity of the Order is in doubt. The empty beds in their novitiates about the world are silent witnesses of their dilemma.

In six years, about fifty novices in the English Province have failed to stay the course. In 1970, the year's intake was seven. In the United States, where the Society is most numerous (7,775), the fall out of novices over five years has been six hundred. In Ignatius's Spain, of all countries, there are now only forty novices in provinces which formerly numbered ten times that number annually. In every nation the Jesuits face a crisis of recruitment except it seems, perhaps significantly, in the officially atheist countries behind the Iron Curtain. In an endeavour to stay the drift from the Order, the Jesuits at their thirty-first congregation, their parliament in session in the sixties in Rome, decided as an experiment to relax certain disciplines, at the discretion of local superiors, which had been a part of their rule since their foundation. Their decision was inspired by the characteristically cloudy conclusions of the ecumenical council of Vatican II which ponderously decided that secular things are not necessarily subservient to spiritual things because they are all part of the universe under God. It was an interpretation of doctrine that the Jesuits were waiting for.

The Jesuits have already taken Marshal McLuhan's message. It has entailed a complete reappraisal of their functions and attitudes. They recognise that their novices belong not to a slow-moving past, but in an immediate, impatient, and highly integrated future. There is no shortage of men with the dedication to serve in their ranks. Indeed, it is probably true that, with wider education, there are more young men than ever eager to accept a lifetime of service. What they are unwilling to accept any more is a vocation in a vacuum. 'I'd sooner make a son than sit on my arse in a schoolroom.'

It is the men who have left the Society, often after as much as seven or eight years, who reveal what have been its inadequacies for them, its tensions and restraints. Notably I only met one who showed any bitterness. The rest, still bound in affectionate ties to the J's, blamed themselves for their failure. No one man told it all. It is only in consensus that a layman can form any sort of impression of a discipline that has flourished for so many centuries; and which, only in recent years, seems to be in decline.

Traditionally, it took about twice as long to make a Jesuit priest as it takes to qualify as a medical man. The first two years of noviceship were a period largely of spiritual formation culminating in the taking of first simple vows. The next two, in what is called the juniorate, concentrated on the classics and modern languages. In the fifth to the seventh year the teaching was philosophy; from the eighth to the ninth, in a phase known as the regency, most of the scholastics were called upon to teach in Jesuit schools. Before or after regency the brighter scholars took university degrees, probably at the Jesuit college of Campion Hall in Oxford. About twelve years on, they studied theology and philosophy for another three years. If they made the grade, they were then ordained priests, only to return for another year's study of theology, final exams, and what is called the tertianship preceding the taking of the final vows of 'voluntary poverty, perpetual chastity and entire obedience'. The tertianship was the ultimate test in which ordained priests, scholars of the highest attainment, men loaded with honours' degrees, were sent back to the life they had known in the novitiate; doing domestic chores, cleaning out the lavatories, preparing vegetables, washing their clothes, devoting themselves once more to the discipline of the thirty-day Long Retreat.

Essentially, the rule is still the same. There has been no relaxation in the training for total service to God. Only the emphasis has altered. Men of mature years and unusual ability serve a shorter apprenticeship. Younger ones are not hived in closed communities but sent to find their feet in industry, social work and the red brick universities. In future, the Jesuits' theological college in Britain will be part of London University.

But, still, the mere curriculum of the Society is forbidding enough. In material terms it is estimated that it costs ten thousand pounds to make a Jesuit priest. In terms of the spirit it is a survival course, and it is meant to be, which only the most determined can see through to the celebration of their first mass and, subsequently, their final avowal. Many break on the way: a few, tragically, lose direction in middle age. The test of scholarship is formidable enough. It is little by comparison with the spiritual involvement it ruthlessly requires.

I asked a first year Jesuit novice, a *primianni* of the Society, who in the outer world would be measuring his day by the girl friends he dated, to list his own. Taking a typical routine he made what the Jesuits would call a *ratio scholarum*. It is ruled hour by hour – no, minute by minute – by a series of bells:

6 a.m. Rise.

6.30 a.m. Morning oblation, the offering of the day to God. Meditation for an hour.

7.30 a.m. Mass.

8 a.m. Breakfast. (*He could scarcely wait for that.*)

8.15 a.m. Shave in cold water, make bed, clean out cubicle, brush gown, and polish shoes.

9–10 a.m. Housekeeping and garden work.

For the rest of the morning activities varied. The shortest, ruled by the bell, was a minute; the longest two hours. For the novices there are relatively few formal studies, apart from classes in scripture, Latin and Greek. There is required reading in Jesuit tradition and, for exercise, ball games. All are assigned their various domestic tasks. Those on kitchen fatigue prepare the dinner.

12.30 p.m. Clear up morning chores.

12.45 p.m. *Examen particulare*, a quarter of an hour's examination of conscience on the first part of the day.

1 p.m. Dinner (self-service).

Follows recreation-time and walks in parties of three in which the senior novice suggests suitable spiritual subjects for conversation. There are conferences and lectures. Some make prison and hospital visits. All must make their salute to the Blessed Sacrament in the chapel every day, say the rosary (often recited on a community walk), and attend to spiritual reading. Brief intervals for general conversation are ruled by the bell. Silence is golden. The seventeen-hour day ends about ten, after a quarter of an hour's preparation for the hour's meditation the following morning. It is also the time, in which those who wish, may go to the confessors of the house to make the confession of their sins. For an outsider it is hard to understand what sins, in the close order of the day, they have time to commit. It may be that they concern explosions of the spirit.

It is not accidental that the novice who outlined his day to me, a day so strictly ordered, left gaps. They are taught early never to ask what happens next, never mind what happens next week. In Ignatius's rule they must obey with 'corpse-like obedience'; in their case the call of the bell. Second year novices, the *secundianni*, are not permitted to teach the newcomers the form. The rule is that every man must be a monastery within himself, rejoicing in a personal withdrawal so complete that he resists even the inclination to closer communion with his fellow novices by the lift of an eyebrow, a smothered laugh, or a shrug of the shoulder.

He must make no special friends. His superiors determine who his company shall be on walks. In threes the names are boarded of novices who may go out together, always with a second year man in charge. 'The conversations we try to make are embarrassingly awful.'

Another rule is known as *Tactus*. No novice is allowed to visit another's room, and no novice may make any physical contact with another. The rule is necessarily relaxed when they are playing ball games; but, in effect, it is adamant. There must be no cliques, no hint of private conspiracy, not the faintest risk of lonely men being drawn together in even latent homosexuality.

A failed American Jesuit, George Reimer,* tells how in his

* *The New Jesuits*, by George Reimer (1971).

novitiate at Florissant, Missouri, there came a day 'when an announcement went up saying that there would be an *exercitum modestiae* at eleven in the morning. No one asked, *"Quid est exercitum modestiae?"* Though the *primianni* stood reading the sign longer than usual, they didn't ask questions. The *secundianni* wouldn't have answered anyway. It was an exercise intended to help each of us to become aware of faults, personality traits, and rule violations that annoyed the community. The novice master asked each man to report his observations as objectively as possible without rancour and warned all not to interpret motives and intentions.'

In the English province, the exercise is called a 'repetition'. One novice kneels in the middle, and the others are asked what fault they have noticed in him. The test in self-abasement is practised, with minor variations, in every Jesuit novitiate throughout the world. Its aim is to prove a man in humble piety. Pride in all but a higher cause is condemned.

Reimer tells from his own experience how a novice complained that 'Brother has a shatteringly loud kind of laugh. He comes too close to your face when he talks'. He remarks how he himself was exasperated by a neighbour clicking a ballpoint pen. Such are the strains of an enclosed society. I am reminded of Bacon's phrase, 'a crowd is not company'. Robert Kee made it the title of a book about his internment in a prisoner-of-war camp. The poet Browning expressed it in his hate verse 'Soliloquy of the Spanish Cloister':

> *GR – R – R – there go, my heart's abhorrence!*
> *Water your damned flower pots, do!*
> *If hate killed men, Brother Lawrence,*
> *God's blood, would not mine kill you!*

Oddly enough, that was one of the favourite verses of a Jesuit father I used to know. Obviously he too had suffered from the enmities born in holy silence. The rule in which vigorous young men are thrown to God is an iron one; none in it more likely to break the spirit, or raise it to greater faith, than what is called the

Long Retreat. A Jesuit novice is pitched into it within weeks of admittance into the Society. In the strangeness of a new gown, and unfamiliar company, he is sent to his Manresa – utter loneliness for thirty days with nothing to comfort him except 'a clothbound book holding exactly 125 four-by-seven pages'. He is given three break days; but, apart from that, he lives under spiritual direction on 'monk's knees' in total meditation and self-scrutiny. The Spiritual Exercises of St Ignatius defy rational analysis. Yet it is proper to add that I have never met a man, who hasn't insisted that it was the most moving mystical experience of his life. It denies review; it offers an intellectual experience which exercitants say is unequalled. I am not one of the initiated. Enough that it is the essential prerequisite of a Jesuit's training and, on ordination, it provides the fulfilment of his vocation.

In a crisis of recruitment it might be supposed that the Jesuits are enlisting every volunteer they can find. In the past they accepted young men, largely from their schools, as young as seventeen. In a different world their neophytes passed smoothly from Jesuit schoolboys to Jesuit novices. It never occurred to many of them to look at another world, or to have any other ambition than to become a Jesuit priest. The pattern has changed. The Society is reluctant to accept beardless boys. They prefer men with university degrees who have seen something of the outside world, and who seek admittance to the Society in mature judgement. A candidate for the Jesuits now has to satisfy a committee, more particular than the committee of even one of the more exclusive London clubs, that his qualifications are unquestionable. One blackball from a panel of enquiring priests, including a psychiatrist, is enough for them to suggest he might well serve God better in another cause. Even if he is tentatively accepted he may be asked to apply again after another sip of the world. If Jesuits are to be fewer, the small company that their founder originally contemplated, they are determined that the quality of their men will be higher than ever before.

The contract that they make with their postulants is more

generous and forgiving than any company in commerce offers. A man who joins them can leave them at any moment he chooses, from the novitiate to old age. Constitutionally he may apply for release from his vows. If he leaves unconstitutionally he will not be forgotten. From the moment he assumes the gown, the Society will act as trustees for any money he has in the bank, or even in his pocket. Some of the men, perhaps the least likely to stay the course, bring enough cash with them to the novitiate to pay their fares home. Men with fortunes, some have brought very large fortunes to the Society, can distribute it as they wish to their relations, or ask that it should be held in their own name. The Jesuits will never use one of their fathers' money except at his particular request. There was one who financed a huge wing at Stonyhurst, insisting that he should see it done to his satisfaction before he died.

But a man who comes to them with no money at all can be equally sure that, if he fails in his vocation, he will be looked after. He will be provided with the finance and amenities to begin again in lay life. It sometimes happens that one of the Jesuit fathers has relations who are in need. Realising that if he weren't serving the Society he might reasonably have been expected to be supporting his family, help in deserving causes is never withheld.

The end product of the Jesuits' rigorous training might be expected to come out like an artifact off an assembly line. What is remarkable is that the Society of Jesus has always displayed such a spectrum of individualists, fearless in their own opinions, widely differing in their talents, conforming only in essentials, united even only in their loyalty to their Order. I have wondered what it is that they all have in common.

Of course, they largely have a communal way of life. They all keep the spiritual rule they adopted as novices. In addition, they read the office which other orders chant; the younger of them in English now. They share a certain eccentricity, the sort of eccentricities which bachelors, without women to keep them in order, tend to develop. In their houses they have a grand tradition of hospitality, love of talk, and a splendid inability to be shocked. But thinking of them as I do, knowing them as I do, I can find just one common denominator. It is in the aura of their gowns.

Novices, as soon as they are admitted to the Society, adopt the gown of their superiors. After their first vows, they wear the Roman collar. In their formative years they look as awkward in their dress as fledglings with undeveloped quills. A reverse collar and a gown are not simply articles of wear. To carry them with effect they call for an attitude of mind.

The head of a made Jesuit rises over his hard white collar like a bust on a plinth. His gown, that graceful attire of learning, is something he assumes with an authority which can only be acquired in scholarship. Our masters at school used their wings to wipe the chalk off the blackboards. It was customary for us to attract their attention by pulling on them as if they were bell cords on a bus. But their gowns were the symbol of their dedication. They wore them with the snobbery which, in the English countryside, goes with very old tweeds with leather patches on the elbows. The greener and greasier the black cloth of them the greater they rejoiced, like wine connoisseurs over an old cork, in the vintage of their education. After the years of study in which they had cut their cloth, they wore it in humbleness, but also in pious pride.

I hope that I haven't left an impression that they were uncouth in their dress. As men do, they just liked old clothes. On formal occasions, in fine frock coats, they could make the rest of us look rather tatty. They clung to their threadbare gowns only in a figurative way. Still by far the most numerous order of the Church they are wondering whether, in another generation, others will wear their cloth so thin.

II

The Dilemma

THE present general of the Jesuit tells that, on assuming office, the holy father gave him the injunction that the greatest task of the Society was to combat atheism. When the general asked 'how?' the pope replied: '*You* must find the answer.' The last of the Bourbon kings, or the fated Stuarts, could scarcely have said anything more defeatist.

Anyhow it is surely untrue that the challenge of our age is atheism. Even in Communist countries, where atheism is official, it is evident that people believe, either in fear or deep mystical conviction, in a Supreme Being. What so many have ceased to have faith in is not God but the human organisations which claim, with divine authority, to instruct us how to reach Him. H. A. L. Fisher, in his *History of Europe*, points out that religions are invented by laymen and organised by priests. Men, as they always have, will continue to look for God. The crisis in religion is that contemporary man has lost faith in God's interpreters on earth. The churches themselves have mislaid the gift of tongues.

Time was when the religious commanded superstitious respect. In social rank priests walked with princes. Their mere ability to read and write conferred on them a station denied to ordinary mortals. Now, they must fight for approbation. The cleric has become increasingly an object of the satirist's wit. Even Jesuits are dismissed as nice people who mustn't be treated too seriously. They are welcome on minority television programmes which so many people don't see. They are good for a paragraph in a gossip column when one of them breaks his vows. It is empty to pretend that they could ever be persecuted again.

Four hundred years ago it was undoubtedly the inspiration of Xavier's mission to the east which brought so many exceptional men into the Society. They came, in adventurous self-sacrifice, in their thousands. As news of their achievements in the uttermost ends of the earth reached Europe the men, willing and anxious to serve even to martyrdom, rose decade after decade. As emissaries of the popes the Jesuits were convinced that their destiny was to hold old Christendom together. In an early exercise in public relations they fought with conviction the cause of the counter-reformation.

All gone. The Jesuits' world-wide mission today, demanding as it still is, has lost its original crusading purpose. Their intellectuals, their preachers and their writers, enjoy a wider platform than they have ever had before. But, in the everyday work of the Society, they have become too largely pedagogues and parish priests. Their modern role, worthy as it is, is out of keeping. They still have their adventurers behind the Iron Curtain, and elsewhere; but, by and large, they are no more extended than the Brigade of Guards would be on traffic duty.

The Jesuits themselves admit openly that they are searching for a new direction in their affairs. So much of the Jesuit rule is a mortgage from the past; so much inhibits them in their present affairs. If I discern the trend correctly they are moving away from their traditional community life. They see their place in the modern world with their men on their own in the universities, the administration, the workshops and the laboratories. It is already happening in the United States where a Jesuit is now a Congressman, a Jesuit is the Kennedy Foundation's first medical ethics scholar, a Jesuit at Harvard has established himself as one of the first senior professors of the electronic media. In Europe a Jesuit is the greatest living expert on agriculture in the Common Market.

All of them are disinclined to accept a rule which is irrelevant to the sort of society we live in now. I doubt if any one of them believes any more in a mediaeval concept in which spirituality needed to be presented in concrete pictures like a tavern sign. It belonged to a time when people were largely illiterate; and so heaven and hell needed full technicolour treatment, with goodies and baddies represented like baddies and goodies in a super picture. The allegories, so many of them so naïve, have no substance in a literate industrial society. It is sad that the papacy is too buried in tradition to rethink anything more radical than whether the patron saint of travellers ought to be excised from the records because there is doubt whether he even existed. They might well look deeper than that. So much more that is improbable passes as 'Faith'. Years pass while prelates in Rome weep for the wickedness of the world, with nothing better to suggest than an appeal to the intervention of the Holy Ghost. How wise the Cardinal Archbishop of Westminster was when he was asked on television what he would do if he were pope. He replied: 'I would write fewer encyclicals.' The Jesuits, first in service to the popes, look like being counted the new pro-testants, They are thinking ahead of Rome.

Their secular problems are still with them. They are bogged with a complex of capital investment in property, locked in trust, which they are unable to exploit. The income is scarcely adequate. So much of their higher cause is lost in sheer ad-ministration. The notion is that it might be handled by lay trustees to free the Jesuits for greater causes.

So much needs rethinking. Even the Jesuits' simple vows of poverty and obedience have lost much of their original meaning, although chastity is as much a discipline as ever. The vow of poverty now simply means that individual Jesuits pay no income tax, no bills, and that they are looked after by their community, in sickness and health, to their graves. In material terms they are the beneficiaries of the most generous of welfare states. Money in modest sums for bus fares and cigarettes is simply something to be requested from the minister; if clothes, credit is provided at the appropriate store. Entire obedience, in practice, is a gentle rule. A provincial would reluctantly order one of his men to undertake a mission against his inclination. Provincials issue prizes, not penalties. If a man breaks the vow of chastity the Society will ease him financially into the outer world. Some who leave it are subsequently overwhelmed by the demands of a different kind of obedience. I remember a Jesuit who told me that he didn't like visiting private houses because he couldn't have a bath when he felt like it. The pattern of the Society today is all too safe.

Theoretically, Jesuits are never supposed to accept elevation in the Church. Yet some of them, some of the most brilliant of them, take a fourth vow in which they undertake, at the drop of a papal hat, to accept any post they are appointed to by the pontiff. Some of them have become archbishops and cardinals. In a sort of way they changed their allegiance. In a sort of way they changed the essential character of the Society. Fighting men should not join the staff.

I wonder whether the Jesuits can pursue their future mission in first service to the popes? Never mind the old men; their feet, like the rector of the novitiate in Edinburgh, are dug too deep in the past. It is the young men who may inspire the reformation in the Catholic Church which is so overdue, who will preach in a language that an industrial world can comprehend.

The Jesuits themselves are thinking ahead of me. They have already changed the order of their novitiates. My own guess, for what it is worth, is that they will ultimately pull out of their material responsibilities, hand over their capital wealth to outside trustees. They are already too involved in business which is not their mission. I believe that they must come to the conclusion that, in community life, they are increasingly ineffective. Their place, as it always was, is in the undiscovered world; this strange new world which calls for a greater mission than any which has gone before.

II

A Personal Confession

'At such love, my love I kindle
'Was there no heaven, still must I love!
'Were there no hell, sin would I shun!
'Were heaven and hell to pass away,
'With their rewards and punishments,
'In me would love for love endure!'

THAT must surely be numbered amongst the noblest sentiments expressed in the name of Christianity. It was conceived by Francis Xavier. I can imagine him struggling with the words, still vivid in translation, to say what lesser men have left unsaid. Leigh Hunt tried in *Abou Ben Adhem,* that essentially shallow verse in which he conferred the love of God on one 'who loved his fellow men'. While I hate the word 'agnostic', with its implication of disbelief, it is undeniable that we are all agnostics. We use words like 'faith' and 'revelation'; but we just don't know. Xavier's thought is the more moving for its utter selflessness.

Perhaps I haven't said enough about the dedicated piety of the Society of Jesus; written too lightly of men who have given their lives to higher causes than most of us have given our own. But piety is a private thing; in public it is a bit of a bore. Try reading the life of that sick Italian Jesuit saint Aloysius or Stanislaus the Pole, and you will see what I mean. The real Jesuits are the important people they are because the display of piety, away from the altar, is not their way. The great Society is so great because, in its hereditary wisdom, it lives with worldlings and doesn't drive sinners too hard. They learnt it from Ignatius and Xavier. They learnt it, in quiet hope, when they were outcasts, banned by the pope, bound together in spiritual hope, scarcely believing that they could rise again.

I have known unhappy ones who have lost their mission. I have known ascetic ones, no doubt men with a deep internal struggle, who have found it difficult to live happily with the world. And I have joyous memories of a day at the Vatican Observatory, in the pope's summer villa at *Castel Gandolfo*, where the Jesuit fathers in charge had clearly found heaven already in the study of the solar galaxies, one of the mysteries of the universe just beyond our own fragmentary part of it.

I am aware that I am one of their unholy children. I make no excuse – the Jesuits, above all, wouldn't expect it from me – for telling what passes for truth in my mind. I have never believed that I myself am important enough for immortality. I have never regretted that death, so far as I understand it, appears to me most likely to lead to the *Nirvana* of Buddhism, a dreamless sleep. Very nice too. Sleep is something I have enjoyed throughout my life.

I believe in God. While I cannot comprehend the theologians' concept that 'God is love', I imagine that I discern the origins of the notion in the wonders of natural life; in simple example in a violet, an ant, a blade of grass, the beauty of a salmon running up a river from the sea. The transcendent marvel of the earth, infinite in its smallness, inexplicable in its beyondness, surely demands the acceptance of a Supreme Being. God is as good a word as any we can make.

When I look at the powder of the stars I wonder how men can be so arrogant as to suppose that only this speck of creation is inhabited by thinking beings. A former Astronomer Royal, let his name be forgotten, had the impudence to suggest just that. A dialectician in the Vatican was more abstruse. He declared that it is proper for Catholics to believe in the existence of thinking beings in other parts of the universe with the proviso that only human beings were born with original sin. The best of Roman luck to him.

Is it too preposterous to suggest that there are beings in what I am told may be a thousand million solar systems, as big as ours, in the Milky Way who could be a thousand or a million years ahead of us in knowledge and engineering? It is a mere fancy of mine that much of the Biblical story makes human sense if you assume just that; that Lucifer was banished for his pride from a more advanced part of the universe; that Adam and Eve disgraced themselves after being introduced to the earth from another place; that Elijah was carried to a better world in a fiery chariot? It is not without interest that what we call 'flying saucers' were known to the ancients as 'fiery shields'. If you only assume an advance as incredible as a journey to the moon seemed to our forebears, it is a technological theory which ought not to be casually dismissed.

At best, I have made a wild guess; but it is no wilder than the doctrines of Christianity which, in respectability, we are called upon to conform to. I can envy those who believe that the way to Paradise is routed like a motor map. If the popular language of religion has got it right, the destination is going to bore me to distraction. I have never been much of a one for holidays. The idea of facing one for eternity, whatever that word means, is intolerable.

I am conscious that, in my thinking, I am a spiritual anarchist; that, in the affairs of mankind, the conventions of religion, like the conventions of politics, are an essential need. Most people are satisfied to be told that, in this world and the hopeful next, everything is arranged for them, like the organisation of a holiday camp. I suppose that it is important, in the name of human happiness, that it should be so.

It seems to be a human need to take sides; whether it's about a football match, Socialists or Tories, Democrats or Republicans, Communism, Fascism and, oh dear, Christianity. The Dominicans can never be forgiven that, carrying the cross before the soldiers of the King of Spain, they condoned the mass slaughter of innocent heathens in the Americas; not in the name of Christ but in the name of their earthly kings for gold, silver and precious stones. Why can't we leave each other alone?

I find that I myself am unable to get hot under the collar about any of the creeds. They are all wrong because, if there were evident truth in any one of them, there would be nothing more to argue about. It happens to be a fallacy that the lower animals don't kill their own species. It is catastrophic that we, who call ourselves the higher ones, go about persecuting our own kind as if there were some moral merit in it.

That silly word 'sin' simply means a crime in the eyes of the hierarchy of the constituted orders of Christianity. The Communists call the offender, according to their rules of the game, 'a reactionary'. We are with them, or against them; and, in the name of a greater cause, always the cause in which they have a built-in interest, they will excommunicate us, march us off to concentration camps, go on strike, and throw up the barricades.

I am coming to the view that there is something in the theory of predestination; not in eternity, but in the sort of people we are born to be. A few, an aggressive few, are born to be bloody nuisances. A larger number, the great ones, are called to give their lives to service; among them priests and artists. The rest, the largest section of society, are predestined to be just decent hardworking people. The vast majority of them are women. The silent majority, as it has come to be called, deserve better of the outsiders.

I am one of the outsiders. I remember Patrick Campbell telling how, when he was struggling to compose an article, two men up a telegraph post watched him through the window with interest as he sat over his typewriter. 'He's not doing anything yet', said one to the other. 'He's still just looking.' I am still looking.

My hope, how much I hope that I am right, rests in that again and again in my life I have been set back on my heels by something approaching a mystical experience, a fleeting touch of another dimension which may represent everything that, in my everyday thinking, has evaded me. Perhaps it is the contact with mystery, the telepathy of knowledge which is called divine grace. Other men, dedicated in spirituality, have spoken to me of it. While I am more than uncertain that it can extend beyond an intellectual twinning of human minds, the fact of premonition is undeniable.

In wandering thought I was driving from London to the coast of Wales. My mother had a house on the way. I argued to myself whether I should stop for supper with her, or join her on my return the following night. Something beyond myself forced me to stop. It was a delightful pause in which my mother had seemed never more ethereally beautiful. I drove on, promising to be with her the next evening. When I turned the swing doors in the hotel in Wales, I heard the insistent double ring of the telephone. It was likely to be a call for anybody; but, as I entered the lobby, I knew beyond a peradventure that it was for me; that it was to tell me that my mother was suddenly dead. It has happened to me, in smaller matters, before and since. Perhaps we are deeper than we know. Perhaps my worldly attitudes are altogether false. Perhaps, as a much-loved Jesuit said to me, I am indeed 'dotty'. Although it may be later than I know, so far I cannot make up my mind.

I have argued, as it seems to me, the improbabilities of formal religion. But the subtleties of the spirit still contain me like a grip on the arm. I know that I am inconsistent in my reasoning; denying this, but emotionally attracted to that. There was a glorious Sunday morning in the *midi* of France when, motoring back from the vineyards of Bordeaux, I sighted the spire of Chartres Cathedral rising out of the plain. I knew that I must attend mass there. It was a high mass. The celebrants at the altar in the centre of the Cathedral, the congregation joined in worship, were bathed in the blue light of the mediaeval glass; that glass shot to pieces by the cannon in the first World War which has been assembled higgledy-piggledy, and yet somehow with more amazing beauty than it might have had when the glass was organised in the lead piping into pictures. In my way I prayed.

It seems to me that human beings, united in thought, combined in devotion, have something in common with the bees. A mob is beastly. An ordered assembly, with a single purpose, lifts the individual into a larger dimension.

At Chartres it came to me that the whole is greater than the part. Although I have tin ears, I have reflected on the phenomenon at concerts of classical music when the orchestra and the audience are joined in the same emotional stream of sound. The conductor is the celebrant. The gift of organised religion, in the Catholic way, is the same. The Roman Church is right to honour music, painting, sculpture, rich vestments, flowers, the delights of this world. I applaud the Pope in his golden litter, with his escort of crimson-clad cardinals, and the waft of ostrich-feather fans. If the pontiff gets too humble in his holy office, he will be making a great mistake.

I recollect taking my wife, a loyal Anglican, to St Peter's for the first time. The usual Sunday carnival was in full spate. In the great edifice babies were being baptised; children in their First Communion dresses, bridal white, were parading to receive the Sacrament. A priest was preaching over there, pilgrims were kissing the well-worn toe of the statue of Peter over here. Fathers were hearing confessions in their boxes in a dozen languages, popping out at intervals to tap a blessing with a stick like a billards cue on the shoulders of importunate children who queued again and again for the fun of it. Organ music filled the basilica. Nice Italian matrons, over-weighted with *pasta* and a surfeit of children, issued food to their broods. At the great entrance of the basilica the Papal Guard in their Renaissance uniforms were politely managing the delicate task of stopping tourists exposing their cameras, and stopping women who, against Vatican ruling, were exposing too much of themselves. Everyone was as noisy and happy as Reilly. All were waiting in the hope to wave their arms and shout '*Viva Papa*'. Religion was fun; religion was life.

I felt a little lonely that I myself have chosen such a solitary path. At the end of the tour my wife said to me wistfully: 'I wish I belonged to this club.'

SELECTED BIBLIOGRAPHY

The standard bibliography of the Jesuits, not quite up to date, runs to eleven volumes. James J. Walsh asserts that nearly one hundred thousand books have been written by the Jesuits themselves, irrespective of the vast literature published by others. Réné Fülop-Miller, in the bibliography of his scholarly work, *Power and Secret of the Jesuits*, lists a thousand reference sources. My own research has been comparatively modest. I have relied more on personal encounter.

JOHN GERARD, S.J., *Centenary History of Stonyhurst College*. Privately printed. 1894.

HUGO RAHNER, S.J. and L. VON MATT, *St. Ignatius*. London. 1956.

RÉNÉ FÜLOP-MILLER, *Power and Secret of the Jesuits*. New York and London. 1930.

VINCENT CRONIN, *The Wise Man from the West*. London. 1955.

H. F. BOULTON, *A Padre on Horseback*. Chicago. 1963.

JAMES J. WALSH, *American Jesuits*. New York. 1934.

R. B. C. CUNNINGHAME GRAHAM, *A Vanished Arcadia*. London and New York. 1924.

GEORGE O'NEILL, S.J., *Golden Years on the Paraguay*. London. 1934.

EDNA KENTON, *Jesuit Relations* (now *Black Gown and Redskins*). London. 1956.

JOHN J. WYNNE, S.J., *The Jesuit Martyrs of North America*. New York. 1925.

BERNARD BASSET, S.J., *The English Jesuits*. London. 1967.

SELECTED BIBLIOGRAPHY

MALACHI MARTIN, *The Encounter: Religions in Crisis*. London and New York. 1970.

GEORGE REIMER, *The New Jesuits*. Boston. 1971.

Constitution of the Jesuits (new English translation) 1970.

Letters and Notices: the visit of the Father General to the English Province 1970. London.

Documents of the 31st Congregation of the Jesuits 1965–66.

Rules of the Society of Jesus (Manresa Press). 1894.

ACKNOWLEDGEMENTS

To the Jesuits, all of them, who in full knowledge of my wayward opinions have opened every door and every book to me; to Mr R. K. Browne, the erudite librarian at 114 Mount Street; to Hugh Kay, a once Jesuit scholastic who was disappointed in his own vocation and who is now happily reunited with the fathers of Farm Street, dealing with importunate questions from people like me; to Harry Hastings of the B.B.C. who directed the documentary 'The Hated Society' and who, as a consequence, indirectly inspired the writing of this; to Caroline Haines, his assistant, who has done so much to assemble the illustrations, and who has good claim to be the first woman to have penetrated places in the Jesuit hierarchy where no woman has ever been permitted before; to Portia Holland, the interpreter of my handwriting; to Jennie Dereham, who made the index: and, finally, to my wife for the powerful reason that, encouragement etc. apart, she is also my publisher.

Illustrations: (*between pages 80–81*) Society of Jesus, British Museum, Douglas Botting (photograph), Mansell Collection; (*between pages 144–145*) Society of Jesus, Radio Times Hulton Picture Library, Mansell Collection; (*between pages 208–209*) Society of Jesus, Radio Times Hulton Picture Library, Mansell Collection, British Broadcasting Corporation.

Index

INDEX

INDEX

INDEX